Call of the Runes

The magic, myth, divination, and spirituality of the Nordic people

By Walter McGrory

First published in the Netherlands by
Walter McGrory, Independent publishing
Helmond

ISBN: 978-90-9036898-6 Paperback

Contents

Introduction

The word Rune itself means mystery, an appropriate definition as a large amount of runic knowledge has been lost. Much of what was written about the runes and the culture surrounding them comes from outside sources. Two primary sources we have are the observations of the Roman historian Tacitus (56 AD- 120 AD) and from a much later date, the stories collected by Snorri Sturluson (1179 AD- 1241 AD). The stories collected by Snorri are known as the Edda's and were written when Christianity was already the dominant religion.

Just as the written accounts are separated by vast gulfs of time and geographical location, the archaeological evidence is scarce and reveals only snippets of insight.

To discover more about the runes, we will take a journey that spans centuries and stretches across the whole of northern Eurasia. When discussing the Nordic culture, we are examining a plethora of tribes, each with its own customs, evolving throughout history.

With the myths, relics, and accounts collected in this book, we will attempt to divine each rune's probable meaning and how they were used. By examining what remains constant from culture to culture, we might lift the veil on the mysteries of the runes. Within this book, all sources are presented in a way that will allow the reader to come to their own conclusions about this mysterious alphabet.

Structure

This book has three parts. The first part focuses on the runes themselves. The runic alphabet this book uses is called the Elder Futhark. The name Futhark is derived from the first six letters of this alphabet F U Th A R and K, just as the standard modern alphabet is named for its first letters, A B. The Elder Futhark is split into three sets of eight runes called Ætt. We look at the rune poems, historical charms, relevant myths, and other cultural information for each rune. Each rune chapter ends with a suggestion of how to experience the rune. Cultural paradigms shift, the concept of ice today does not have the same connotation to us as it would a thousand years ago. In experiencing the runes, several exercises are recommended to familiarise yourself with how the people originally would have interpreted the archetypes the runes represent.

The second part of the book will focus on magic and ritual. In this section, several historical charms, spells, and amulets are examined and compared to show how the Nordic cultures used magic. There are also step-by-step guides on creating charms following the same ancient formula.

The final part of this book focuses on divination. Divination is one of the most popular modern uses of the runes and the use with the least amount of historical data. This section will explore the historical precedence of runic divination and how it can be practiced in a modern setting. This chapter also includes real-world examples of rune readings broken down step by step, with tips on practicing and giving rune readings yourself.

The runic alphabets

The runes used in this book are the Elder Futhark. Just like the name Alphabet comes from the first two letters Alfa and Beta, the Name of the Futhark comes from its first six letters Fehu, Uruz, Thurisaz, Ansuz, Raidho, and Kenaz. In total, the Elder Futhark has twenty-four runes.

The oldest known complete line of Elder Futhark runes, the Klyver stone [G88], is found in Sweden. This rune stone dates back to about 400AD.

Figure 1: Futhark rune row as inscribed on the Klyver stone [G88]

The Elder Futhark was used from around the second century until the eighth century in Scandinavia and is the oldest runic alphabet and most probably originated in what is now Denmark (Rausing, 1992). As seen in the Klyver stone rune row, the runes show slight variations to how the runes are depicted in this book. Some of this is because of wear on the stone, but other runes like Sowilo with an extra branch and the reversed Berkana rune are variations. The shape of the runes could have differed due to artistic use or based on region. The Elder Futhark was used to write in Proto-Norse (Sean & Klaus , 1995), there is no surviving rune poem of these runes, and the names of the runes are, therefore, reconstructions based on the names of the runes in later texts.

The Younger Futhark was used between the ninth and the eleventh century in Norway, Sweden, Denmark, and Iceland. The younger Futhark was a slimmed-down version of the Elder Futhark and contained only 16 runes. The Younger Futhark runes are named and described in the Icelandic and Norwegian rune poems. Because the Younger Futhark is eight runes shorter than the Elder Futhark, eight runes from the Elder Futhark have no Icelandic or Norwegian rune poem.

The Futhork was a later variation on the Elder Futhark that was first used in Denmark. Starting from the fifth century, we see this simplified alphabet slowly replace the Elder futhark in archaeological finds. Around the eighth century, the Futhork had entirely replaced the Elder Futhark. The Futhork stayed used until around the eleventh century in the British Isles and Frisia. This runic alphabet has several iterations and contains between twenty-nine and thirty-three runes, depending on the time. The Anglo-Saxon rune poems cover the names and meanings of these runes.

The so-called medieval runes were used in Scandinavia from the twelfth until the fifteenth century. The medieval runes add multiple runes to the Younger Futhark to account for both the sounds lost from the Elder Futhark and to allow for writing in Latin (Lars, 2011).

This book focuses on the Elder Futhark, the oldest of the runes. All texts in this book are transcribed in the Elder Futhark, even when the original text was written in another runic alphabet. This is done for simplicities sake so that the reader of this book does not have to remember multiple symbols for each rune. In this book, there are figures which include a photo or a drawing of runic artifacts with the original runic alphabet inscribed. Underneath each of these figures will be a transcription written in Elder Futhark.

The next page overviews the different types of runes and their phonetic value within their runic alphabet. Each runic alphabet had local and artistic variations, meaning that the overview sometimes deviates from runic artifacts.

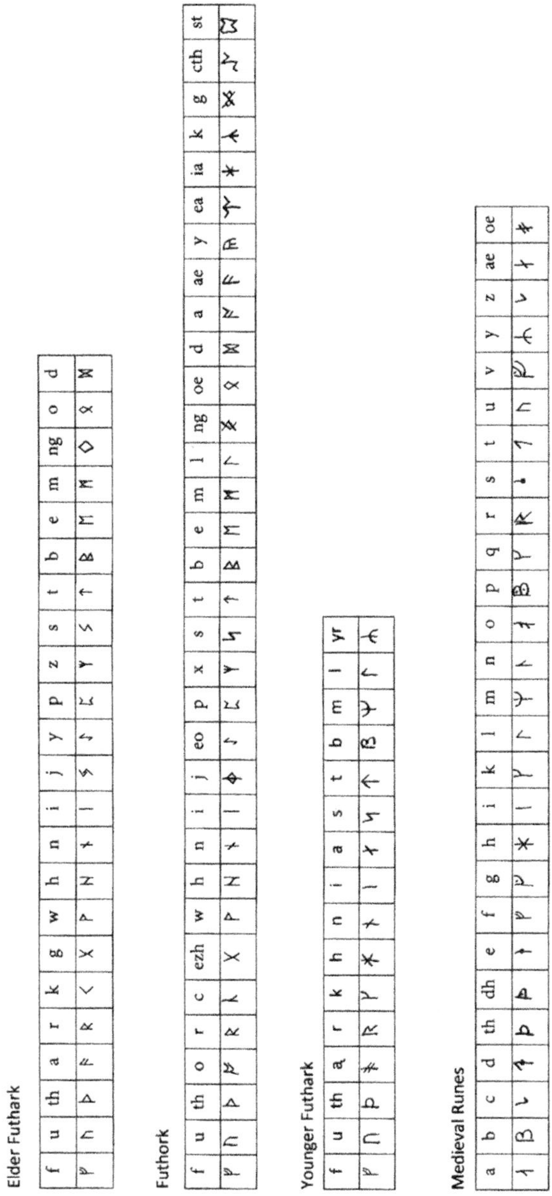

Figure 2: Runic alphabets comparison

The rune poems

Every chapter about a rune references one or more rune poems. The rune poems each describe the name and meaning of the rune in a stanza. There are three known sets of rune poems, the Icelandic, Norwegian, and Anglo-Saxon rune poems. Each set has a separate verse form and interpretation, but all overlap in theme when speaking about the same rune.

Based on literary analyses, the Anglo-Saxon rune poems were probably already around during the end of the 7th century (Van Renterghem, 2014). The oldest know manuscript dates from the tenth century and is only known as the Cotton Otho b.x 165. The name is so because it was found in the Cotton Library in London in the Otho Bookshelf at location B.x 165. The Cotton library in London burned to the ground in 1731. Fortunately, the rune poems were copied by George Hickes in 1705, and this version still exists today. The text consists of 29 stanzas, including all the Elder Futhark runes. Of all the rune poems, the Anglo-Saxon rune poems are most strongly influenced by Christianity and make use of Christian imagery.

The Norwegian poem's origin is roughly placed in the early 13th century (Louis-Jensen, 2010). An early copy found its way into the collection of Ole Worm[1] , a Danish scholar, and collector of runic lore and artifacts. The original thirteenth century source is lost, but in 1636 Ole Worm published" Runir seu Danica literatura antiquissima" a bundled collection of his collected runic manuscripts, and the runic poems survive here. There are Norwegian rune poems for each of the 16 Younger Futhark runes.

The Icelandic rune poems are presumed to be the youngest poems dating from the late 13th century (Louis-Jensen, 2010). Ironically oldest

---

[1] Ole Worm is also know under his latinised name Olaus Wormius. The writer H.P Lovecraft names Olaus Wormius as the translator of the most complete edition of the Necronomicon within his fictional universe.

known surviving manuscript containing rune poems contains the Icelandic rune poems. The manuscript was written around the fifteenth century and is found in the "Handritasafn Árna Magnússonar," a collection of historical documents collected by the Icelandic Árni Magnússon. Árni was the Secretary of the Royal Archives and Professor of Danish Antiquities at the University of Copenhagen and compiled a vast collection of historical documents from his native Iceland. When he passed away in 1730, he left his collection to the university of Copenhagen. In 1965 a new law was passed, and all pieces important to Icelandic culture were returned to Iceland, where the rune poems now reside in the Árni Magnússon Institute for Icelandic Studies.

The RuneS Database

The Runic artifacts used in this book all have a code attached to them, like the G 88 from the Klyver stone in figure 2. These codes reference the RuneS DB, a database of runic objects throughout Europe.

The Runic database started in 1986 at Upsala university and was initially focused on objects found in Sweden for use by the language department. In 1992, the "Axel and Margaret Ax:son Johnson Foundation for Public Benefit" gave a grant to expand the Runic database beyond Swedish objects. This idea had been around for longer but could not be afforded. The funding ran out in 1997, and work has continued on a volunteer base. The most recent version of the Runic database was released in 2008 with over 6500 objects, and work is underway on a 3.0 version.

Each object starts with a letter showing the location it was found. For instance, the G in G 88 means the object originates from Götland. This is followed by either an object number or a reference to its location in publishing. If you are interested in a specific object in this book, you can use its reference number to find more information.

Translations and limitations

The translation of runic manuscripts and runic artifacts is not without its difficulties. The old Scandinavian languages are dead languages, and only a limited amount of material has survived. This means there is no complete dictionary of the whole language, and sometimes the meaning of words has to be guessed from context or by comparing them to modern Scandinavian or Germanic words. Grammatical rules were also less strict, adding to the difficulty of interpreting a sentence.

The manuscripts containing the rune poems are all not original sources but copies. There is some debate if, during the copying, errors were made. The manuscripts we have are hundreds of years old, causing the ink to fade, and the pages were not always handled with the greatest care. Runic artifacts have the same problems, runes can be partly worn away over the centuries or lost altogether, leaving only old drawings that might lack detail.

When considering that translators of runic artifacts are trying to translate only partially readable texts written in a dead language, where both the runes and the grammar vary depending on the author, it is then understandable that there is not always consensus about the translations.

Care has gone into selecting the translations used in this book, but it should be mentioned that different, sometimes conflicting translations exist.

Ætts

The runes' chapters are separated into three sections, each of 8 runes. A set of eight runes is called a Ætt but is comelily spelled as Aett. Ætt translates to "those that are related" and means a clan.

In the Futhark, there are three such Ætt. Sometimes the Ætt are given names like Freya's Ætt, Heimdall's Ætt, and Tir's Ætt, but no historical sources name them. Each rune has a specific place in each Ætt, for example, Uruz is the second rune of the first Ætt, and Mannaz is the fourth rune of the third Ætt.

This is important because the people who used the runes liked to create elaborate codes where the runes were hidden in numbers. Each chapter on the runes will start with its name, its meaning, and its location in the Ætt.

For example, the first chapter on Wunjo starts
1.8 Wunjo – Joy
As it's the eighth rune of the first Ætt, its meaning is joy.

Notes for the experienced rune practitioner

This book includes many original sources, which cannot be found in most other rune books. However, there are two things you will not find in this book outside of this introduction the merkstave and the blank rune. You will probably have encountered these if you have read several rune books.

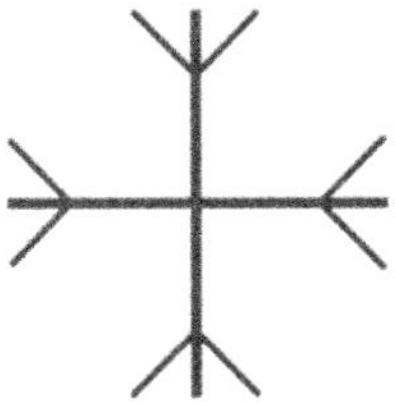

Figure 3: Ægishjálmr

The merkstave "reversed runes": some books connect separate meanings to the runes depending on the direction the runes are facing, similar to reversed cards in tarot. I have not included these in this book because there is no evidence for merkstave runes. In amulets or writing, we can see that this is not how runes were used. Sometimes runes were given different directions in writing to draw attention to the word, but the meaning and pronunciation stayed the same, the same goes for amulets.

One of the most famous runic magical symbols is the Ægishjálmr or Helm of Awe(fig .3). This symbol, in its simplest form, is a combination of four Algiz runes, each pointing in a different direction. If reversing a rune would also reverse its meaning, this common talisman would be four runes canceling each other out. For this reason, I have not included any further speculation on merkstave runes.

The blank rune: the blank rune, Odin's rune, or the Wyrd rune, is a blank runestone or stave sometimes used in rune readings, included in rune sets, or written about in rune books. The first written account of the rune comes from Ralph Blum, who used the rune in his book, *The book of runes(*1984). The idea came from a runestone set he acquired that included a blank stone. If you wish to use the runes to write a blank symbol is very impractical as you can't distinguish between a blank rune and a blank piece of paper. It would not be feasible to create charms using a blank symbol as each amulet, article of clothing, shield, etc., has potentially an infinite number of blank symbols on it.

Because this book aims to give a cohesive historical view of the runes and is not just focused on divination, neither Merkstave runes nor the blank rune will be mentioned outside this Introduction.

Acknowledgments

The most common sources used in the book will be acknowledged here and in the bibliography but not in the text itself. This helps the readability by not having every Havmal or Tacitus quote be followed by a reference. Sources used less often will be quoted in the text and the bibliography.

Rune Poem translations:

Dickens, B. (1915). Runic and Heroic Poems of the Old Teutonic Peoples. Edinburg, Scotland: Cambridge University Press

Poetic Edda translations:

Bellows, H.A. (1936). The Poetic Edda's. New York, America : New York The American-Scandinavian Foundation

Prose Edda translations:

Brodeur, A.G. (1916). The Prosse Edda. New York, America: New York The American-Scandinavian Foundation

Tacitus Germania translations:

Church, A.J .& Brodribb, W.J. (1876). Germania. Cambridge, England: Macmillen and Co.

Gallic War translation:

McDevitte, W. A. & Bohn, W.S. (1869). C. Julius Caesar. Caesar's Gallic War. New York. Harper & Brothers.

Egils Saga translations:

Green, W.C. (1893). The story of Egil Skallagrimson. London, England: Paternoster row E.C.

The Runes

The first ætt

ᚠ

1.1 Fehu - Cattle

Germanic	Gothic	Old English	Old Norse	Sound
Fehu	Faihu	Foeh	Fe	F

Fehu is the first rune of the first Ætt, and it is here that we begin our runic journey. Fehu is a rune of wealth, which is now represented with money and, in the old days, was represented with cattle. Wealth is a form of power but a fleeting one, it can only be spent once, and then it's gone. In this way, Fehu represents the opportunities that wealth can bring. The rune is often also linked to the Vanir Frey and Freya, whose name begins with the sound of Fehu.

The rune poems

Norwegian

ᚠᛖ·ᚠᚨᛖᛚᛞᚱ·ᚠᚱᚨᛖᚾᛞᚨ·ᚱᛟᚷᛖ·ᚠᛟᛞᚺᛖᛊᚲ·ᚢᛚᚠᚱ·ᛁ·ᛊᚲᛟᚷᛖ·

Fé vældr frænda róge; føðesk ulfr í skóge.

Wealth is a source of discord among kinsmen;
the wolf lives in the forest

The first line of the Norwegian rune poem shows us what will become a recurring theme throughout the myths and the sagas of the North. Incredible piles of wealth, especially when hoarded, lead to strife.

The most famous example of this is the saga of Sigurd: The story centers on a cursed hoard of gold guarded by a dragon called Fafnir. The curse has corrupted Fafnir and corrupts everyone around it with greed, turning brother against brother and friend against friend. Sigurd famously slays Fafnir. Unfortunately, this does not end the curse. The curse is not lifted until the treasure is thrown into the Rein river. The story of Sigurd shows that hoarding treasure can lead to great misfortune, and the best path is to let it go.

If wealth a man has won for himself,
Let him never want more;
Oft he saves for a foe what he plans for a friend,
For much goes worse than we wish.
- Hávamál 39

The *Hávamál* is a poem from the Edda detailing the advice Odin gives to mortals. One piece of wisdom shared by Odin in the *Hávamál* shows the same sentiment as the saga of Sigurd did, greedily amassing wealth leads to trouble.

The wolf's image is often used to symbolize an outcast from society and the hardships following this banishment. Úlfer in old Norse and Wulf in Old English both mean wolf but are also used to describe thieves and outlaws (Szőke, 2018).

The wolf living in the forest in the second line is a warning: those who give in to greed will have to live alone outside of society in the woods to fend for themselves.

ᚠᛖ·ᛖᚱ·ᚠᚱᚨᛖᚾᛞᚨ·ᚱᛟᚷ·ᛟᚲ·ᚠᛚᚨᛖᛞᚺᚨᚱ·ᚠᛁᛏᛁ·ᛟᚲ·ᚷᚱᚨᚠᛊᛖᛁᛞᚺᛊ
ᚷᚨᛏᚨ·ᚨᚢᚱᚢᛗ·ᚠᛇᛚᚲᛁᚱ·

Icelandic

Fé er frænda róg ok flæðar viti ok grafseiðs gata aurum fylkir.

Wealth Source of discord among kinsmen and fire of the sea and path of the serpent.

The Icelandic rune poem echoes the Norwegian rune poem's warning about the potential discord that great wealth can bring.

A kenning is a metaphorical description of a conventional term, often rooted in mythology. Kennings are commonly used in Nordic Poetry and are widely known because of their repeated use.

In this poem, *fire of the sea* is a kenning for gold. The Sea Jotünn Aegir frequently holds elaborate dinner parties for the Gods in his underwater domain. Wood does not burn underwater, so Aegir uses enchanted gold that burns eternally to light and warms his halls. This is the origin of the kenning *fire of the sea.*

Part of the reason why gold is so valuable is that it doesn't oxidize and so doesn't naturally decay, remaining shining and splendid forever. Gold can generally be understood as a symbol of immortality in the sagas.

In Edda's, there is a poem called Volüspá. In this poem, Odin summons a seer from the dead to question her about the past, present, and future. At the start of their conversation, they talk about the war of the Gods where the Vanir and Aesir battled. Gullveig, meaning intoxicated by gold, is a Goddess who belongs to the Vanir(one of the two major clans of Norse Gods). The Vanir sent her to parlay with the Aesir. the Aesir killed her three times, and each time she was reborn.

Later in Volüspá, Odin and the seer speak about the future and what will happen after Ragnarök, the final battle of the Gods. In the aftermath of Ragnarök, the seer prophesies the only thing the surviving Gods will have left of their possessions are the golden game pieces that they played with at the start of creation.The repeating theme here is that what is made of gold endures for all time.

There is one exception to this rule. In the myth Lokasenna, Loki crashes one of Aegir's parties, mad that he was not invited while the other Gods were. He insults all the attending Gods individually and then swears that Aegir's golden fires will burn out and be destroyed. When a God makes a declaration like this, it has a habit of coming true in myths.

Gold in almost all Nordic poetry is forever, with the notable deviation being the specific gold that is referenced with the kenning *fire of the sea.* Keeping this in mind, it seems like a warning not to put too much trust in wealth because it is not as reliable as it might seem.

The last line, the path of the serpent, is an allusion to the myth of Sigurd. Fafnir, the great dragon Sigurd slays, was not always a dragon. Before the curse of greed, woven into the treasure, hooked his heart and caused him to kill his brother, Fafnir was a dwarf. The corruption of accumulated wealth and hoarding is the path that led Fafnir to become a serpent.

ᚠᛖᚩᚻ·ᛒᚣᚦ·ᚠᚱᚩᚠᚢᚱ·ᚠᛁᚱᚪ·ᚷᛖᚻᚹᚣᛚᚳᚢᛗ·ᛋᚳᛖᚪᛚ·ᛞᛖᚪᚻ·ᛗᚪᚾᚾᚪ
·ᚷᛖᚻᚹᚣᛚᚳ·ᛗᛁᚳᛚᚢᚾ·ᚻᚣᛏ·ᛞᚫᛚᚪᚾ·ᚷᛁᚠ·ᚻᛖ·ᚹᛁᛚᛖ·ᚠᚩᚱ·ᛞᚱᛁᚻᛏᚾᛖ·
ᛞᚩᛗᛖᛋ·ᚻᛚᛖᚩᛏᚪᚾ·

Feoh byþ frofur fira gehwylcum; sceal ðeah manna gehwylc miclun hyt dælan gif he wile for drihtne domes hleotan.

Wealth is a comfort to all men; yet must every man bestow it freely, if he wish to gain honour in the sight of the Lord.

The Anglo-Saxon rune poem is the most positive, and this is logical because the Saxons were not known as ascetics. Although the previous two rune poems warn against hoarding, that does not means owning property is a sin.

Better a house, though a hut it be,
A man is master at home;
His heart is bleeding who needs must beg
When food he fain would have.
- Hávamál 37

Being able to be self-sufficient was seen as a virtue, as reflected in the stanza from *Hávamál* above.

The second and third lines of the Anglo-Saxon rune poem reinforce the warning against miserly behavior. Furthermore, it introduces a second important virtue from Norse culture, Generosity. We will delve deeper into generosity and hospitality in the chapters on Gebo and Mannaz. For now, it is important to know that hospitality and sharing of material gifts were held in high esteem

There is some debate about the Lord's identity in the poem's last line. A common theory is that due to the Christianisation of the poem, the original God's name was replaced by the word Lord, a common epithet for JHWH.

However, Lord could also be a literal translation of Freyr, whose name translates to Lord. Snorri, the author of the Poetic Edda, introduces and describes Freyr as follows.

Freyr is the most renowned of the Æsir; he rules over the rain and the shining of the sun, and therewithal the fruit of the earth; and it is good to call on him for fruitful seasons and peace. He governs also the prosperity of men.

- Gylfaginning 24

While Freyr is more strongly associated with agriculture than with cattle, the fact that he governs the prosperity of men makes him a likely candidate for the lord of this poem. Another clue that Freyr might be the Lord is that his name starts with the Fehu sound, as well as his sister Freya's, who is strongly associated with gold. Freya's name, in turn, means Lady. Therefore the Brother and Sister can represent the two sides of Fehu, successful farming and riches.

Historic use in charms and amulets

The following inscription can be found on a meat cleaver in a woman's grave from the 4th century in Floksand, Norway.

KJ37

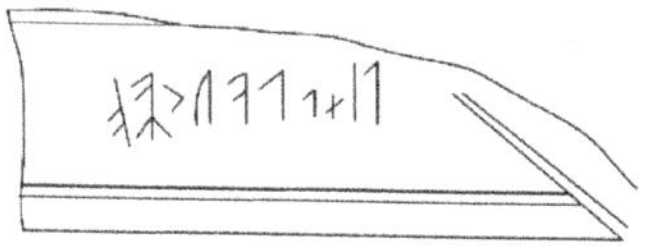

Figure 4: Floksand meatcleaver

ᛚᛁᚾᚨ·ᛚᚨᚢᚲᚨᛉ·ᚠ

Lïna, Laukaz, F(ehu)

Linnen, Leek, Cattle / wealth

(Antonson, 1975)

Linen and leek are two charm words used in many amulets, especially fertility charms. Their meaning will be discussed in the chapter on

Laukaz and the chapter on amulets more thoroughly. For now, it is enough to say that they enhance the magical effect of the amulet. The single Fehu rune then is the core of this amulet, the woman who used this knife hoped to attract wealth to her household.

Another excellent example of the historical use of Fehu for wealth magic is a standing stone found near where the village of Gummarp used to be. The inscription reads:

DR 358

Figure 6: the Gummarp rune stone

Figure 5: the Gummarp rune stone

ᚺᚨ ᚦᚢᚹᚢᛚᚠᚨᛉ·ᛊᚨᛏᛏᛖ
HaþuwulfaR satte
Hathawulf set
(Arntz, 1944)

ᛊᛏᚨᛒᚨ· ᚦᚱᛁᚨ·ᚠᚠᚠ
staba þria fff.
Three staves fff

Here we see a different type of magic using the authority of the runemaster as a source of power instead of charm formulas. The desired effect remains the same, Wealth. Practically this rune stone says: I Hathawulf wrote three runes here Fehu Fehu Fehu. Hathawulf is adding his power or authority to the rune stone by adding his name. The effect that he wanted to achieve was the triple Fehu rune or wealth. Writing a rune repeatedly was a formula on many amulets for focusing attention and increasing its magical potency.

Cultural relevance

In the old days, few people would deal in silver or gold, let alone have a hoard of it.

While there might not seem to be an apparent connection between the words cattle and wealth for us today, it must be remembered that the size of a man's cattle herd was very much a measure of his wealth. Etymologically the link can still be seen, where the word 'fee' refers to an amount of money in English, and the Dutch word 'vee' means cattle.

Like all runes, this rune must be understood in the context of the people who first used it. This was before banks and harsh winters without well-insulated houses or stables. Hoarding great piles of gold and silver was to invite robbers, and the only cattle that would survive a harsh winter were the cattle you could take into your house. Wealth was even more fleeting than it is these days; the more you had, the more difficult it was to keep.

The North had a strong seafaring tradition for trade, fishing, exploration, and raiding, for which they are most known. While their goal was to bring riches back home, they also took the young, strong men and women with them. This left a diminished workforce for caring for the livestock and defending the village.

In this light, it is easy to see the worth of Odin's advice from the *Hávamál*:

A better burden may no man bear
For wanderings wide than wisdom;
It is better than wealth on unknown ways,
And in grief a refuge it gives.
-Hávamál 10

It was better to spend your wealth generously than to hoard it. The man who shares his wealth enjoys it and gains a good reputation in hard times that might be worth more than any gold.

Conclusion

Fehu represents financial strength and all the benefits and pitfalls that come with it. In modern days this has become more dominant than it was in the old North. Because of this, we sometimes forget that financial strength is not the only strength a man can have. Financial stability is a great boon and something we would all like to achieve as long as we realize it is not our only source of worth or our only goal.

In readings: on its own, Fehu represents wealth or financial gain. Depending on its position in the spread or other runes nearby, it might mean wealth in a different sphere, a wealth of knowledge with Ansuz(Odin's rune), or a wealth of friends with Mannaz(humankind rune). If the rune is in an unfavorable position in the reading, it could represent financial loss, but more likely, the path of the serpent, greed.

In advice and counseling: the rune by itself calls for temperance. Take stock of the riches you have, they might be more significant than you think, and guard against greed. It is always worth it to reflect on the treasures in your life, both material and immaterial. Het *Hávamál* says

Among Fitjung's sons saw I well-stocked folds,
Now bear they the beggar's staff;
Wealth is as swift as a winking eye,
Of friends the falsest it is.
- Hávamál 76

In magic and ritual: Fehu is mainly used for wealth and fertility. Used on its own for material wealth or in combination with other runes for wealth in other areaands. The rune can also be used as a symbolic representation of either Freyr or Freya in your ritual or spellwork

Experiencing the runes

There are several ways to experience the ideas of Fehu in our modern lives so that we might get a better understanding of what the rune would have meant in the old world.

Hoard: While studying Fehu, it is also a perfect moment to take stock of your wealth. What are the things you treasure most, and what do you still want? First, start with making a list of all the things you have and treasure. They can be material, like property, money, or nonmaterial, like an education, friends, or a job that gives a lot of satisfaction.

Second, make a list in the same manner of things that you really want, both material and non-material. Put the two lists next to each other and see if there are any things you would like to add or take away after comparing the two. We will use them again in the other experiencing the rune's sections.

Wealth: To truly experience wealth, one has to spend it. Indulge in something more luxurious that you would typically not get for yourself. You can use the list you made as your inspiration. This could be an experience like an extravagant spa day or a high-quality item. Try to take in as much as possible, and use all your senses as if you are experiencing it for the first time. Savor the smells, sights, and feelings. If it is an item, feel the textures and admire the quality. Watch out not to overspend. Know your limits.

Generosity: Riches and wealth are best when shared. While studying this rune, treat your friends or family for an evening or day. This need not be lavish, buy an extra round in the pub, invite people over for dinner, or give a small gift just because.

No great thing needs a man to give,
Oft little will purchase praise;
With half a loaf and a half-filled cup

A friend full fast I made.
- Hávamál 52

Freyr & Freya: The last of these exercises is a dedication to the sibling Gods associated with this rune. Set up a small altar for Freyr and Frey using a Fehu rune as the focus. You can add other appropriate items to the altar. First, start with a Blót to give thanks for the things on your list that you treasure.

Secondly, you could make another offering and ask for something from the list of things you desire that is out of your reach. The Gods don't always work directly but help those that help themselves. Look for opportunities that might open up and act on them.

Thirdly, if you have made an amulet for prosperity or fertility, as described in the chapter on magic, you can ask Freyr and Freya to bless the amulet.

Figure 7: Freya

ᚢ

1.2 Uruz - Primal Ox

Germanic	Gothic	Old English	Old Norse	Sound
Uruz	Urus	Ur	Ur	U

Uruz is the second rune of the first Ætt. It symbolizes the raw power of creation, unbridled and ever-moving. Uruz is a compound word created from the words 'ur' and 'uz.' The prefix 'ur' is still used in Germany and the Dutch 'oer' as the word for primal. The German 'ochse' and the Dutch 'os' are still pronounced similarly as the 'uz' in Uruz, which means 'Ox.' This rune is often understood as referencing the primal cow Auðumbla who played a role in the Norse creation myths.

The rune poems

ᚢᚱ·ᛖᚱ·ᚨᚠ·ᛁᛚᛚᚢ·ᛃᚨᚱᚾᛖ·ᛟᛈᛏ·ᛚᛟᛇᛈᚱ·ᚱᚨᛖᛁᚾᚾ·ᚨ·ᚺᛃᚨᚱᚾᛖ·

Norwegian

Úr er af illu jarne; opt løypr ræinn á hjarne.

Ur Dross comes from bad iron; the reindeer often races over the frozen snow.

Dross is a waste product created during the process of smelting iron ore. The lower the quality of the iron, the more dross will be produced as a by-product. It is worth noting that, etymologically, the word 'ore' is related to the German 'ur' and the Dutch 'oer.' Both have a double meaning, meaning both primal and ore.

In the Icelandic rune poem for Fehu, we saw *fire of the sea* as a kenning for gold; now, we have dross as a kenning for waste. These are kennings or euphemisms that often find their roots in mythology.

Without the Edda's as a frame of reference, the Norwegian and Icelandic rune poems might seem very confusing. Therefore, we will take a quick detour through the edda's to better understand some of the mythological foundations of Uruz.

In the Eddas, there is a poem called Gylfaginning, and in it, Gylfi, the king of the land now called Sweden, finds himself challenged to a test of knowledge. Gylfi hosts ask the king to show his wisdom by asking them questions, and each question concerns Norse cosmology or how the Norse thought the universe fits together. In the following excerpt, Gyli uses the pseudonym Gangleri because he does not trust his hosts.

Gangleri asked: "How were things wrought, ere the races were and the tribes of men increased?"[2]

Then said Hárr: "The streams called Ice-waves, those which were so long come from the fountain-heads that the yeasty venom upon them had hardened like the slag that runs out of the fire,--these then became ice; and when the ice halted and ceased to run, then it froze over above. But the drizzling rain that rose from the venom congealed to rime, and the rime increased, frost over frost, each over the other, even into Ginnungagap, the Yawning Void.[3]*"*

---

[2] The question then is what is the origin of the universe?

[3] *Ginnungagap (yawning void)* is the promethean void that exists between Niffilheim and Muspelheim.

Then spake Jafnhárr: "Ginnungagap, which faced toward the northern quarter, became filled with heaviness, and masses of ice and rime, and from within, drizzling rain and gusts; but the southern part of the Yawning Void was lighted by those sparks and glowing masses which flew out of Múspellheim[4]."

And Thridi said: "Just as cold arose out of Niflheim[5], and all terrible things, so also all that looked toward Múspellheim became hot and glowing; but Ginnungagap was as mild as windless air, and when the breath of heat met the rime, so that it melted and dripped, life was quickened from the yeast-drops, by the power of that which sent the heat, and became a man's form. And that man is named Ymir[6], but the Rime-Jotun call him Aurgelimir;

-Gylfaginning 5

In the Gylfaginning, we see another kenning related to smelting by-products, slag instead of dross. What is interesting is that the word slag is used as a euphemism for a hard layer of frost. The hard layer created by the icy cold, hard enough for a reindeer to run over, Juxtaposes the hard coating formed from the fiery smelting process.

It could be that both lines of the rune poem refer to frost or just poetic license.

The Norwegian poem is a play on words using 'ur' both to refer to the raw materials needed to create iron and the primal moment where fire and earth created the universe.

---

[4] One of the two first worlds in the Norse cosmology that exist in the Ginnungagap *Musphelheim* (world ender) is the world of fire.

[5] One of the two first worlds in the Norse cosmology that exist in the Ginnungagap *Niffelheim* (world of mist) is the world of ice.

[6] Ymir is the forefather of all the Jotun, later he is slain by Odin and his brothers who create the other worlds out of his body.

ᚢᚱ·ᛖᚱ·ᛊᚲᛇᛃᚨ·ᚷᚱᚨᛏᚱ·ᛟᚲ·ᛊᚲᚨᚱᚨ·ᚦᚹᛖᚱᚱᛁᚱ·ᛟᚲ·ᚺᛁᚱᛞᚺᛁᛊ·ᚺᚨᛏᚱ·
ᚢᛗᛒᚱᛖ·ᚹᛁᛊᛁ·

Úr er skýja grátr ok skára þverrir ok hirðis hatr. umbre vísi

Shower lamentation of the clouds and ruin of the hay harvest
and abomination of the shepherd.

The Icelandic rune poem is less mysterious than the Norwegian one. Rain is the lamentation of the clouds. If it rains while the hay is drying, it can ruin the drying hay causing it to rot. A ruined hay harvest makes it so the shepherd cannot feed his flock through the winter, causing them to starve.

The First thing that stands out in this rune poem is that while most of us these days have a negative association with rain, that is unless we are sitting comfortably inside in front of a roaring fireplace, in a farming society, rain is more favorable and would even be prayed for.

What is also remarkable is that this poem does not describe a winter storm. when the rain is so cold, it bites the skin like daggers. The hay harvest takes place in the late spring or early summer. This means that we are talking here about a spring or summer shower. For a farming community, these are incredibly important for the fall harvest. The question is then, why does this poem frame rain in such a negative way? My interpretation is that this poem's purpose is to show that there is a negative side to even a generally positive natural phenomenon. That nature is indifferent and that rain will fall regardless of the effect.

ᚢᚱ᛫ᛒᛇᚦ᛫ᚪᚾᛗᛟᛞ᛫ᛟᚾᛞ᛫ᛟᚠᛖᚱᚻᛇᚱᚾᛖᛞ᛫ᚠᛖᛚᚪᚠᚱᛖᚳᚾᛖ᛫ᛞᛖᛟᚱ᛫ᚠᛖ
ᛟᚻᛏᛖᚦ᛫ᛗᛁᛞ᛫ᚻᛟᚱᚾᚢᛗ᛫ᛗᚪᛖᛖᚱᛖ᛫ᛗᛟᚱᛋᛏᚪᛈᚪ᛫ᚦᚪᛖᛏ᛫ᛁᛋ᛫ᛗᛟᛞᛁᚷ᛫ᚹᚢ
ᚻᛏ᛫

Ur byþ anmod ond oferhyrned, felafrecne deor, feohteþ mid hornum mære morstapa; þæt is modig wuht.

The aurochs is proud and has great horns; it is a very savage beast and fights with its horns; a great ranger of the moors, it is a creature of mettle.

The Anglo-Saxon rune describes the aurochs, a species of giant bovine that went extinct in the early 17th century. For perspective, the average cow weighs roughly 1200lb, but the average aurochs weigh over 3000lb. These behemoths were seen throughout Europe as a symbol of great strength and barbarous untameable nature. In the East of Europe, both drunk men and strong men are sometimes called auroch.

Julius Caesar, in *Gaelic wars,* describes the auroch as follows:

"...those animals which are called uri. These are a little below the elephant in size, and of the appearance, colour, and shape of a bull. Their strength and speed are extraordinary; they spare neither man nor wild beast which they have espied. These the Germans take with much pains in pits and kill them. The young men harden themselves with this exercise, and practice themselves in this sort of hunting, and those who have slain the greatest number of them, having produced the horns in public, to serve as evidence, receive great praise. But not even when taken very young can they be rendered familiar to men and tamed. The size, shape, and appearance of their horns differ much from the horns of our oxen. These they anxiously seek.

after, and bind at the tips with silver, and use as cups at their most sumptuous entertainments."

- Gaelic Wars Chapter 6.28

For the Nordic people killing an auroch single-handedly was a symbol of strength. The horns were kept as a token of a successful hunt and were often prized possessions. This is reflected in the rune poem; the first and the second lines talk about the quality of auroch horns. A proud, savage, and brave creature indeed.

Historic use in charms and amulets

There are no surviving examples of the Uruz rune used in an amulet or a spell. The auroch itself seems to have been at the center of ritual since prehistoric times. However, we only have a tiny fragment of spells and amulets. This means it is historically likely that Uruz was used in charms or amulets that we have yet to uncover.

The aurochs are well represented in cave paintings, and in many cases, their bones were found with clear signs of ritual use, dating as far back as 4000BC.

Figure 8: Cave painting of an Auroch (caves of Lascaux)

Cultural relevance

The stanza of Gylfaginning, which we discussed earlier in this chapter, describes the first moment of creation. Unlike the conscious creation ex nihilo[7] of the Abrahamic religions, the Nordic universe is not empty at the dawn of creation. Two opposing forces already exist in the universe, Niflheim: the realm of cold, Muspelheim: the realm of heat, and between these two lies the Ginnungagap: the Great Void.

From Nifelheim flows a never-ending stream of ice and snow and from Muspelheim flows a never-ending stream of lava and fire. The crucible where these two meet is the Ginnungagap, and creation blooms from the clash of these two opposing forces.

The idea that the world does not originate out of the plans of a perfect divine being but from spontaneous opposing forces implies a less restrained worldview. If creation fits together like a clock, every gear perfectly in place, there is little room for change. In such a universe, customs, rituals, and your place in society are divinely decreed without the possibility of improvement.

A worldview that does not include a fixed, perfect design leaves more room to be changed for the better and personal responsibility. Although, it doesn't bring the security that the belief in a divine plan can give.

Then said Gangleri: "Where dwelt Ymir, or wherein did he find sustenance?" Hárr answered: "Straightway after the rime dripped, there sprang from it the cow called Auðumbla a; four streams of milk ran from her udders, and she nourished Ymir." Then asked Gangleri: "Wherewithal was the cow nourished?" And Hárr made answer:

---

[7] Ex nihilio means out of nothing, in the Norse mythology there are the world of fire and ice.

"She licked the ice-blocks, which were salty; and the first day that she licked the blocks, there came forth from the blocks in the evening a man's hair; the second day, a man's head; the third day the whole man was there.

He is named Búri: he was fair of feature, great and mighty. He begat a son called Borr, who wedded the woman named Bestla, daughter of Bölthorn the giant; and they had three sons: one was Odin, the second Vili, the third Vé. And this is my belief, that he, Odin, with his brothers, must be ruler of heaven and earth; we hold that he must be so called; so is that man called whom we know to be mightiest and most worthy of honor, and ye do well to let him be so called."
-Gylfaginning 4

The stanza above describes Ymir coming into being. Ymir is the first of all the Jötun; he and his kin represent destructive chaos. In this stanza, Auðumbla[8], the first cow, comes into being and from her udders flows a never-ending stream of milk that sustains Ymir. She licks the ice of Niflheim, releasing Búri, Odin's grandfather. In this way, the Gods and the Jötun owe their existence to Auðumbla.

Conclusion

Uruz represents uncontrolled energy. Auðumbla sustained the Jötun (trolls) and the Gods(the forces of chaos and order in the Nordic pantheon) with her milk. It was not a conscious decision to feed them, but the four rivers of milk flow from her regardless. She did not free Búri because she was trying to create a God but because she wanted the salty ice for her sustenance.

Like the auroch, the energy of this rune is great but untameable. It is a force of unbridled strength and creation, neither good nor evil.

---

[8] Meaning "Hornless cow rich in milk".

In readings: this rune on its own represents that untameable energy. In questions about work or a new project it might mean that the enthusiasm and the energy are there, but they are unfocused.

Combined with other runes, it shows what are energies flowing uncontrollably strong. In combination with Pertho (luck rune), for instance, it might suggest a gambling problem. Combined with Yera (year rune) it might indicate incredibly potent returns for what you have sown. Combined with Mannaz (humankind rune), it might mean a strong person who is out of control.

In advice and counseling: this rune represents a powerful flow of energy that is easy to get swept up in, getting lost in your work, or bursting with motivation. While the abundance of energy is very positive, you have to take care to control of it, or it will control you. Conquer your inner auroch.

In magic and ritual: this rune can be used in combination with other runes or in a bind rune to increase energy and add from the well of raw creation to your spell. It can be used in amulets or spells to help promote a new start or as a focus for meditation when trying to tap into the primal source.

Experiencing the runes

Drizzle: Uruz represents the natural forces beyond the control of humanity. Those forces are needed for our survival but are indifferent to it. To experience those forces, I invite you to go outside in a summer rainstorm and feel yourself get soaked. Try to comprehend the incredible phenomenon of water pouring from the sky.

Ginnungagap: what we do with our life is of our own making, but the circumstances that influence our lives are sometimes out of our control. Make a list of those forces influencing your life over which you have little or no control. How many of these forces are necessary for you in your life?

Horns of the aurochs: pick a physical goal you have been thinking about and conquer it. This could be a long-distance walk, climbing a mountain, or setting an exercise goal and keeping to it. Make sure that your goal is realistic but challenging and has a clear start and finish. Once you complete your goal share your success on social media, like showing off your hard-fought horns.

Figure 9: Auðumbla licking Búri free from the ice, four rivers of milk flowing from her uthers.

ᚦ

1.3 Thurizas - Troll

Germanic	Gothic	Old English	Old Norse	Sound
Thurisaz	Thiuth	Thors	Thurs	Th

Thurisaz is the third rune of the first Ætt. Depending on the region, this rune can mean Troll or Thorn, two seemingly very different concepts. In both cases, this is a rune of obstacles and opposition. This is also the first rune on the list that does not have a phonetic equivalent in the western alphabet. Instead, it represents the 'Th' sound pronounced like the start of Thorn. This rune is often used as part of curses, both historically and in the sagas.

The rune poems

ᚦᚢᚱᛋ·ᚡᚨᛖᛚᛞᚱ·ᚲᚡᛁᚾᚾᚨ·ᚲᚡᛁᛚᛚᚢ·ᚲᚨᛏᚱ·ᚡᚨᛖᚱᛞᚺᚱ·ᚡᚨᚱ·ᚨᚡ·ᛁᛚᛚᚢ·

Norwegian

Þurs vældr kvinna kvillu kátr værðr fár af illu.

Thurs giant causes anguish to women; Misfortune makes few men cheerful.

The second line of this Rune is easily explained if you understand the role of Thurs in Norse mythology.

Both the word Jötun and the word Thur are used interchangeably to describe various creatures in the sagas. For example, they often refer to Trolls, Orges, Etinns, and Giant. The word giant brings to mind towering monsters, but in the sagas, they are mostly the same size as the humans or Gods. Fenrir, the world serpent, and a whole host of other monsters and spirits also fall under the category Jötun and Thurs.

Etymologically, the term 'Jötun' is related to the old English 'eoten,' the origin of both the modern English 'eat' and 'ettin'; you can hear this clearly in the English eaten and the Dutch eten meaning; 'to eat.' 'Thurs,' on the other hand, is related to the English 'thirst' and is the origin of the word 'troll.'

From this, we can see the general role that the Jötun play in Norse mythology. The flames of the eldjötnar[9] will consume the world tree at the end of days. The Fenrir wolf will devour Odin. Skoll and Hati[10] will eat the moon and the sun, so all things will end.

In the stories where both humans and Jötun appear, the Jötun are always antagonistic. They are not only the monsters of myth but also held accountable for natural disasters, sickness, and other hardships. For instance, the nine daughters of Aegir swallow sailors into the sea like the sirens of Greek mythology. The following healing charm was found in a scribbled in the margin of a manuscript in England from 1073 AD. In it is a clear example of an Ogre that was held responsible for the infection of wounds.

---

9 Name for the Fire Giants.

10 Two giants wolves, their names mean "one that mocks" and "one that hates".

ᚷᛇᚱᛁᛚ·ᛋᚨᚱᛞᚺᚠᚨᚱᚨ·ᚠᚨᚱ·ᚦᚢ·ᚾᚢ·ᚠᚢᚾᛞᛁᚾᚾ·ᛖᛋ·ᛏᚢ·ᚦᛟᚱᚱ·ᚠᛁ̄ᚷᛁ·ᚦᛁᚲ··
ᚦᚢᚱᛋᚨ·ᛞᚱᛟᛏᛏᛁᚾᚾ·ᚷᛇᚱᛁᛚ·ᛋᚨᚱᛞᚺᚠᚨᚱᚨ·ᚠᛁᛞᚺᚱ·ᚨᛖᛞᚺᚱᚨᚠᚨᚱᛁ

Gyril sārðvara, far þū nū! Fundinn es-tū. Þōrr vīgi þik, þursa drōttinn! Gyril sārðvara. Viðr æðravari

Gyril[11] *wound-causer, go now! You are found. May Thor bless you, lord of Thurs! Gyril wound-causer. Against bloodvessel pus* (Macleod & Bernard, 2006).

The blessing of Thor here might be interpreted as a swift blow to the back of the skull with Mjolnir[12]. Thor and the Jötun have a strong connection which we will explore further in the following rune poem.

Therefore, "Misfortune that makes few men cheerful" is almost certainly the baleful influence of trolls and giants.

The first line is a bit more elusive, especially since we will see it echoed in the Icelandic rune poem. The poem then references the anguish brought to women by giants. Giants can bring misery to women and men, beasts and Gods, so why are women singled out? There are three possible answers.

Firstly, the Thurs rune was famously used in a curse by Skirnir[13] to force Gerd[14] to marry Freyr. Therefore, it is plausible that this rune had a special connection to curses aimed at blackmailing women into marriage.

[11] The name of the wound causing troll

[12] Thor's magical hammer

[13] the messenger of Freyr,

[14] a giant maiden of great beauty

Secondly, the giants made several attempts to coerce Freya, the most beautiful of the Gods, into marrying one of them.

In Gylfaginning 42, it is told that a giant offered to build a wall around Asgard[15] that would make it impenetrable to enemy forces in exchange for Freya. The Gods impose a time limit for construction. Thanks to some trickery from Loki, the giant misses the deadline and gets a blessing to the skull from Thor.

In Þrymskviða,[16] the Jötun steal Thor's hammer and will only give it back in exchange for Freya's hand in marriage. Freya refuses, leading to Thor dressing up as Freya, marrying the Giant, and then as soon as he recovers his hammer, giving every giant a blessing on the skull. Jötun stealing women seems to be a recurring theme

Figure 10: Thor getting dressed up as a bride

Thirdly, Unexplained medical problems often were attributed to Jötun. It is plausible that the cramps and discomforts of menstruation were seen as the work of Jötun. Men did not suffer these discomforts; therefore, women would be prone to attack by Jötun.

While these are all possible explanations, there is not enough evidence for any of them to be definitive.

---

[15] The realm of the Gods

[16] One of the most popular poems from the Edda's

ᚦᚢᚱᛊ·ᛖᚱ·ᚲᚹᛖᚾᚾᚨ·ᚲᚹᛟᛚ·ᛟᚲ·ᚲᛚᛖᛏᛏᚨ·ᛒᚢᛁ·ᛟᚲ·ᚹᚨᚱᛞᚱᚢᚾᚨᚱ·ᚹᛖ
ᚱᚱ· ᛊᚨᛏᚢᚱᚾᚢᛊ·ᚦᛖᚾᚷᛁᛚᛚ·

Þurs er kvenna kvöl ok kletta búi ok varðrúnar verr. Saturnus þengill.

Thurs - Giant torture of women and cliff-dweller and husband of a giantess.

The Icelandic poem's first line resembles the Norwegian poem's first line. It shows us that the Jötun's role as a torturer of women was very significant, making the mystery of its true meaning even greater.

The second line is based on the description of Jötun in Skaldic poetry. Any character that lives in a cave or among rocks is almost certainly a Jötun. This indicates the strong connection between Jötun and the earth.

When this world came into being, the first living thing was the Jötun Ymir. When Odin and his brothers Vili and Ve killed Ymir, they created the earth from his flesh, the trees from his hair, the clouds from his brains, and the mountains from his bones. The foundation from which the physical world was created is a Jötun given shape by the Gods. Further strengthening the connection between Jötun and the earth.

In other Sagas, Jörð, the mother of Thor, is referred to as the personification of the earth. She is a Jötun and is a mistress of Odin, Thor's father. Jörð translates to earth in old Norse. She is the personification of mother earth and is responsible for the growth of plants and trees.

These stories also illustrate that the line between Jötun and God is thin. Some Gods even have Jötun spouses, and others have Jötun ancestors. Mimir and Loki[17] are full-blood Jötun.

If it were not for the poem's explicit references to the jötun, the third line, Husband of a giantess, could refer to several of the Gods.

The relationship between the Gods and Jötun is a very complicated one. In most myths, the Jötun are the antagonists, only there to be outwitted or bested by the Gods. In these myths, the Jötun are dangerous enemies, equal in both wit and strength. In contrast to this hostility, the Gods are in some sagas welcomed at Jötun banquets.

The most precise distinction that can be made between the Jötun and Gods is that generally, the Gods represent order as well as creation, whereas the Jötun represent chaos and destruction.

ᛞᛟᚱᚾ·ᛒᛇᚦᛞᚻᛖᚨᚱᛚᛖ·ᛋᚳᛖᚨᚱᛈ·ᛞᚻᛖᚷᚾᚨ·ᚷᛖᚻᚹᛇᛚᚳᚢᛗ·ᚨᚾᚠᛖᚾᚷ
·ᛇᛋ·ᛇᚠᛇᛚ·ᚢᚾᚷᛖᛗᛖᛏᚢᛗ·ᚱᛖᚦᛖ·ᛗᚨᚾᚾᚨ·ᚷᛖᚻᚹᛖᛚᚳᚢᛗ·ᛞᚻᛖ·ᚻᛁᛗ·
ᛗᛁᛞ·ᚱᛖᛋᛏᛖᛞᚻ·

Đorn byþ ðearle scearp; ðegna gehwylcum anfeng ys yfyl,
ungemetum reþe manna gehwelcum, ðe him mid resteð.

The thorn is exceedingly sharp, an evil thing for any thane to grasp, uncommonly severe on all who sit among them.

The poem above interprets Thurisaz as a thorn and not as a troll. These two concepts might seem far removed, but some pertinent connections exist. For instance, one of the grandfathers of Odin, a Jötun, was called Bölþorn or evil thorn.

---

[17] Mimir is a Aesir of Jotun desent associated with wisdom Loki is a Jotun who becomes a blood brother of Odin and so he becomes a Aesir.

Also, there is a condition called elf-shot, referenced in Anglo-Saxon medical texts, and was believed to be caused by nature spirits shooting a tiny cursed needle into its victim. Sometimes this needle was made from a thorn of a plant. This idea is very similar to the idea that Jötun cause all diseases, as mentioned earlier.

A spell appears in several sagas called Sventhorn or sleeping thorn. As the name suggests, the purpose of this spell is to put people to sleep.

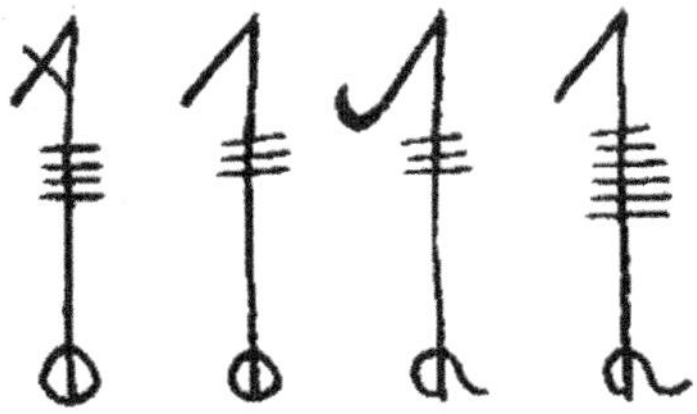

Figure 11: the Sventhorn

The method of casting a Sventhorn is described differently in different sources. In Gongu-Hrolf's Saga, a cursed thorn is physically pricked into Hrolf, and it is not until the thorn is dislodged that he is awakened.

Here we can see the similarities to sleeping beauty, pricking herself and falling asleep connected with the wall of thorns. It is also in line with the use of Thurisaz as a Curse rune, as seen in the historical use.

The poem itself is pretty straightforward. A Thorn is very sharp, but it cuts only those who try to grasp it.

Historic use in charms and amulets

One famous use of Thurisaz is from Skirnir[18], who Freyr sent to fetch the Jötun Gerd to be his bride. At first, Skirnir promises riches, but this fails, then he threatens with violence and disgrace, but this does not

---

[18] A servant of the God Freyr.

sway her either. Finally, he revealed to have cut three Thurisaz runes in the bark of a tree. These runes are part of a curse that would make Gerd's life a living hell, but if she agrees to marry Freyr, he will remove the runes. After hearing this, Gerd breaks down and promises to give her love to Freyr.

A copper disk found near Sigtuna in Sweden dating from the twelfth century bears a similar curse with the following inscription.

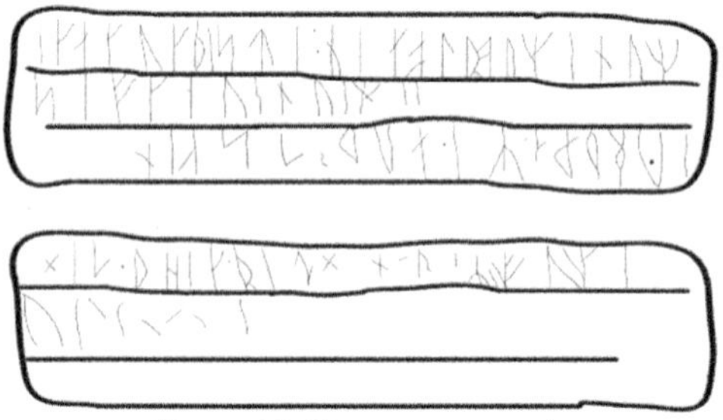

Figure 12: Sigtuna copper plate

U Fv1933;134

ᛁᚲ᛫ᚨᚲ᛫ᚢᚲ᛫ᚱᛁᛊ᛫ᚦᚢ᛫ᛁ᛫ᚠᛖᚷ᛫ᚢᚾᛞᛁᚱ᛫ᛏᚢᚾᚷᛚᚢᚾᚢᛗ᛫ᛊᛁᚠᚷᛖᚠᚾᚢ
ᛗ᛫ᛟᚱ᛫ᚦᚨᛏ᛫ᚨᚾᚷᛁ᛫ᛖᛇᛞᚢ᛫ᚦᚨᛏ᛫ᛊᚲᛁᚾ᛫ᛖᚲ᛫ᚦ᛫ᛊᛖᚷ᛫ᚦᚱᛁᚢ᛫ᚾᚨᚢ
ᛞᚺᚱ᛫ᚾᛁᚢ᛫ᚠᛁᚢᚱᚱ᛫ᚾᚨᚾ᛫ᚲ

Ik ak uk. Ris þū ī veg undir tunglunum, sifgefnum! Ør þat angi! Eyð þat skīn! Ek þ seg þriu, Nauðr nīu. Vīurr nān 'k

The text roughly translates to:
'leave under these evil stars, get confused in the mist, your light be destroyed.

I speak three Thurs (Thurisaz) and nine needs (Naudiz), Ansuz(a single rune representing Odin) Lord of the sanctuary I call on you (Samnordic Rune Text database, 1993).'

The combination of a repeating Ansuz rune followed by a repeating Naudiz rune ending with runes depicting the desired effect is found on many rune charms. In this case, the desired result is three times Thurisaz, which is always a curse. We will delve deeper into runic amulets in the chapters on rune magic.

Cultural relevance

The Jötun are not so much evil in the sense that the demons of the Abrahamic religions are evil, but it is more accurate to say they are uncaring. In the best cases, their thoughts and desires and thoughts run parallel to those of humankind; in the worst cases, they run contrary to humanity's best interests.

The Jötun represent a force of nature in its rawest form. For example, Jörð makes the plants and trees grow; this helps humanity but is not done for their benefit. A city is a small tamed piece of the earth; the moment we stop maintaining these such places, the wild will creep back in and, over time, swallow them. The forces of nature do not act out of malice but with simple disregard for humanity; this indifference is echoed by the Jötun when they cause earthquakes, floods, storms, and other natural disasters.

No absolute distinction can be made between the Gods and Jötunar other than the name. The same is true for Alfar[19] and Landvættir[20] compared to the Jötun. Not only did the Northerners make offerings to the Gods but also to the beings who controlled nature.

Even though the Jötun are naturally ambivalent to humanity, they are powerful, and it does not hurt to make an offering to those forces.

---

[19] Elves

[20] Land spirits

Conclusion

Where Uruz is an unlimited force of creation, Thurisaz is one of destruction. In some rune books, this rune is described as a rune of Thor and is therefore associated with protection. However, historically there does not seem to be any link between this rune and Thor or protection. The only possible exception is that the first rune of Thor's name is Thurisaz. It is a rune used to curse one's enemies, of uncaring giants leaving only destruction and misery in their wake, and it is a rune of thorns that rend the flesh.

In readings: this rune represents opposition. On its own, it can represent many different obstacles. It is important to note that these obstacles are outside forces like the Jötun are to humankind. Although these forces might not be deliberate in design, it is essential to analyze their effect. Sometimes it is easier to find a new path and go with the flow than to rage against the storm. Thurisaz's position in a reading could shed light on where the obstacle will come from. For instance, paired with Tiwaz (justice rune), it could be legal problems, or when paired with Isa (ice rune), it could indicate that your obstacle will remain frozen for a while.

In advice and counseling: this rune represents the obstacles in your life. The *Hávamál* says:

The lame rides a horse, / the handless is herdsman,
The deaf in battle is bold;
The blind man is better / than one that is burned,
No good can come of a corpse.
-Hávamál 71

This poem illustrates that: Whatever your situation, you can find a way forward as long as you are not dead. Everyone has obstacles that define their life, some of which are out of our control. Life's challenges are unfair, but we must take responsibility for what we can control and try to improve our situation. Life owes us nothing; look at your obstacles and try to understand them. Find the best way to play the hand you are dealt.

In magic and ritual: this rune is used in curses and curse amulets, usually in threes or multiples of three. Potentially, this rune could be used in ceremonies to represent the Jötunar. However, Before doing a ritual involving the Jötunar, think hard about why you want to draw the attention of such powerful uncaring forces.

Experiencing the runes

Releasing the thorn: A thorn is an evil thing for any thane to grasp. Sometimes the trouble in our life is the trouble we create for ourselves.

Make a list of five things that give you the most stress. For each one, write the root of the obstacle next to it. Decide whether or not each obstacle is worth the effort or stress of fighting against. Maybe there is a way around to the goal, or it is not worth the price you have to pay.

Slaying the giant: Some Giants cannot be avoided. Pick one of the obstacles on your list that cannot be ignored. Make a plan on how you are going to overcome this obstacle. List the options that you have and strengths that you can use.

Figure 13:The jötun Hyrrokkin riding on a wolf with vipers as reins

Jotunheim: Visit a wild place, go off the beaten find a good spot. Leave a small offering of fruit or honey for the Landvættir. Sit quietly for a while and see what you experience.

ᚨ

1.4 Ansuz - Odin

Germanic	Gothic	Old English	Old Norse	Sound
Ansuz	Ansuz	Ós	Áss	A

Ansuz is the fourth rune of the first Ætt and directly ties to one of the Norse Gods. Ansuz represents Odin, the father of the runes. This is also the rune of the Aesir, the clan of Gods of which Odin is chieftain. Odin is a God with many faces, and throughout the sagas, he is referred to by over 200 different names and titles, each representing another aspect of the All-father. This rune is focused on Odin's wisdom, leadership, and eloquence.

The rune poems

Norwegian

ᛟᛋᛋ᛫ᛖᚱ᛫ᚠᛚᚨᛖᛋᛏᚱᚨ᛫ᚠᚨᛖᚱᛞᚺᚨ᛫ᚠǫᚱ᛫ᛖᚾ᛫ᛋᚲᚨᛚᛈᚱ᛫ᛖᚱ᛫ᛋᚠᚨᛖᚱᛞᚺᚨ᛫

Óss er flæstra færða fǫr; en skalpr er sværða.

river mouth is the way of most journeys; but a scabbard of swords.

The river mouth is where the river flows into the sea, and this may be literal, but it may also be a metaphor describing speech or storytelling. The river mouth is a part of many journeys for the seafaring Norsemen; as we shall discover in the Anglo-Saxon poem, this rune is also interpreted as just 'mouth.' Boastful tales of high adventure are found at the end of most journeys and are the inspiration for journeys yet to begin.

The second line describes the river mouth as '*a scabbard of swords*'. While telling stories and making boasts might be the way to adventure, a good orator can also soothe rising tempers. Diplomacy might sometimes avert war, and a good moderator can keep swords in their scabbards when emotions run high.

Odin, the undisputed leader of the Aesir, is not necessarily the strongest warrior among the Gods; that honor is reserved for Thor. In Skáldskaparmál,[21] Odin challenges the giant Hrungnir to a horse race, and Odin wins, but as a result, the giant enters Asgard[22]. The rules of hospitality forbid the Gods from killing the giant, who is making a nuisance of himself. Instead, Odin has Thor challenge Hrungnir, known as the mightiest Jötun. After a short but intense battle, Hrungnir receives Thor's blessing to the skull. When the Gods resort to violence, they always send Thor as their champion.

Odin is the God of wisdom and strategy, and his victories are usually won without weapons. In most of Odin's adventures, he outsmarts his opponents or tricks them. That swords remain in the scabbard does not mean there is only peace! Many a battle is won or lost before the first sword is unsheathed.

---

[21] A poem from the Prose Eddas where Bragi and Ægir discus Norse mythology.

[22] Literally translates to the garden of the Gods, here the Aesir have their halls.

The *Hávamál* has several sayings, warning to watch your words

A man shall not boast / of his keenness of mind,
But keep it close in his breast;
To the silent and wise / does ill come seldom
When he goes as guest to a house;

The knowing guest / who goes to the feast,
In silent attention sits;
With his ears he hears, / with his eyes he watches,
Thus wary are wise men all.
-Hávamál 6-7

ᛟᛊᛊ·ᛖᚱ·ᚨᛚᚷᛁᚾᚷᚨᚢᛏᚱ·ᛟᚲ·ᚨᛊᚷᚨᚱᛞᛊ·ᛃᛟᚠᚢᚱᚱ·ᛟᚲ·ᚠᚨᛚᚺᚨᛚᛚᚨ
ᚱ·ᚠᛁᛊᛁ·ᛃᚢᛈᛁᛏᛖᚱ·ᛟᛞᛞᚠᛁᛏᛁ·

Óss er algingautr ok ásgarðs jöfurr, ok valhallar vísi. Jupiter oddviti.

God Aged Gautr and chieftan of Ásgardr and lord of
Vallhalla.

In the Icelandic poem, all three lines are kennings for Odin. Gautr is one of the many names of Odin used in the sagas and roughly translates to shaper or originator. Sometimes Gautr is only part of his name; for example, in Balders Draumar, Odin is called Aldagautr[23]. Gautr is also the origin of the name of the Geats, a Germanic tribe from the 12th and 13th centuries.

The line 'chieftain of Ásgard' shows Odin in his role as the ruler of the Aesir, the most prominent of Gods. Nordic cosmology is divided into nine realms, each connected by Yggdrasil, the world tree. The Aesir live in the realm of Asgard, at the top of the world tree. Asgard is a

---

[23] Shaper of men, a name he earned as creator of mankind.

compound word built from the word 'Áss' or God, and 'gard' meaning garden.

Ásgard is a vast realm, and just like Midgard, the middle garden where humanity resides it is split up into different domains. In the realm of Iðavöllr[24] lies the province of Glaðsheimr[25]. Glaðsheimr houses Valhalla and the 13 high seats where the most important Gods hold council. Valhalla is a compound word built from 'val' and 'halla,' which translates to 'the hall of the fallen.' It is a magnificent hall of mind-boggling proportions; the roof is made of golden shields, the rafters of mighty spears, and the walls are gleaming white. Valhalla has 540 doors, each wide enough for 800 men to leave simultaneously. Within Valhalla is Thor's hall Bilskirnir and it has 540 rooms.

Half of the people who die noble deaths are picked by Freya and taken to Fólkvangr. Odin chooses the other half to reside in Valhalla. These are the Einherjar[26], the warriors who died gloriously in battle.

On top of Valhalla stands the goat Heiðrún who gives no milk but instead the best mead in the world, enough for all the Einherjer. In the hall lives the Giant Boar Sæhrímnir, who is each day slaughtered, eaten, and then reborn the next day.

In the saga GylfaginningIn, Gangleri says:

"You say that all men who have fallen in battle from the beginning of the world are now with Odin in Valhalla. With what does he feed them? I should think the crowd there is large." High responds that this is indeed true, that a huge amount are already in Valhalla, but yet this amount will seem to be too few when "the wolf comes."

-GylfaginningIn 38

---

[24] The splendid plains.

[25] The bright homes.

[26] Those that fight alone or one man army.

Every day the Einherjer train and duel, those that die during the harsh training are reborn again the next day. The Einherjer serve as Odin's elite army and will fight at his side during the events of Ragnarök[27].

ᛟᛋ·ᛒᛇᚦ·ᛟᚱᛞᚠᚱᚢᛗᚪ·ᚫᛖᛚᛖᚱᛖ·ᛋᛈᚱᚫᛖᚳᛖ·ᚹᛁᛋᛞᛟᛗᛋ·ᚹᚱᚪᚦᚢ·ᛟᚾᛞ·
ᚹᛁᛏᛖᚾᚪ·ᚠᚱᛟᚠᚢᚱ·ᚪᚾᛞ·ᛖᛟᚱᛚᚪ·ᚷᛖᚻᚹᚪᛗ·ᛖᚪᛞᚾᛇᛋ·ᛟᚾᛞ·ᛏᛟᚻᛁᚻᛏ·

Os byþ ordfruma ælere spræce, wisdomes wraþu ond witena
frofur and eorla gehwam eadnys ond tohiht.

The mouth is the source of all language, a pillar of wisdom and a comfort to wise men, a blessing and a joy to every thane.

The first line of the Anglo-Saxon rune poem reads: 'The mouth is the source of all language' The connection between language and Odin is strong. In the Ynglinga saga, Snorri observes that Odin only speaks in verse, accentuating the All-father's complete control of language.

In the saga Skáldskaparmál, a story is told of how Odin stole the skáldskapar mjaðar[28] from the Jötun Suttungr through trickery. The skáldskapar mjaðar was made from the blood of the God KvÆsir, who was so wise he could answer all questions. KvÆsir[29] was murdered by the dwarfs Fjalar and Galar, who mixed his blood with honey to make the skáldskapar mjaðar.

After committing a string of murders, the dwarfs were caught by Suttungr, and they were forced to give him the skáldskapar mjaðar as compensation. Whoever drinks the mead is said to become either a Poet

---

[27] The end of the world.

[28] The mead of poetry.

[29] This name might be a pun based on the Proto-Germanic kvass meaning to squeeze [juice out] and Aesir. Making him the squeezed god.

or a scholar. Odin, of course, has had his fill of the mead. He bestows it on humanity, giving them the gift of poetry and wisdom.

The mouth might be the source of all language, but it is not the only way language is used. In the *Hávamál*, Odin tells of how he hung himself from Yggdrasil for nine days and nine nights. In that time, he did not eat or drink and pierced himself with Gungir[30]. In this way, he made an offering of himself to himself. After the ninth day, he gained the runes. With this sacrifice, Odin brought the written alphabet into the world. One of Odin's many names is Rúnatýr, or God of Runes. Nordic philosophy states a gift demands a gift; this will be discussed later in the chapter on Gebo. The high price that Odin had to pay to gain the runes shows their worth.

The relationship between speech and the comfort of Wiseman, as expressed in the second line of the Anglo-Saxon poem a more complicated equation. Wisdom could be measured through skill in speech, and there are many examples in the sagas where people play riddle games, sometimes with life or death stakes.

The *Hávamál* says:

Though glad at home, / and merry with guests,
A man shall be wary and wise;
The sage and shrewd, / wide wisdom seeking,
Must see that his speech be fair;
A fool is he named / who nought can say,
For such is the way of the witless.
-Hávamál 103

This stanza implies that speaking well, not too much or too little, is the wise man's hallmark. However, a person who cannot contribute to the conversation is considered a fool.

---

[30] Odin's magic spear, that never misses.

The *Hávamál* also warns that no one likes a smartass and that it is often wiser to hold your tongue than to boast, as explained in the following stanza

A man shall not boast / of his keenness of mind,
But keep it close in his breast;
To the silent and wise / does ill come seldom
When he goes as guest to a house;
-Hávamál 6

The last line of the Anglo-Saxon poem speaks of the blessing and joy of language for Thanes. A Thane is a freeman but not a ruler; the word means servant. For Thanes, the gift of a story or wise counsel from his more educated superiors is cause for joy. It is important to remember that this refers to speech, wisdom, and advice that the spoken word can deliver. Wisdom for the ruling class could be a heavier burden to carry. Odin is the wisest of Gods, and he gained his wisdom through great sacrifice. He drank from the mead of poetry, gained the runes, and gave one of his eyes to achieve a single sip from the well of Mimir, granting him even greater wisdom.

However, this wisdom comes at a cost; Odin knows Ragnarök is coming and knows his ultimate fate during those dark days. With this in mind, Odin's advice in the *Hávamál* is as follows.

A measure of wisdom / each man shall have,
But never too much let him know;
For the wise man's heart / is seldom happy,
If wisdom too great he has won.
-Hávamál 55

Historic use in charms and amulets

Many formulaic rune charms contain the word 'alu,' commonly translated as dedicated or blessed. Figure 8 below is a charm found in Lindholmen, Denmark, that uses the Alu charm word.

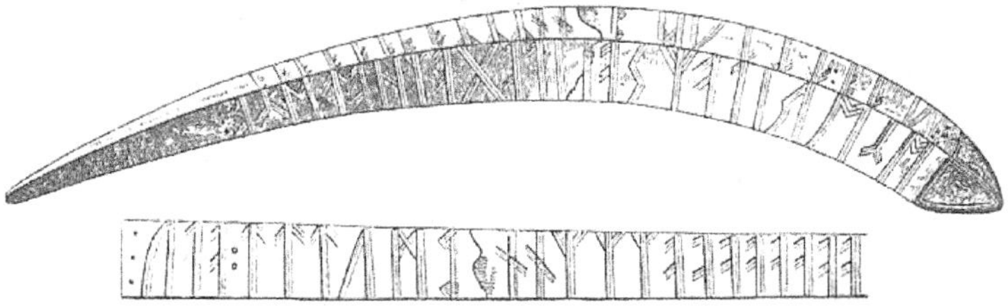

DR261

Figure 14: drawing of the Lindholm amulet

ᛖᚲ᛫ᛖᚱᛁᛚᚨᛉ᛫ᛊᚨᚹᛁᛚᚨᚷᚨᛉ᛫ᚺᚨᛏᛖᚲᚨ᛫
ᚨᚨᚨᚨᚨᚨᚨᚨᛉᛉᛉᚾᚾᚾ᛫ᛒᛗᚢᛏᛏᛏ᛫ᚨᛚᚢ

Ek Erilaz Sawilagaz hateka aaaaaaaazzznnn bmuttt alu

The first line translates to:

"I the Erilaz, I am called Sawilagaz"[31].

The second line is more formulaic and has the word alu at the end. The rune charm in the chapter about Thurisaz contained the line: " I speak three Thurs (Thurisaz) and nine needs (Naudiz), Ansuz(a single rune representing Odin) (Flowers, 2006).'

[31] Sawilagaz means "the sunny" one or "the willy one".

The figure above shows a similar structure, but this time is written in individual runes: eight Ansuz runes, three Alghiz runes, and three Naudiz runes.

The eight Ansuz runes call upon the Gods, Odin lord of the runes specifically. The three Naudiz runes represent fate, binding the desired effect into destiny. Algiz is a rune of protection; this way, the three Algiz signify that the goal of this charm was protection for Sawaligaz.

My opinion is that 'alu' function in the same way as the Ansuz rune. Both are used to draw the Gods' attention and give the charm power. In this, we can see the power of the Ansuz rune as a representation of a link to the Aesir in general and Odin specifically.

Figure 15: Odin

Cultural relevance

In later Christian sources, the Vikings are commonly depicted as bloodthirsty barbarians respecting only strength. But the role of Odin shows us that the virtues of eloquence and wisdom were highly regarded. It is interesting to note that not Thor, the strongest of warriors, or Tyr, the brave lord of justice but Odin, the poet, the sage, and the mystic is the supreme deity.

Drinking the mead of poetry would make you a sage or a skald[32]. In modern days most people think of a poet as a person who can make art with words, but for the Vikings, a skald was even more. Poets were the ones that remembered the stories and songs and kept history alive. They composed new events into songs so that they could be spread amongst the kingdom.

Vikings believed that speaking the right words in the right way could change the past, the present, and the future. Words, both spoken and written, are not only vessels to contain the truth, but they shape the truth. Many runic amulets are nothing more than "Name says that this will happen" complemented with the correct symbols or written in the proper formulaic structure.

One of the two most common forms of magic practiced in the North was Galdr, literally translated to chanting; it was seen as a higher form of magic. The lesser form of magic was called Seidr and was more akin to shamanistic magic. Whereas, in the Abrahamic religions, we see the "let there be light," and there was light; in Nordic magic, it is more akin to "There is light," and there is light. If written and spoken runes form the basis for reality, then it is not hard to understand why Odin, the lord of both the runes and poetry, is the All-Father.

---

[32] A skald is a poet or bard

Conclusion

Ansuz is a rune of Odin, language, and wisdom. Therefore, it is in some ways, the rune representing all runes. Similar to Odin Himself, it is a symbol of mystery and magic.

In readings: Odin, with his many names, is multi-faceted, just like this rune. Depending on the question, the rune can represent Odin, language, or wisdom. Ansuz combined with Ehwaz (horse rune), for example, can represent Sleipnir, Odin's steed, symbolizing rapid, storming movement between situations. Ansuz, combined with Eihwaz (yew tree rune), symbolizes Odin's sacrifice for the runes, so it could represent that sacrifices are needed. However, combined with Tiwaz (justice rune), Ansuz could be interpreted as counseling or mediation to gain justice.

In advice and counseling: this rune urges you to look at your narrative. Recent studies in Psychology have shown that our memories are sometimes more story than fact. Just as Odin is a God with many facets, so can your life be viewed from many angles, yielding dramatically different vistas.

What would you like the story of your life to be? When you meet your ancestors, what song would the Skalds sing? Do not only look at what you have to achieve to get there but try to see your past deeds and see how they lead up to this song. Frame your past failures and struggles as the stepping stones to your destiny. This is by no means easy, but it can be a potent tool for self-realization.

In magic and ritual: This is a rune used in many amulets and can represent the Father of the runes. By inscribing this rune, you symbolically link the object to the Aesir and call their attention. Odin inscribed a rune in the mouth of his son Baldr to grant him great eloquence. While I do not advise carving runes in your mouth, spells for greater power of eloquence can be an application of the Ansuz rune. In ritual, you can use this rune to represent Odin, potentially, on an altar.

Experiencing the runes

Words of the High One: Throughout this book, you will find a lot of quotes from myth and saga, but what is quoted the most is the *Hávamál*, "the words of the High One." These are the poems given by Odin, lord of wisdom, as advice. take some time to find and read a translation of the *Hávamál.* Let the words sink in; what advice is given? What does this tell you about the Viking age?

The Father of Runes: One of Odin's many names is the father of Runes. If you have not yet done so, now is an excellent time to try to do your first rune reading. You can do a reading for yourself or a relative or find someone online to do a reading for. Head over to the chapter on divination and try out the first spread.

Prayer to the one-eyed God: While studying Ansuz, it is an excellent time to get better acquainted with the God that rules this rune. Again you can use the rune on your altar as a focus for your blot. Odin is the Chieftain of the Gods, the father of runes, and much more. Think well about what you would like to say to the Ruler of the Gods, what you would ask of him and what you offer in return. As the lord of poetry, any prayer spoken in verse would surely be appreciated.

Figure 16: Drawing of Odin hanging himself in the world tree

ᚱ

1.5 Raidho - Wagon

Germanic	Gothic	Old English	Old Norse	Sound
Raidho	Raidha	Rádh	Reidh	R

Raidho is the fifth rune of the first Ætt. It symbolizes journeying. The rune Raidho is about the conscious decision to get from A to B and the method you plan to use to get there. The Dutch word 'rijden'[33] and the German 'reiten'[34] are etymologically linked to Raidho and imply being in control of your destination.

The rune poems

Norwegian

ᚱᚨᛖᛁᛞᚺ·ᚲᚹᛖᛞᚺᚨ·ᚱᛟᛋᛋᛟᛗ·ᚹᚨᛖᛋᛏᚨ·ᚱᛖᚷᛁᚾᚾ·ᛋᛚᛟ·ᛋᚹᚨᛖᚱᛞᚺᛖᛏ·
ᛒᚨᛖᛉᛏᚨ·

Ræið kveða rossom væsta; Reginn sló sværðet bæzta.

Riding is said to be the worse for horses; Reginn forged the finest sword.

[33] with the 'ij' pronounced as 'ai' meaning to drive.

[34] here the 'ei' is pronounced as the 'ai' meaning to ride.

The finest sword is Gramr; in the Volsong saga, a stranger, later to be revealed as Odin, crashes the wedding party of Signy[35]. At the end of the party, the stranger plants Gramr into the tree growing through the center of the hall. He proclaims that whoever can pull the sword out of the tree can keep it and then disappears. All the men try to pull the sword out of the tree but to no avail until Sigmund, the bride's brother, tries. He dislodges Gramr without any effort at all.

The sword proves a mixed blessing. While the sword is the finest ever made, it also earns him the envy of king Siggeir. The sword helps Sigmund win many battles until he comes across the stranger again and attacks him. During the battle, the Gramr is broken by the stranger, who is still Odin in disguise. Sigmund dies, and the pieces of the sword pass to his son Sigurd, who comes under the foster care of the dwarf Reginn.

Reginn raises Sigurd well. He teaches him languages, the runes, and sports, making him mentally and physically strong. At one point, Reginn convinces Sigurd that he needs a horse of his own to be taken seriously. After getting advice from a hermit in the forest, again Odin in disguise, Sigurd manages to acquire Grani. Grani is a descendant of Odin's Horse Sleipnir and the best of Horses in Midgard.

After this, Reginn tells Sigurd about his brothers, Fafnir and Otr. Otr could shapeshift into an otter and, in this form, was murdered by Loki for his pelt. Reginn, Fafnir, and their father Hreidmar confronted the Aesir and got him to pay a great treasure as compensation. Loki is a spiteful God; as part of the treasure, he adds a cursed ring. The ring overwhelms Fafnir with greed. This causes him to steal all the treasure for himself. Hreidmar tries to stop him but gets killed in the process.

Reginn asks Sigurd to avenge his father but warns Sigurd that the curse has transformed Fafnir into a mighty dragon. Sigurd agrees on the condition that Reginn forges a sword for him capable of slaying such a

---

[35] Signy is the sister of Sigmund who is the father of Sigurd.

beast. Two times Reginn forges a sword, two times Sigurd strikes it to an anvil to test its strength, and two times the sword shatters. The third time Reginn forges a sword from the remains of Gramr. This time when Sigurd strikes the anvil, it slices straight through. This shows that Reginn forged the best of swords, just as described in the last line of the rune poem.

In Sigurd's story, the sword Gramr and the horse Grani are acquired by him as tools, Not just tools but the best of tools. Good tools make the work go easier because they do part of the work for you. If we are talking about traveling by horse, the journey should be smooth for the rider. The horse should be responsible for most of the effort. This might explain the rune poem's first line, "riding can be said to be the worst for the horse." A good tool always takes the brunt of the work out of your hands, regardless if it is a horse, axe, or computer.

Horses played many roles in Nordic mythology, messenger, virility symbol, guardian spirit, and shamanic journey. We will expand on these roles in the chapter on Ehwaz, the horse rune. When analyzing the poem, we see that Reginn and Reið is not just a convenient alliteration. Reginn not only facilitates Sigurd getting Gramr but also the horse Grani tying it back to the first line of the poem. With this in mind, we can explain the Norwegian rune poem as advice to work with good tools.

Icelandic

ᚱᛖᛁᛞᚺ·ᛖᚱ·ᛊᛁᛏᛃᚨᚾᛞᛁ·ᛊᚨᛖᛚᚨ·ᛟᚲ·ᛊᚾᚢᛞᚺᛁᚷ·ᚠᛖᚱᛞᚺ·ᛟᚲ·ᛃᛟᚱᛊ·ᛖᚱ
ᚠᛁᛞᚺᛁ·ᛁᛏᛖᚱ·ᚱᚨᛖᛊᛁᚱ·

Reið er sitjandi sæla ok snúðig ferð ok jórs erfiði. iter ræsir.

Riding Joy of the horsemen and speedy journey and toil of the steed.

Akin to the previous poem, this rune poem also tells us that riding is the struggle of the steed. However, this poem also more clearly adds the benefits of this labor to the rider. The horse's toil gives the horsemen joy and adds speed to his journey.

The horse as a tool is also referenced in the *Hávamál*

The lame rides a horse, / the handless is herdsman,
The deaf in battle is bold;
The blind man is better / than one that is burned,
No good can come of a corpse.
- Hávamál 71

In this verse, we see that each man must follow his path. In this aspect, 'one that is burned' refers to someone being cremated, not someone with burn marks. Each of us has to find a path in life that works with the tool we have.

ᚱᚪᛞ·ᛒᛇᚦ·ᚩᚾ·ᚱᛖᚳᛇᛞᛖ·ᚱᛁᚾᚳᚪ·ᚷᛖᚻᚹᛇᛚᚳᚢᛗ·ᛋᛖᚠᛏᛖ·ᚩᚾᛞ·ᛋᚹᛁᚦ
ᚻᚹᚪᛖᛏ·ᛞᚻᚪᛗᛞᚻᛖ·ᛋᛁᛏᛏᛖᚦ·ᚩᚾ·ᚢᚠᚪᚾ·ᛗᛖᚪᚱᛖ·ᛗᚪᛖᚷᛖᚾᚻᛖᚪᚱᛞᚢ
ᛗ·ᚩᚠᛖᚱ·ᛗᛁᛚᛈᚪᚦᚪᛋ·

Rad byþ on recyde rinca gehwylcum sefte ond swiþhwæt, ðamðe
sitteþ on ufan meare mægenheardum ofer milpaþas.

Riding seems easy to every warrior while he is indoors and very courageous to him who traverses the high-roads on the back of a stout horse.

The Anglo-Saxon rune poem also talks about the ease that riding brings but adds an interesting detail. The practice of riding when actually on the road might be much more demanding than it looked from the comfort of one's hall.

The Dutch have a saying: "The best Helmsmen stay on shore." From the shore, it is easy to criticize and second guess, but to sail a boat is a whole different story. Similarly, researching this book took many years, and I assumed that when I started writing it, it would all be smooth sailing, but this was unfortunately not the case.

Making a plan or observing someone from the comfort of your home is one thing, but following through is another.

Historic use in charms and amulets

There are no surviving examples of the Raidho rune being used in either amulet or spell. However, we only have a tiny fragment of all spells, and amulets survived. This means it is not historically unlikely that Raidho was often used in either charms or amulets.

Figure 17: Solar Wheel.

One of the oldest symbols used by humanity is the Solar wheel, with Germanic artifacts bearing this symbol dating back well over 4000 years ago. In Nordic mythology, a Goddess named sol carries the sun across the sky in a cart. One of the leading theories about the origin of the symbol of the solar wheel is that it represents the wheel of the wagon that carries the Sun.

There are many accounts of the ceremonial use of wagons in Nordic culture. This gives the wagon and the rune that represents it a solid foundation in mythic symbology.

As a side note, the solar wheel has been appropriated by white supremacists, but the symbol dates back to prehistoric times and can be found in cultures worldwide. The term swastika comes from the Sanskrit 'su,' meaning good, and 'asti,' meaning existing. Together they are best translated to 'all is well.' During the second world war, the Nazis used this symbol and called it the Hakenkreuz[36]. The Swastika is either the precursor or a derivative of the solar wheel. If you Imagine the breaks in the outer rim of the solar wheel, you see the symbol becomes a swastika.

White-supremacist and anti-semitic groups often borrow symbols from Norse mythology, butchering their meaning or disregarding their origin. This perverted definition has given an undeserved negative connotation to most Nordic symbolism.

Cultural relevance

In the following excerpt, the Roman historian Tacitus describes a ritual he witnessed being performed by a group of Germanic tribes.

None of these tribes have any noteworthy feature, except their common worship of Nerthus, or mother-Earth, and their belief that she interposes in human affairs, and visits the nations in her car. In an island of the ocean there is a sacred grove, and within it a consecrated chariot, covered over with a garment. Only one priest is permitted to touch it. He can perceive the presence of the goddess in this sacred recess, and walks by her side with the utmost reverence as she is drawn along by heifers. It is a season of rejoicing, and festivity reigns wherever she deigns to go and be received. They do not go to battle or wear arms; every weapon is under lock; peace and quiet are known and welcomed only at these times, till the goddess, weary of human intercourse, is at length restored by the same priest to her temple. Afterwards the car, the vestments, and, if you like to believe it, the divinity herself, are purified in a secret lake. Slaves perform the rite, who are instantly swallowed up by its waters. Hence arises a mysterious terror and a pious ignorance concerning the nature of that which is seen only by men doomed to die.
-Germania 40

---

[36] Meaning the hooked cross.

More than a thousand years later, we see almost the same story penned by Christian hands. In the 14th century Flateyjarbók, an Icelandic book of myths, we find the tale called Ögmundar þáttr dytts. The story tells of how a statue of Freyr was transported through Sweden. Again, the cart was tended by a priestess, and wherever the wagon passed, grand celebrations were held.

Comparing these two stories shows the same ritual more than a millennium apart. Tacitus mentions the worship of Nerthus, the feminized version of Njord, who is the father of Freyr.

Both Njord and Freyr were members of the Vanir. The Vanir are nature Gods; their sphere of influence included things like the seasons and the harvest. It is no surprise that these customs tied to the Vanir seem to have been very cyclical. The wagon ritual marks the passage from summer into fall or winter into spring.

There are more examples of the image of the God on a wagon being used in rituals throughout the sagas. In addition, archaeological sites have also yielded evidence of these ritual wagons. This shows that the practice must have been widespread.

Gods Sol and Mani, The Goddess of the sun and the God of the moon may not be Vanir but are also cyclical wagon Gods. The concept of the sun and the moon riding in a wagon is ancient, as proven by the Sun wagon from Trundelhelm, 1700 BCE.

Figure 18: Stylistic rendition of the Sun Wagon of Trundelhelm

Conclusion

Raidho is a rune of wagons and roads. It is a multi-faceted Rune, both the vessel of travel and the plotted course. It is the rune of the farmer bringing in his harvest on his cart, the longboats sailing out with the tide, and the sun and the moon's great cycles marking time and bringing structure to life.

The wagon and the horse can be interpreted as tools, and the better the tool, the easier the job. Every tool has its purpose; however, if we use them outside their intended jobs, they might work counterproductively. Thus, the wagon rune helps us reach our goals and forces us to follow the road we have chosen.

In readings: Just as the wheel's turning pushes us forwards on our path, so does this rune represent structured movement. On its own, this might indicate planned travel, like a vacation or moving to a new location. It could also figuratively mean a study where you progress on the road to knowledge through a structured curriculum.

Raidho, in combination with Jera(year rune), strongly emphasizes the natural circles of life, the road that all living things must follow from birth to death. Raidho, in combination with Thurisaz(troll rune), might represent self-destructive cycles in one's life, dark paths that we keep returning to.

In advice and counseling: In the chapter on Naudiz, we will discuss Wyrd, the Nordic concept of fate. Wyrd is not the same as predestination but the idea that your current situation is created from your past actions, and your future status will be made from your present actions.

Our lives are mostly lived on a path of our creation. Our choices have paved it, and our actions push us along with a certain momentum. On these travels, we often find ourselves looping back to familiar paths, both happy and dark. This rune counsels you to examine the paths you choose to tread.

In magic and ritual: This rune can be used in spells and charms related to planning and travel. Combined with Ansuz(Odin's rune), this rune can be used to help with your academic path. Combine this rune with Ehwaz(horse rune), and you can make a charm for safe travels. In rituals, this rune can be used to represent the wagons of the sun and the moon during celebrations of the equinox or the solstice.

Experiencing the runes

A blessing to Sol and Mani: Sol and Mani are the charioteers that pull the sun and the moon across the sky. Their jobs are to map out day, night, months, and years. In other words, they represent the ordered progression of the universe. Forever chasing the two are the wolves Hati and Skoll. When the wolves finally catch up to the sun and the moon, it will be the beginning of Ragnarök, the end of everything.
You can inscribe this rune on a piece of paper or, better yet, on a small chariot. This will create an altar to ask the Gods to bring stability to the universe and your life

Forging the path: It might be a good idea to take stock of what direction you want your life to go by studying this rune. Whether striving for a long-term goal or forging a new path, there will be challenges. Once the wheels start turning, they will slowly wear away the dirt to reveal new tracks, and progressing along that path will become more accessible and manageable. Pick up a piece of paper and plan what your new road should be. It could be as simple as studying the runes, a path you have by now made a good amount of progress on. Those who have ever encountered road work on their way to work know that no road is built in a day. After deciding on a course of action, stick to it for at least eight weeks. After you have worn away the dirt to reveal the path, you can evaluate if it is the right road for you.

Making a map: We all have our favorite haunts and roads we walk daily. Some roads are our way home or work, and some are darker paths. Take a notepad with you for the next week and scribble down what you do during the day and any thoughts you feel are worth writing down. After a couple of weeks, examine your notes and find your patterns. Look for recurring themes, what makes you happy, what makes you angry, what is efficient, and what could you do without? What are the ever-returning seasons of your life?

Figure 19: Sol and Mani being chased

ᚲ

1.6 Kenaz - Torch

Germanic	Gothic	Old English	Old Norse	Sound
Kenaz	Kusma	Cén	Kaub	K

Kenaz is the sixth rune of the first Ætt. It is a rune of heat and fire; depending on the region, the heat either manifests as the welcoming fires of the homestead or the burning heat of a heavy fever. Both hearth fire and the heat of a fever held a much greater significance for the Vikings. Without fire, you would freeze to death in the icy winters, and a fever was a much more severe threat without penicillin.

The rune poems

Norwegian

ᚲᚨᚢᚾ·ᛖᚱ·ᛒᚨᚱᚾᚨ·ᛒᛟᛚᚹᚨᚾ·ᛒᛟᛚ·ᚷᛟᚱᚹᛖᚱ·ᚾᚨᚾ·ᚠᛟᛚᚹᚨᚾ·

Kaun er barna bolvan bol gorver nán folvan.

Ulcer is fatal to children; death makes a corpse pale.

Child mortality was much higher in the Viking age than it is now in the age of modern medicine. At that time one in every three children would not live to the age of fifteen. There are few records of the cause of this high child mortality rate in Scandinavia. However, we can make an educated guess based on the records kept by the clergy from the rest of Europe. Fever was given as the common cause of death.

The second line shows the contrast between the hot, feverish child and the pale, cold corpse the sickness can leave behind. Odin or Freya would choose those who died in battle to serve in their retinue, but those who died from illness or old age went to Hel. Hel was the name of the underworld and the Goddess who ruled it. The Christian word 'hell' originates from this Nordic use.

Under the pens of Christian historians, Hell became a dark place, but historical evidence suggests that this was not always the case. The hall of Hel was most probably as respected as Odin's hall. Hella was a Goddess of two faces; her left side was a beautiful woman, her right side a blackened rotting corpse. It is worth noting that the spirits of the dead were often portrayed as black as night in early mythology. Portrayals of these dark spirits can still be seen in current-day Pagan celebrations throughout Europe.

The Eddas tell us that Hella is the daughter of Loki and the giantess Angrboða[37].

Some historians tie her to the frau Hulla who appears in the fairy tales from The Brothers Grimm but the similarities go further than a similar-sounding name. Frau Hulla was the goddess guiding dead children,

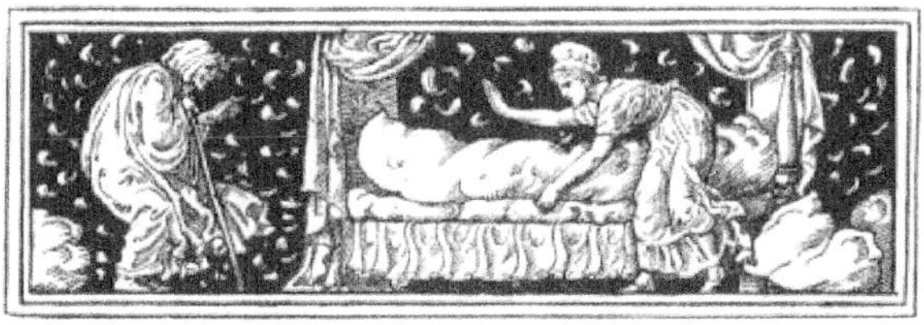

Figure 20: Mother Hulda

[37] She who brings suffering.

earning her the nicknames 'Dunkle Großmutter[38]' and 'Weisse Frau'[39]. The nicknames echo the image of Hell, with her dark and light sides. Frau Hulla is a Goddess of weaving and winter. Therefore, she must have been a significant deity before the rise of the Aesir, possibly one of the Vanir.

Fire, even in sickness, is life. Frau Hulla is a Goddess of snow, and Hella lives deep within the frozen wastes of Nifelheim. Once the fire leaves your body, it is clear you have passed into their realm, and the fire burns brightest just before the end

---

ᚲᚨᚢᚾ·ᛖᚱ·ᛒᚨᚱᚾᚨ·ᛒᛟᛚ·ᛟᚲ·ᛒᚨᚱᛞᚨᚷᚨ·ᛟᚲ·ᚺᛟᛚᛞᚠᚢᚨᚺᚢᛊ·ᚠᛚᚨᚷ
ᛖᛚᛚᚨ·ᚲᛟᚾᚢᚾᚷᚱ·

Kaun er barna böl ok bardaga ok holdfúa hús. flagella konungr.

Disease fatal to children and painful spot and abode of mortification.

The Icelandic rune poem touches on the same themes as the Norwegian poem. There is also an interesting parallel between Kenaz and Thurisaz, the troll rune. One of the kennings for death is 'joy of the troll-woman'; the troll woman, in this case, refers to the Goddess Hella. Both of these runes have a strong connection with death and suffering. However, while Thurisaz relates to woman's suffering, Kenaz deals with the suffering of children.

The 'abode of mortification' potentially refers to a Viking funeral custom witnessed by the Arab explorer Ibn Fadlan. After a chieftain has died, he is first placed into an underground barrow for ten days. During this time, funeral preparations are made, and the corpse can dry out.

---

[38] Dark grandmother

[39] White lady

According to Ibn Fadlan, the corpse's flesh has a black hue when it is finally removed from the barrow. Afterward, they drink intoxicating drinks, the chieftain is dressed in new clothes, and a slave girl is picked to accompany her lord to the next world. The final rituals are performed by an old lady called the 'angel of death' guarded by a group of warrior women.

In the end, the Chieftain is burned, and the ashes are buried. The burning of the deceased assist in speeding their transition into the afterlife. Once more, we see the connection between fire and death.

Anglo-Saxon

ᚳᛖᚾ·ᛒᚣᚦ·ᚳᚹᛁᚳᛖᚱᚪ·ᚷᛖᚻᚹᚪᛗ·ᚳᚢᚦ·ᛟᚾ·ᚠᚣᚱᛖ·ᛒᛚᚪᚳ·ᛟᚾᛞ·ᛒᛖᛟᚱ
ᚻᛏᛚᛁᚳ·ᛒᚣᚱᚾᛖᚦ·ᛟᚠᛏᚢᛋᛏ·ᛞᚻᚪᛖᚱ·ᚻᛁ·ᚪᛖ.ᚦᛖᛚᛁᚾᚷᚪᛋ·ᛁᚾᚾᛖ·ᚱᛖᛋᛏ
ᚪᚦ·

Cen byþ cwicera gehwam, cuþ on fyre blac ond
beorhtlic, byrneþ oftust ðær hi æþelingas inne restaþ.

The torch is known to every living man by its pale, bright flame; it always burns where princes sit within.

The Anglo-Saxon rune poem focuses on the more positive aspect of fire. It calls to mind a mighty hall belonging to a prince where warm fires that never fail burn invitingly inside. This same image can be found in the *Hávamál.*

Fire for men / is the fairest gift,
And power to see the sun;
Health as well, / if a man may have it,
And a life not stained with sin.
Hávamál 68

In this excerpt, we see the connection the Nordic people made between fire and health. A resource is always more valued if it is scarce and warmth is lacking in the frozen winters of the deep North. To have a great hall where warmth and fire could be shared is as much a sign of wealth and power for a prince as gold or silver.

Fire he needs / who with frozen knees
Has come from the cold without;
Food and clothes / must the farer have,
The man from the mountains come.
-Hávamál 3

This poem can have multiple meanings. The most obvious one is the importance of hospitality and the basic needs of survival, nourishment, and fire. It is the last line that is open for interpretation. The line either references a man coming down from his mountain home and finding kinship or the man has just escaped troll country. In the kennings, trolls are most often described as living in or under mountains or rocks. In the chapter on Thurisaz, we saw that trolls were often associated with sickness. If the last line describes a man leaving troll country, the poem could be about a man regaining his health.

In Nordic culture, the hearth was the center of every household, where the family gathered socially, and family spirits were worshipped. We can see the last remains of these traditions in the American Christmas or the European saint Nicholas day. In both traditions, offerings are made by the fireplace in exchange for gifts. Therefore heart fire can still be seen as a potent symbol for home and family.

Historic use in charms and amulets

There are no surviving historical charms or amulets that specifically center around Kenaz. However, there is an ancient ritual that makes use of a physical torch. After moving to a new piece of land, it was customary to take ownership of that land ritualistically. The ritual involved walking around the property with a torch to mark its boundaries and then making an offering to the Landvættir.

Cultural relevance

The firelight and the torch are common themes in Nordic mythology. When controlled, fire is a boon and a blessing. Inviting someone to the hearth is a sign of hospitality. The hearth is the place for offerings, and without its warmth, none could hope to survive the Scandinavian winters.

For earth cures drink, / and fire cures ills,
The oak cures tightness, / the ear cures magic,
Rye cures rupture, / the moon cures rage,
Grass cures the scab, / and runes the sword-cut
- Hávamál 137

In this stanza, fire is listed as the cure for all ills. Echoing the sentiment that fire is life, the corpse grows cold after the fire has left it.

It is better to live / than to lie a corpse,
The live man catches the cow;
I saw flames rise / for the rich man's pyre,
And before his door he lay dead.
- Hávamál 70

Fire is mysterious; it consumes and transforms all that it touches. In that sense, the fire could be seen as a gateway to the unknown. When we stare into the flame and let our minds wander, we can echo this feeling just like the shamans of old. Perhaps that is why offerings and the dead were so often burned.

In a breaking bow / or a burning flame,
A ravening wolf / or a croaking raven,
In a grunting boar, / a tree with roots broken,
In billowy seas / or a bubbling kettle,
- Hávamál 85

Fire is also meant to be feared. The poem above is a short excerpt of a more extensive verse listing things not to be trusted. While Ragnarök begins with ice, it ends in fire. During Ragnarök, the flame giant Sutr sets the world tree ablaze, bringing creation to its inevitable end. The world will burn out in the dying days just as a man in the throes of his last high fever.

Conclusion

Kenaz is a complicated rune of sickness and health, life and death, safety and danger. In that way, it is also a rune of boundaries and gateways. It keeps the dark and cold at bay during long dark winter nights and ferries us to the next life after death. Kenaz is a powerful rune that benefits from clear intentions.

In readings: On its own, it might represent inflammation. Remember, inflammation is your body trying to fight off something; it is not the real problem. Depending on the question, different things could be trying to keep you safe. In combination with Thurisaz(troll rune), it might indicate an actual physical illness. If paired with Othala(ancestors rune), it might mean a safe haven. Lastly, in the *Hávamál*, the words of learning are compared with the sparks of fire. Coupled with Ansuz, this rune talks of shared wisdom, knowledge, and words that can set a mind ablaze.

In advice and counseling: In holistic medicine, the human body and mind are seen as a whole. When diagnosing a patient with this philosophy, it is not just the biomedical aspect that is treated but the patient in their environment. Tiredness, paranoia, ulcers, muscle spasms, and more can be caused by stress or social anxiety. We talked about the meaning of inflammation, but there can also be a symbolic aspect of inflammation. When the stress and social pressures in your life boil over, that can also lead to medical problems; thus, it is vital to assess your quality of life and take a deeper look at what other issues might be influencing you as a whole.

In magic and ritual: Flame and fire are powerful ritualistic tools. Flame and the Kenaz rune can be symbolically used to burn away impurities. Kenaz can be used to create protective amulets against the cold. It can also stoke the flames of life in sickness, to burn through the fever.

Experiencing the runes

Border flames: There is a significant difference between a home and a house. Many cultures have used fire and smoke as a ritual way of purifying a house, appeasing the local spirits, and symbolically claiming the space as a home. Find a good size wooden branch and paint Kenaz and Othala on the wood. Next, dip strips of linen in molten candle wax and wrap these around one end of the branch. Make sure that the candle wax is not too hot, it only has to be just melting. An excellent way to melt candles is au bain marie. Keep wrapping strips of linen around the branch until you have a good fist-size top. After sunset, light the torch and walk around the outside of your property. This can only be done with free-standing properties. Let each member of the household lay a hand on the torch.

After finishing your round, place the torch in the ground and make offerings to the Landvættir and whatever God you feel is appropriate. Grain, honey, spirits, meat, and cream are time-tested offerings. The offering should be burned. The best way to do this is a small campfire. Make sure you keep fire safety in mind. After you are done, put out the torch and either bury it or save it for another ritual.

Sweating it out: Many shamanistic cultures, including the Norse, have applied hot and cold to gain ecstatic knowledge. Attempting a full sweat lodge ritual without training or someone to supervise is not recommended. However, a slightly toned-down version of this ritual can be experienced in the sauna. Find a good sauna in your neighborhood and experience both the heat of the sauna and the cold of the cooling-down pool. Go through several cycles, and try to evaluate your thought process, what changes can you feel?

Hospitality: Kenaz is also the rune of the hearth fire. Invite some people over and light a roaring fire if you have a fireplace. Light a fire pit in your backyard if you do not have a fireplace. It is important symbolically for this event to be held on your property. Make sure there is enough to eat and drink for everybody.

Figure 21: Drawing of Hella leading a child

ᚷ

1.7 Gebo - Gift

Germanic	Gothic	Old English	Old Norse	Sound
Gebo	Giba	Gyfa	Gipt	G

Gebo is the seventh rune of the first Ætt. It is a rune of giving, receiving, and the exchange's dynamics. This rune does not come with the full complement of three rune poems. Not all runes appear in all versions of the runic alphabet. Norway and Iceland used the younger futhark from the eighth century, which did not include Gebo.

The rune poems

Anglo-Saxon

ᚷᛇᚠ·ᚷᚢᛗᛖᚾᚪ·ᛒᛇᚦ·ᚷᛚᛖᚾᚷ·ᚪᚾᛞ·ᚻᛖᚱᛖᚾᛇᛋ·ᚹᚱᚪᚦᚢ·ᚪᚾᛞ·ᚹᛇᚱᚦ
ᛋᚳᛇᛈᛖ·ᚪᚾᛞ·ᚹᚱᚪᛖᚳᚾ·ᚪ·ᚷᛖᚻᚹᚪᛗ·ᚪᚱ·ᚪᚾᛞ·ᚪᛖᛏᚹᛁᛋᛏ·ᛞᚻᛖ·ᛒᛇᚦ·
ᛟᚦᚱᚪ·ᛚᛖᚪᛋ·

Gyfu gumena byþ gleng and herenys, wraþu and wyrþscype and wræcna gehwam ar and ætwist, ðe byþ oþra leas.

Generosity brings credit and honour, which support one's dignity; it furnishes help and subsistence to all broken men who are devoid of aught else.

In the chapter on Fehu, we discussed the importance of generosity in Norse culture. This chapter will further analyze how deeply this concept is ingrained in the Nordic mindset.

Friends shall gladden each other / with arms and garments,
As each for himself can see;
Gift-givers' friendships / are longest found,
If fair their fates may be.

To his friend a man / a friend shall prove,
And gifts with gifts requite;
But men shall mocking / with mockery answer,
And fraud with falsehood meet.
- Hávamál 41,42

Hospitality and kinship often become two of the most important virtues in cultures that arise in harsh climates, hot or cold. In the *Hávamál* quote above, Odin advises that gift-giving is the basis for friendship. This must not be confused with bribery. In the harsh Scandinavian climate, people shared what they could and expected others to do the same, returning a gift for a gift.

Victory in battle, Successful harvest, happiness in love, great wealth, or many children are all gifts from the Gods. A gift not reciprocated becomes sour. Those who received the gifts from the Gods are expected to pay it forwards.

Figure 22: Drawing of the Skepptuna standing stone

Historic use in charms and amulets

A rune stone in the tiny Swedish town of Skepptunaears the enigmatic text: *"kiftiʀ 'mina ' ik-ktiʀ nu ' "*this translates to gift of mine (Samnordic Rune Text database, 1993). There are several possible interpretations for the function of this stone. The first is that this is a place where blót[40] was given to the Landvættir or the Gods. The second option is that this stone was a blót or a sign of respect to the Landvættir. The final option is that this is a remembrance stone for a departed family member.

Departed ancestors were still thought to influence the living in several ways. Children were named after illustrious ancestors in the hope that they would gain the same courage and prowess. An Ancestor could bestow his Fylgja[41] on one of his descendants and grant a blessed life in that way.

There is a story in the Flateyjarbók[42] from the Þáttr Þorleifs Jarlaskálds[43] that tells of Hallbjörn, the shepherd. Hallbjörn sits on the grave of Þorleifr the skald, trying to compose a poem in Þorleifr's honor. Unfortunately, Hallbjörn is not a great poet and eventually falls asleep without progress. While sleeping, the poet Þorleifr comes to the shepherd and gifts him with the gift of poetry. This story shows three things, an ancestor's grave turning into a place of spiritual power, the ancestors passing their destiny on after death, and the idea that poetry is a divine gift.

Each Family had a collective guardian spirit called the Hamingja. in Surrson's saga, such spirits visit Gisli. They take the shape of two ancestors. These both advise him on what they feel is the best course of action.

A particularly renowned man or woman could draw in sacrifices to their grave from more than just their family. Over time such a person could develop a cult status similar to that of a Landvættir or Alfar.

---

[40] Offerings.

[41] Guardian spirit representing luck and destiny.

[42] An Icelandic manuscript from the 14th century.

[43] Poem from the Flateyjarbók

This example shows that the Gebo concept was not limited to the Mortal realms. The idea of gifts as social lubrication, relying heavily on reciprocation to keep civilization turning, permeates all levels of life and death in Norse culture.

Cultural relevance

The exchanging of gifts in the Nordic countries was so prevalent that Tacitus made the following note:

No people are more addicted to social entertainments, or more liberal in the exercise of hospitality. To refuse any person whatever admittance under their roof, is accounted flagitious. . . . No one makes a distinction with respect to the rights of hospitality, between a stranger and an acquaintance. The departing guest is presented with whatever he may ask for; and with the same freedom a boon is desired in return. They are pleased with presents; but think no obligation incurred when they give or receive.

-Germania 21

While this might be an outsider's exaggeration, the sagas and poems tell us clearly that a gift demands a gift in return. This excerpt from the Germania underlines what a central role gifting must have played.

When the winters are harsh, and the land yields less bounty, exchanging gifts is essential to ensure everybody has enough to get through the winter. Moreover, it is a custom that promotes fellowship and ties between families.

It is no coincidence that the old Norse word for Gebo, 'Gipt,' can mean three things. Firstly, it can mean a literal gift one person gives to another. Secondly, it can mean a natural gift, like the gift of poetry given by the Gods, and lastly, it can mean a wedding. In the Norse context, all three are social commitments, and a gift demands a gift. Social responsibility to your neighbors shows that you will stand together. A social bond with the Gods that assures us their bounty. Finally, the social commitment of marriage makes two families one.

Conclusion

Gebo is a rune of balance, the balance in giving and receiving. In doing so kinship grows in the community and in the relationship between humanity and the spirits. The exact shape of Gebo, with its symmetry, echoes this balance.

In readings: On its own, this rune means a gift is due. Based on the question, this can mean the querent will receive something or that they still have a debt to pay. Gifts do not always have to be material. Money, lending a hand, advice, or kinship are all gifts we need now and again and should repay in kind. Combining it with other runes can better indicate which direction we can expect the gift to come from. Combined with Tiwaz(justice rune), it can mean that a legal dispute is balanced. When paired with Berkana(birch rune), this can indicate either a child on its way or the bond with a parent. When combined with Fehu(cattle rune), this rune might mark a financial gift coming your way.

In advice and counseling: No man is an island, as the famous John Donne poem tells us. This is not a rune of relationships that is the domain of Mannaz(humankind rune). This rune accentuates the social etiquette that facilitates a community. A shared hobby, beliefs, colleagues at work, and many other connections make you part of a community. In society, each member is always expected to do their part. The question you should be asking yourself is, what connections do I possess, and is there balance in what I gain versus what I take?

Remember, for the Nordic people, this meant giving the needy food and shelter so they would survive the winter. This was not a debt but a security they could count on one another in the long run.

In magic and ritual: Sacrifice is one of the core principles of most rituals. We gift the Gods with praise and offerings to both thank them and show the bonds between us. A true sacrifice is not about the amount of physical things thrown into a fire but about what the sacrifice means to you. Are your intentions to forge a bond, or are they to get something in return? How much does losing your sacrifice affect you? These are questions that you have to answer.

The rune Gebo can also be used in wedding ceremonies inscribed on the gifts to show that the gifts represent the merging of the two families.

In other rituals, you can use Gebo with Othala(ancestors rune) to strengthen family ties, Mannaz(humankind rune) to strengthen the relationship between friends, or Ansuz(Odin's rune) in rituals to strengthen your connection with the divine.

Experiencing the runes

Gifting: Gebo is one of the easiest runes to experience. Gifting is an action that can manifest in many forms. You can bring food and drinks to your next gathering of friends or kin, gift a friend, co-worker or loved one with a token of your appreciation, or give to the homeless. Note what the giving does to you and what it does for the other person.

The Landvættir: Create an altar for the Landvættir that dwell there in your garden or nearby piece of nature. The Landvættir come in many different shapes and sizes. Take a moment and meditate. Try to empty your mind and get a picture of the spirits in that location. My previous residence was in a highly urban area, so when I tried to visualize the Landvættir, they would appear to me as pigeons and earthworms.

One day, as I was coming home unexpectedly to some awful news, my door was covered in earthworms. Until that day, I had no idea that earthworms could climb vertical surfaces. This happened three times more, and I knew to steel myself for bad news each time.

Create a small sacred space in your garden, and now and again, leave offerings for the Landvættir. Honey, milk, cream, nuts, and pastry are all excellent offerings. See if you can notice any differences in how your garden grows and feels and local animals' behavior.

Family gifts: Like the Fylgja, some gifts come to you from family. Not all achievements are your own. Take a day to talk to a patriarch or matriarch in your family. Talk about the accomplishments of those that came before you. See if you can find similarities in character and traits.

If ancestors have passed away with qualities that you find admirable, ask for their help to develop those qualities in yourself.

Figure 23: veatirr

ᚹ

1.8 Wunjo - Joy

Germanic	Gothic	Old English	Old Norse	Sound
Wunjo	Winja	Wynn	Vend	W

Wunjo is the eighth and last rune of the first Ætt. It is a rune of joy, bliss, and harmony. It is also a rune of Odin in his Shamanistic forms. It represents connecting to the cosmos and ecstatic understanding. One of Odin's many names is Njótr, which means he who experiences joy.

The rune poems

ᚹᛖᚾᚾᛖ·ᛒᚱᚢᚳᛖ·ᛞᚻᛖ·ᚳᚪᚾ·ᚹᛖᚪᚾᚪ·ᛚᛇᛏ·ᛋᚪᚱᛖᛋ·ᚪᚾᛞ·ᛋᛟᚱᚷᛖ·ᚪᚾᛞ·ᚻᛁᛗ·ᛋᛇᛚᚠ
ᚪ·ᚻᚪᛖᚠ·ᛒᛚᚪᛖᛞ·ᚪᚾᛞ·ᛒᛚᛇᛋᛋᛖ·ᚪᚾᛞ·ᛖᚪᚳ·ᛒᛇᚱᚷᚪ·ᚷᛖᚾᛁᚻᛏ·

Anglo-Saxon

Wenne bruceþ, ðe can weana lyt sares and sorge and him sylfa hæfþ blæd and blysse and eac byrga geniht.

Bliss he enjoys who knows not suffering, sorrow nor anxiety,
and has prosperity and happiness and a good enough house.

What is most prominent in this poem is its clear emphasis on bliss being a state of mind. The poem defines bliss as the absence of suffering, sorrow, and anxiety. The last part of the last line is the most noteworthy.

It states that bliss can be achieved if one has a "good enough house." The emphasis here is on enough. The only physical requirement for bliss is not a great or beautiful house, just a house that does the job. This sentiment is echoed in the *Hávamál.*

Better a house, / though a hut it be,
A man is master at home;
A pair of goats / and a patched-up roof
Are better far than begging.
- Hávamál 36

For a people mostly known for their expeditions raiding and plundering treasure, the people from the North were, as seen by this rune and by Fehu, surprisingly non-materialistic. Beautiful things and drinking copious amounts of alcohol were pleasant but not considered the foundation of a good life. Housing, food, and clothing were seen as enough for bliss.

Figure 24: A Norse homestead

Historic use in charms and amulets

There was a brooch found in the village of Bezenye in Hungary. It was part of a set of two Brooches probably belonging to two women. The inscription was as follows:

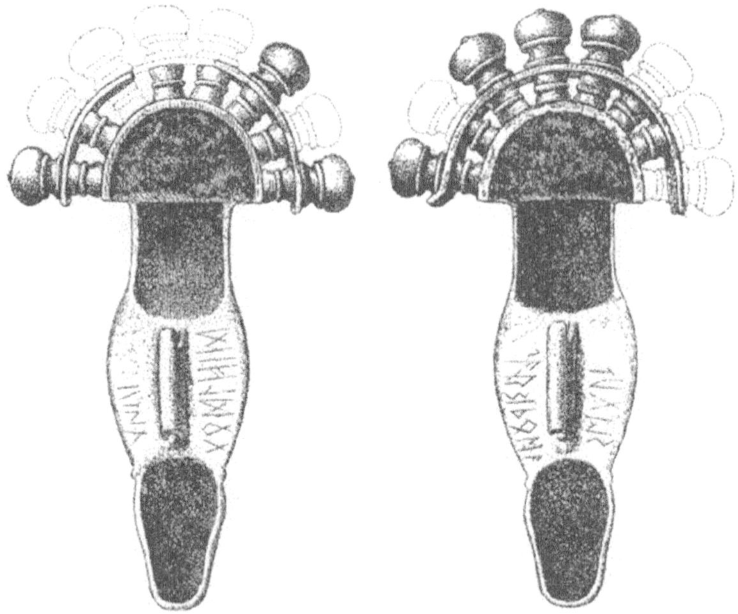

KJ166

Figure 25: drawing of the Bezenye, bow brooch (a)

ᚷᛟᛞᚨᚺᛁᛞ·ᚢᚾᛃᚨ

Godahid (w)unja

Godahild, Joy (Krause & Jankuhn, 1966)

A simple charm wishing happiness to Godahild. Most rune charms are not more than a statement of intent; the same is true for the Bezenye brooch. The second brooch found on the same site had a similar inscription, "*Arsiboda, blessing*" (Krause & Jankuhn, 1966). These two inscriptions show that not all runic charms were long and full of hidden depth.

In the saga Sigdrifumál, there is an exchange between Sigurd and the Valkyrie Brunnhilde where she teaches Sigurd some of her runic magic. One stanza reads:

"Beer I bring thee, / tree of battle,
Mingled of strength / and mighty fame;
Charms it holds / and healing signs,
Spells full good, / and Joy-runes."
Sigdrifumál 5

Tree of battle is a name referring to Sigurd. Brunnhilde brings him a draught full of magic charms that increase health, strength, and joy. The story includes more runic drinks and ends its explanation with the following:

"Shaved off were the runes / that of old were written,
And mixed with the holy mead"
Sigdrifumál 18

From this exchange, we can infer that one of the ways rune magic was performed was by inscribing the rune on a piece of wood and then scratched off into the drink. We can also conclude that Wunjo was used in beneficial draughts.

Cultural relevance

The word Wunjo is Etymologically related to the German 'wonne' (bliss) and 'wunch' (wish). In early Germanic poetry, the word wish has a much broader meaning than it has today. Wish is an almost conscious force that blooms into reality as divine providence. In this way, Wunjo is a rune of a moment when the divine is perfectly aligned with reality, a rune of a skald's inspiration, a shamanistic trance, and a beautiful sunny afternoon when the sun is out, and the breeze is just perfect.

Ansuz, contrary to Wunjo, is the rune of scholarly knowledge and eloquent truths. According to Nordic traditions, wisdom can be born from ecstatic revelation as well as from rigorous study. The moment where the sage walks the thin line between madness and revelation, propelled into other realms on a wave of bliss, is what defines Nordic shamanism.

The name Odin most likely comes from the word '*Odr*' (Inspiration or ecstasy) and '*inn*', a suffix meaning masculine. His name then translates to the man of inspiration or man of bliss. The name Odin represents his shamanistic role in the sagas.

The *Hávamál* has many sections underlining the importance of learning from experience, travel and listening to the wisdom of others. Yet much of Odin's wisdom comes to him from more extraordinary sources.

Odin's knowledge of the happenings in the nine worlds comes to him from his two spirit animals, Huginn en Muninn. His knowledge of the runes comes from a ritual where he passed through death, a common theme among shamanistic cultures. Odin's eloquence and prophetic poetry stem from his intoxication by the mead of poetry. Intoxication is a common method to gain wisdom in the sagas.

Lastly, Odin is known for his ability to travel the nine worlds. Traveling between the worlds across the world tree is a practice mirrored in many shamanistic cultures worldwide. Ecstatic joy can be seen as a connection to the divine.

Conclusion

Wunjo, in its simplicity, is sometimes hard to grasp. We all understand the word joy, but defining it is more complicated. What brings joy, and how do you know when you have it?

A measure of wisdom / each man shall have,
But never too much let him think;
For the wise man's heart / is seldom happy,
If wisdom too great he has won.
- Hávamál 55

Paradoxically reaching for wisdom might be the thing that keeps you from experiencing joy. For the Nordic people, joy was that perfect moment, without thought or effort, when the universe seemed to click, a feeling beyond thought or reason.

In readings: A very fortunate rune to draw with almost any question or situation. It represents an effortless and favorable outcome or resolution.

Other runes can give more clarity on what the meaning of Wunjo is in the context. Combined with Ansuz (Odin's rune), this rune can represent poetry or storytelling. If it is next to Ehwaz (horse rune) or Eihwaz (yew tree rune), it suggests shamanistic communication with the spirits or other worlds. Combinations with Mannaz (humankind rune) or Berkana (birch rune) represent joy's more social side, such as happiness among friends and good relations between children and their parents.

In advice and counseling: This rune tells you that what keeps you away from joy is sometimes your desire to achieve it. What are you overthinking? Why can't you relax? This rune is not about what you need to feel joy. There is nothing you need, but it can raise the question of what is keeping you from it.

In magic and ritual: Sigdrifumál shows us that this rune was used for enchanting joy into drinks. That makes this an excellent rune to use at gatherings for friends and family. Not just to be infused into mead, but this rune can be worn or embroidered on wedding or anniversary celebrations.

Experiencing the runes

Feast of joy: Joy can be experienced but not described. Many stories warn of the paradoxical nature of joy; those that try to attain it lose it forever. The feast of joy works on the other paradoxical aspect of joy, that joy shared is joy doubled.

Hold a grand celebration of something positive in your life, a wedding, a birthday, an anniversary, etc. Carve or burn the runes Wunjo (joy rune) and Mannaz (humankind rune) on a piece of birch wood (make sure the wood has not been treated with chemicals and you use a non-toxic wood if you do not use birch). Use a small carving knife or file to scrape some of the runes off and infuse them into the drink.
Alternatively, inscribe the runes on bottles and containers for the drinks.

The road of the shaman: Similarly, the spiritual side of joy cannot be described. Mystics and shamans of all traditions and walks of life have difficulty expressing spiritual joy.

There are many paths in shamanism, and we will visit a few in the chapter on magic. Here we will try one of the simplest ways: meditation.

Light a candle and place it about arm's length away at eye level. Your sitting position is not important as long as your spine is straight. Focus on the flame and only on the flame. Your attention will wander, but acknowledge your thoughts and return to the flame. Don't get frustrated; focus takes practice.

Try this each day for about 5 minutes (longer if you feel like it) for a week. After the week, see if you feel any difference while meditating or the rest of the day. Keep up the practice if you feel it brings you joy.

The wish father: One of Odin's many names is *Óski* God of wishes. As discussed earlier, Wunjo is etymologically related to the German 'wunch' (Wish). Wunjo is then a rune tied to Odin in its meaning of divine bliss and receiving what you want.

Think of a thing you wish for and make a stave or a paper charm to achieve it. Place the stave or charm in a prominent place in your house. If you have an idol of Odin, place it next to the charm. Make a small offering to Odin and keep the charm or stave there for a week and then burn it.

Did you receive (partly) what you desired? Were there opportunities for you to grasp that you did not take?

Figure 26: Dissarblot celebration

The second ætt

ᚺ

2.1 Hagalaz - Hail

Germanic	Gothic	Old English	Old Norse	Sound
Hagalaz	Hagl	Heagl	Hagall	H

With Wunjo, we finished the first Ætt. Now we turn to Hagalaz, the first rune of the second Ætt. From Wunjo's warm embrace, we move into the frigid cold. Hagalaz represents the destructive force of a hailstorm. We might not notice a hailstorm from the comfort of our modern home, but in Nordic times, a hailstorm could flatten an entire harvest, leaving the village to starve.

The rune poems

Norwegian

ᚺᚨᚷᚨᛚᛚ·ᛖᚱ·ᚲᚨᛚᛞᚨᛊᛏᚱ·ᚲᛟᚱᚾᚨ·ᚲᚱᛁᛊᛏᚱ·ᛊᚲᛟᛈ·ᚺᚨᛖᛁᛗᛖᚾᚾ·ᚠᛟ
ᚱᚾᚨ·

Hagall er kaldastr korna; Kristr skóp hæimenn forna.

Hagall Hail is the coldest of grain; Christ created the world of old.

Cold grain, ice grain, and ice egg are all kennings for hail commonly used in stories and poetry. The egg, seed, or grain are symbols of emerging life and the potential of creation. It is not surprising, then, that in the past, this rune poem has been described as a rune of creation. This can also be seen in the second line about Christ creating the world.

It is interesting to note here that in Christian mythology, the father aspect of God, not Christ, created the world. It is not unlikely that the poem has been Christianised and that Kristr was a good poetic match for the original God's name in the poem. Kjalarr, one of Odin's names, would be a good fit, and Kjalarr's literal meaning, "the nourisher" would fit well with the theme of cold grain. On top of that, the world was created out of the primal fire and ice in Nordic myth.

However, there is another interpretation. The other rune poems and runic amulets found containing Hagalaz show it as a much more destructive force. Because of that, it seems logical to see if the Norwegian poem can be interpreted similarly.

If an apple tree is born from an Appleseed, then a frozen field grows from a seed of ice. The world was created from frost and fire, but in those barren lands, no mortal can survive. We, humans, live in Midgard, the place made by "the creator." Niflheim, the land of ice, is the home of the dead and the cursed. Through that lens, we can see hail as a seed of death, a harbinger of the ice covering the world during the end times.

ᚺᚨᚷᚨᛚᛚ·ᛖᚱ·ᚲᚨᛚᛞᚨᚲᛟᚱᚾ··ᛟᚲ·ᚲᚱᚨᛈᚨᛞᚱᛁᚠᚨ·ᛟᚲ·ᛊᚾᚨᚲᚨ·ᛊᛟᛏᛏ·
ᚷᚱᚨᚾᛞᛟ·ᚺᛁᛚᛞᛁᚾᚷᚱ·

Hagall er kaldakorn ok krapadrífa ok snáka sótt. grando hildingr.

Hail is cold grain and shower of sleet and sickness of serpents.

This verse also opens with hail described as cold grain. Instead of mentioning a god of creation, this verse continues with more frost. Hail is a shower of sleet. Even now, sleet can be a significant problem in Scandinavia, bringing traffic to a halt.

More telling still is the sickness of serpents, a kenning for serpent venom. The idea that ice is venomous is reflected in other myths as well. In the saga, Gylfaginning, the ice that flows from Nifelheim is called venomous several times. The assumption that ice is poison is not that farfetched because every year, the Nordic people would see how the growing cold and frost would slowly seemingly kill all plant life. Not to mention frostbite or hypothermia.

One legendary serpent lives in the frost of Nifelheim, gnawing on the world tree's roots. Its name is Níðhǫggr[44] , and when it breaks free from its prison in the roots of the world tree, it will be one of the signs that Ragnarök has begun. The word Níð means someone who has lost their honor. The dishonored dead were trapped with Níðhǫggr in his prison of ice on the tree's root. When the serpent breaks free, the dishonored dead will fly with him.

The sickness of serpents is not just the poison of the world-ending dragon but the social destruction that oath breakers and murderers bring.

Figure 27: Níðhǫggr

[44] malicious striker.

ᚻᚫᛖᚷᛚ·ᛒᛇᚦ·ᚻᚹᛁᛏᚢᛋᛏ·ᚳᛟᚱᚾᚪ·ᚻᚹᛇᚱᚠᛏ·ᚻᛁᛏ·ᛟᚠ·ᚻᛖᛟᚠᛟᚾᛖᛋ·ᛚᛇ
ᚠᛏᛖ·ᚹᛖᚪᛚᚳᚪᚦ·ᚻᛁᛏ·ᚹᛁᚾᛞᛖᛋ·ᛋᚳᚢᚱᚪ·ᚹᛖᛟᚱᚦᛖᚦ·ᚻᛁᛏ·ᛏᛟ·ᚹᚫᛏᛖ
ᚱᛖ·ᛋᛇᛞᚻᛞᚻᚪᚾ·

Hægl byþ hwitust corna; hwyrft hit of heofones lyfte,
wealcaþ hit windes scura; weorþeþ hit to wætere syððan.

Hail is the whitest of grain; it is whirled from the vault of heaven and is tossed about by gusts of wind and then it melts into water.

The last of the three rune poems starts again with a variation on the grain of ice. It then goes on to describe the whirling chaos of a hailstorm. This can be interpreted as the pandemonium left in the wake of the destruction that Hagalaz represents.

Laying waste to the crops is not the only destruction the hail storm brings. Destroyed crops lead to a winter of famine, and the reduced immunity from starving can lead to a plague. Destruction ripples out from the point of impact.

The rune poem ends with a hopeful message where the hail melts into water. All things pass in the end, even the raw destruction of Hagalaz.

Historic use in charms and amulets

This first example comes from the kragahul spear (DR 196 U), a 5th-century spear shaft found in Funen, Denmark.

Figure 28: kragahul spear

DR 196 U

ᛖᚲ·ᛖᚱᛁᛚᚨᛉ·ᚨᚾᛊᚢᛁᛊᚨᛚᚨᛊ·ᛗᚢᚺᚨ·ᚺᚨᛁᛏᛖ·ᚷᚨᚷᚨᚷᚨ·ᚷᛁᚾᚢ·ᚷᚨᚺᛖᛚᛚᛁ
ᛃᚨ·ᚺᚨᚷᚨᛚᚨ·ᚹᛁᛃᚢ·ᛒᛁ·ᚷ·

Ek Erilaz Ansuïsalas Müha haite. Gagaga Gïnu gahellija, hagala wïju bi g...

I am Called Earl Muha, Ansugisal. I cry a roar resoundingly; I invoke hail in the spear (Macleod & Bernard, 2006).

The construction of this charm is formulaic. The second line heavily uses alliteration and mirrors the third line, where the statement of intent is given. (Gagaga with hagala and Ginu with winju), These last two lines have the same formulaic structure as Galdr (magic) chant. See the chapter on magic for more information on Galdr. The shaft also makes use of bind runes but whether this is for magical reasons or because of limited space is unclear. See the chapter on magic for more information on bind runes. The statement of intent invokes the power of Hagalaz into the spear. Channelling the power of the hailstorm into the spear to increase its destructive power.

The second example of Hagalaz being used in war is the Thorsberg shield buckle. The inscription was made on the backside of the shield buckle, invisible when the buckle was attached to the wooden shield. A hidden inscription is not decorative, so it stands to reason that it was either magical or personally religious. It bears the following inscription:

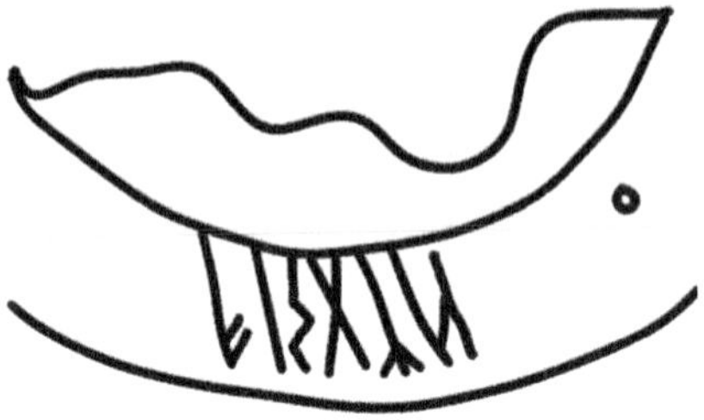

DR 8

Figure 29: Drawing of the Thorsbergshield buckle

ᚨᛁᛊᚷᛉ·ᚺ

Aisgz h

Challenger (of) Hagallaz (hail) (Antonson, 1975)

The interpretation of this runic inscription is difficult, but as it is found on a shield, it might be designed to challenge harmful strikes or arrows by magically enhancing the shield.

Cultural relevance

The first of the stories in the poetic Edda is Völuspá. The translation of this title is prophecies of the Völva or priestess. In it, Odin is told the whole history of the world

An ash I know, / Yggdrasil its name,
With water white / is the great tree wet;
Thence come the dews / that fall in the dales,
Green by Urth's well / does it ever grow.
-Voluspo 19

The story echoes the Anglo-Saxon rune poem. First, there is hail (water white), then it melts away, and growth begins. At the foot of the tree live the three Norns, fate spirits who weave destiny. Of the three sisters, Urth represents the past. Her well is nourished by the past's melting hail, representing the good times after a hard time.

Conclusion

Hagalaz is the rapid strike of the hailstone. If you have ever been in a severe hailstorm, you know how it can strike without warning, shatter glass, rip branches from trees and flatten crops, then disappear in a few minutes, leaving a clear sky behind. After half an hour, the only evidence left is the destruction and slight dampness of the ground.

In readings: rarely a fortunate rune to draw. It denotes a time of change not born out of wish or effort but through outside influence. The change will be sudden and unfavorable, and while the instigating event might be over quickly, its effects will linger around. Ultimately, there is no choice but to go through the hardship and hope better things can be found on the other side.

The other runes that are drawn together with Hagalaz can give a hint as to where the blow will fall. Hagalaz, in combination with Fehu (wealth rune), might indicate financial problems. Hagalaz paired with Tiwaz (justice rune), on the other hand, might suggests legal difficulties. More positively, Hagalaz, paired with Algiz (protection rune), can show that you will weather the storm unscathed.

In advice and counseling: life can deal some harsh blows, and this is the rune of vicious blows. The message of this rune is that after the hail has stopped and melted away, you still have to pick up the pieces. The immediate pain will stop, but it is up to you to pull your life back together.

In magic and ritual: Hagalaz can be used to curse and destroy. We have already discussed using Hagalaz on weapons to enhance their striking power. Just the symbol of Hagalaz might be used to cause destruction. Hagalaz can also be used to break through blockades as long as you are ready to clean up the rubble afterward. As a curse, it can be buried in a runic charm with Naudiz(destiny rune) and Ansuz(Odin's rune) on the location you want to curse, or it can be attached to a symbolic representation of the person or object you want to curse.

Experiencing the runes

Experiencing the storm: Take a walk in the forest after a large storm. Where the Vanir represent the positive aspects of nature, the Jötun represent its destructive side. After such a violent event, room is made for new things to grow. Contemplate that life continues after such an event, but it must continue in a new form. What has come before is dead and destroyed.

Unbind: The following ritual is used to destroy obstacles in your path. Be warned the force of Hagalaz is explosive and will leave a mess in its wake. For the ceremony, you will need a large rock inscribed with a large Hagalaz with red paint, a piece of cloth, and a couple of ice cubes.

Place one of the ice cubes on the cloth and name it the problem or obstacle in your life that you want to destroy. Close your eyes and visualize the name you gave the ice cube taking shape in the ice cube.

Close the cloth over the ice cube and thoroughly smash the ice cube with the rock. Continue doing this as often as desired. Afterward, let the ice shards melt away like hail stones and bury the cloth you used.

Seeking shelter: Knowing where the blow will strike can help you prepare. The blow will come but picking up the pieces afterward might be more manageable. Draw the Hagalaz rune on a piece of paper. Now draw three runes from a rune bag and place the first under the Hagalaz. This rune represents the storm that is coming. The second rune is placed left of Hagalaz. This rune represents the cause of the storm. The last rune is put to the right of Hagalaz. This represents what will help move past the storm.

Figure 30: Drawing of a knight being turned around by evil weather

ᚾ

2.2 Naudiz - Need

Germanic	Gothic	Old English	Old Norse	Sound
Naudhiz	Nauths	Nyd	Naudhr	N

Naudiz is the second rune of the second Ætt. We leave the chaotic forces of the hailstorm to visit the Norns, who weave the destiny and doom of all living things. Naudiz is a rune of destiny and the etymological root for both the English word '*need*' and the Dutch word '*noodlot*' (meaning unfortunate inescapable events). Destiny is what must come to pass as the Gods stuck on their path to Ragnarök. Knowing your future can bring either peace of mind or the despair of being trapped in an unfavorable situation.

The rune poems

Norwegian

ᚾᚨᚢᛞᚺᚱ·ᚷᛖᚱᛖᚱ·ᚾᚨᛖᛈᛈᚨ·ᚲᛟᛊᛏᛖ·ᚾᛟᚲᛏᚨᚾ·ᚲᚨᛖᛚᚱ·ᛁ·ᚠᚱᛟᛊᛏᛖ·

Nauðr gerer næppa koste; nøktan kælr í froste.

Constraint gives scant choice; a naked man is chilled by the frost.

The Norwegian rune poem gives a concise summary of the Nordic views on predestination versus free choice. At birth, many things are fixed, family, geographical location, genetic gifts, and genetic disadvantages. The Nordic people believed that your choices in life could not change destiny. Contrary to the Western paradigm that believes we are entirely in charge of our fate.

Your choices set you on a path and limit your choices in the future. One is never completely free. Opportunities are constrained by outside influences such as social and economic climate and the choices of others. Those are the constraints referred to in the first line of the poem.

The second line echoes the meaning of the first. A naked man cannot choose whether or not to be chilled by the frost.

When studying the meaning of Naudiz, two words are essential, Wyrd and Öorlog. Wyrd comes from the same root as the German word '*werden*' and the Dutch '*worden*' (meaning to become).

Wyrd is the force that moves you from who you are to who you will become based on your choices. The saga's heroes say they do not fear battle because the day they die is already written. This implies that you cannot change your destiny. However, Wyrd is how you live under the constraints you have been given.
The poet Robert Bolt said: "*death comes to us all,*" but how you live is yet to be determined. You cannot escape your Wyrd, the result of your actions, but you can influence your life's direction with your choices.

Öorlog is a composite word consisting of both Ur (meaning primal) and log (meaning law). Öorlog is the universal order. What goes up must come down. Öorlog is the destiny woven for us at the time of our birth by the Norns.

If we contrast the two, Öorlog is the constraint referred to in the Norwegian rune poem. Wyrd is the consequence of the choices we make within those constraints. The fact that a naked man gets chilled by the frost is inescapable, but the choices that led to that outcome are not yet set in stone. Wyrd means that his choices in the present may change his fate for better or worse.

ᚾᚨᚢᛞᚺ·ᛖᚱ·ᚦᛇᛃᚨᚱ·ᚦᚱᚨ·ᛟᚲ·ᚦᚢᚾᚷᚱ·ᚲᛟᛊᛏᚱ·ᛟᚲ·ᚹᚨᛊᛊᚨᛗᛚᛁᚷ·ᚹᛖ
ᚱᚲ·ᛟᛈᛖᚱᚨ·ᚾᛁᚠᛚᚢᚾᚷᚱ.

Nauð er Þýjar þrá ok þungr kostr ok vássamlig verk. opera niflungr.

Constraint grief of the thrall-maid and state of oppression and toilsome work.

The constraint referred to in the Icelandic rune poem is also Öorlog. To the Nordic people, the status one was born in and the rules governing that class were as much a natural law as gravity or the changing of the seasons. The thralls were the lowest of the three casts within the Nordic social structure, and they worked as slaves.

There were several ways one could end up as a thrall. For instance, they could be captured on raids, they could not pay their debts, or they were born into that class. Thralls were expected to do the hard and unforgiving work that came with the class without reward.

However, Nordic society allowed for social mobility in a limited amount. Wyrd can enable you to alter your social standing in life. The existence of the various social classes was considered natural law, and each came with its own constraints.

ᚾᛇᛞ·ᛒᛇᚦ·ᚾᛖᚪᚱᚢ·ᛟᚾ·ᛒᚱᛖᛟᛋᛏᚪᚾ·ᚹᛖᛟᚱᚦᛖᚦ·ᚻᛁ·ᚦᛖᚪᚻ·ᛟᚠᛏ·ᚾᛁ
ᚦᚪ·ᛒᛖᚪᚱᚾᚢᛗ·ᛏᛟ·ᚻᛖᛚᛈᛖ·ᚪᚾᛞ·ᛏᛟ·ᚻᚪᛖᛚᛖ·ᚷᛖᚻᚹᚪᛖᚦᚱᛖ·ᚷᛁᚠ·
ᚻᛁ·ᚻᛁᛋ·ᚻᛚᛇᛋᛏᚪᚦ·ᚪᛖᚱᛟᚱ·

Nyd byþ nearu on breostan; weorþeþ hi þeah oft niþa bearnum to helpe and to hæle gehwæþre, gif hi his hlystaþ æror.

Trouble is oppressive to the heart; yet often it proves a source of help and salvation to the children of men, to everyone who heeds it betimes

---

Goethe wrote: "In limitation, the master reveals himself." Meaning that under constraints, the strong will excel. The Anglo-Saxon rune poem shows a more positive side to this rune in the same spirit.

A life without hardship will not be sung about in the sagas, and will not earn a seat in Odin's hall. Hardship was not seen as a punishment of the Gods to be suffered meekly but instead as a test of true character. Nordic people believed that through hardship, we become stronger and wiser. In the end, our response to suffering reveals who we truly are.

The Nordic people had a stern view of life, as illustrated in the *Hávamál*:

Cattle die, / and kinsmen die,
And so one dies one's self;
But a noble name / will never die,
If good renown one gets.
- Hávamál 77

Almost all the sagas end in hardship, and even the reign of the Gods will end with their deaths at Ragnarök. It is not self-sacrifice that is celebrated but trying every step of the way with full knowledge that the step may be the last. During Ragnarök, the Gods know that they will lose and that the world tree will burn. The final battle is not the last ditch attempt to foil destiny or to buy time for a final plan. The Gods know there is no hope, yet they chose to face their end by fighting a heroic last battle instead of being crippled by fear.

Historic use in charms and amulets

As a rune of Öorlog, the force that fixes destiny in its place, it is an obvious choice for those who want to use the runes to guide the ebb and flow of fate.

Naudiz also shows up in the chapter about Thurisaz and Ansuz because Naudiz is used in the Ansuz-Naudiz desire formula on many different spells. However, Naudiz was not only used in combination with Ansuz but also written on charms on its own.

In Sigrdrífumál, the valkyrie Brynhildr teaches Sigurth, the hero of the poem, both wisdom and rune magic. Most of the runic secrets are not fully explained, and the exact way of working with them can only be guessed based on the clues we have.

However, Naudiz is explicitly named:

Ale-runes learn, / that with lies the wife
Of another betray not thy trust;
On the horn thou shalt write, / and the backs of thy hands,
And Naudiz shalt mark on thy nails.
Thou shalt bless the draught, / and danger escape,
And cast a leek in the cup;
- Sigrdrífumál 7

The text that poem refers to, on the cup and the hand is unknown, but Naudiz must be inscribed on the nails to make the spell work. The writer of *The Poetic Eddas*, from which this story is taken, was Snorri Sturluson. He lived in Iceland in the 12th century when the conversion to Christianity was almost complete. Snorri did not write these texts because he believed in them but out of historical curiosity. In his works, he even proposes Odin was a powerful king of old, whose story, through retelling over the centuries, transformed into stories about a God.

Perhaps the sagas contained more details about the writing on the hands and cup, or maybe it was assumed to be common knowledge. However, Naudiz is still mentioned in several sagas, implying that even after Christianity took over, the use of Naudiz in magic was common knowledge.

Cultural relevance

In Nordic tradition, destiny and femininity were strongly tied. Tacitus, the Roman historian, describes in his book *Histories* the account of the prophetess Veleda as follows:

Veleda, a maiden of the tribe of the Bructeri, who possessed extensive dominion; for by ancient usage the Germans attributed to many of their women prophetic powers and, as the superstition grew in strength, even actual divinity. The authority of Veleda was then at its height, because she had foretold the success of the Germans and the destruction of the legions.
- Germania 61

We can find a similar account penned down by Julius Ceasar in his *Commentarii de Bello Gallico*, a history of the war against the Gauls:

When Caesar inquired of his prisoners, wherefore Ariovistus did not come to an engagement, he discovered this to be the reason-that among the Germans it was the custom for their matrons to pronounce from lots and divination, whether it were expedient that the battle should be engaged in or not; that they had said, "that it was not the will of heaven that the Germans should conquer, if they engaged in battle before the new moon.".
- Commentaries on the Gallic war 1:50

These women referred to in these quotes were called Völva in the Nordic cultures and were prophetesses but also practitioners of the magic called seiðr, which was reserved for women.

Völvas travelled with their retinue from village to village to offer their services. We know the Volva were highly respected and generously compensated for their assistance from the sagas and archaeological finds. In Eirík's saga Rauða, the arriving Völva is offered the high seat usually reserved for the Jarl or king of that tribe. In Volspula, even Odin visits a Völva to seek knowledge of the future.

Not just in Völvas do we see the connection between the feminine and destiny. The Norns, weavers of Öorlog, were all female, and so were all the other Disir (the spirits of Wyrd and Öorlog).

However, fortune-telling is not solely the province of the feminine. Tacitus makes the following observation about the Nordic tribe's obsession with destiny.

They attach the highest importance to the taking of auspices and casting lots. Their usual procedure with the lot is simple. They cut off a branch from a nut-bearing tree and slice it into strips these they mark with different signs and throw them at random onto a white cloth. Then the state's priest, if it is an official consultation, or the father of the family, in a private one, offers prayer to the gods and looking up towards heaven picks up three strips, one at a time, and, according to which sign they have previously been marked with, makes his interpretation. If the lots forbid an undertaking, there is no deliberation that day about the matter in question. If they allow it, further confirmation is required by taking auspices.

- Germania 10

Destiny was a real force for the Nordic people, not only for heroes and kings but for the common folk as well.

Conclusion

Naudiz is a rune of Öorlog, that which must come to pass, the very fundamental laws that govern the universe. The rune represents the boundaries that constrain us and force us into action. These limitations allow us to find orientation to where we want to go, and in this way, it is also the rune of the Norns.

In readings: Naudiz represents the external restraints on your life that limit your options. It could also mean that pivotal predestined points in your life are approaching. This rune on its own is hard to read for many questions as it just refers to the inevitability of certain events.

In combination with Tiwaz (justice rune), for example, it can point to constraints imposed by law, or with Othala (ancestors rune), it can imply inescapable events flowing out of your family or heritage.

Naudiz does not necessarily have to mean that hardship is coming. Naudiz, combined with Wunjo (joy rune), would suggest that inescapable joy is coming your way.

In advice and counseling: Shit happens. Will you drown in it, or will you fertilize your garden? Naudiz, in counseling, asks you to look at your restraints and then, within your limitations, see possibilities.

In magic and ritual: Naudiz is used in amulet magic to weave a charm into the tapestry of fate. The three Norns, Skuld, Verdandi, and Urdr, are the primary guardians of the tapestry of fate but hardly the only ones. All the races have their Norns capable of looming destiny. Mortal users of Galdr or Seidh were also thought to have the power to change the weave.

The Naudiz rune is used in several types of magic and amulets as a charm word. This way, Naudiz can be used in staves, runic charms, bind runes, runic rows, and chants. In ritual, the rune can also be used (in three repetitions) to represent the Norns.

Experiencing the runes

Spá: Spá is the Norse name for the art of prophecy; Völva were also called Spákonna (meaning spa woman or seeing woman). You did a general reading in the chapter on Ansuz, and now it is time to do a specific reading. Go to the divination section and look up a lay that fits the question you want to ask. Make sure it is a question you know the outcome of in a week or two. Write down your casting and interpretation. Afterward, re-examine your answer. Was it significant? Do you see a different interpretation with the new perspective?

Dísablót: Once a year, the Dísablót was held. A great festival where people gather from far and wide. The gathering was political and religious but also resembled a fair and lasted about a week. During this time, sacrifices were made to ensure good fortune.

Dísablót was held with the return of spring, but an offering to the Norns can always be made. Use the Naudiz rune to represent the three sisters and their kin and present them with an offering.

Weaving the loom: The Naudiz rune is not only used to read the loom of destiny but also to influence it. One of the easiest charms to create is the rune row. Create a simple rune row charm (see the chapter on magic for examples) and carry it with you for a week. After a week, see if you noticed any results and write them down.

Figure 31: The Norns weaving

ᛁ

2.3 Isa - Ice

Germanic	Gothic	Old English	Old Norse	Sound
Isa	Eis	Is	Íss	I

Isa is the third rune of the second Ætt. Like Hagalaz, this is a rune of frost, but unlike the hailstorm's sudden destructiveness, Isa represents winter's long standstill. Isa is also the rune of constraints; however, unlike the call of destiny (Naudiz), the ice will melt on its own when the time comes.

The rune poems

Norwegian

ᛁᛊ᛫ᚲᛟᛚᛚᚢᛗ᛫ᛒᚱᚢ᛫ᛒᚱᚨᛖᛁᛞᚺᚨ᛫ᛒᛚᛁᚾᛞᚨᚾ᛫ᚦᚨᚱᚠ᛫ᚨᛏ᛫ᛚᚨᛖᛁᛞᚺᚨ᛫

Ís kollum brú bræiða;blindan þarf at læiða.

Ice we call the broad bridge; the blind man must be led.

A kenning for ice is the broad bridge, referencing a river that has frozen over. In the winter, when it is so cold the rivers are frozen, life was at its most brutal in the Nordic countries. The second line referencing a blind man being led does not just apply to the blind but to all those who need help during such times. A community can only survive if they are ready to support each other. Ice is treacherous because it is not a permanent state. The *Hávamál* warns:

Give praise to the day at evening, / to a woman on her pyre,
To a weapon which is tried, / to a maid at wedlock,
To ice when it is crossed, / to ale that is drunk.

- Hávamál 71

This poem cautions against rash action. A wise person does not cross the ice without testing it, nor do they trust a weapon that has not been tried. However, the poem below suggests that ice is not universally treacherous but instead advises taking advantage of the right moment.

By the fire drink ale, / over ice go on skates;
Buy a steed that is lean, / and a sword when tarnished,
The horse at home fatten, / the hound in thy dwelling.
- Hávamál 83

ᛁᛊᛊ·ᛖᚱ·ᚨᚱᛒᛟᚱᚲᚱ·ᛟᚲ·ᚢᚾᚾᚨᚱ·ᚦᚨᚲ·ᛟᚲ·ᚠᛖᛁᚷᚱᚨ·ᛗᚨᚾᚾᚨ·ᚠᚨᚱ·ᚷᛚ
ᚨᚲᛁᛖᛊ·ᛃᛟᚠᚢᚱᚱ·

Icelandic

Íss er árbörkr ok unnar þak ok feigra manna fár. glacies jöfurr.

Ice Bark of rivers and roof of the wave and destruction of the doomed.

Like the Norwegian poem, the Icelandic rune poem also gives us kennings for ice. All these kennings, the broad bridge, the bark of rivers, and the roof of the wave perfectly show the transient nature of ice. Water freezes into solid ground, and the rushing river turns quiet and still; however it is not permanent. Under the seemingly solid ice, the river still flows.

The ice of winter brings respite to farmers and warriors alike. No crops are sown or harvested, and the cold and the snow bring temporary peace to any war. The warrior who is not prepared will fall, as will the farmer who has not rationed will starve. Eventually, the snow and ice will disappear, and only those who were decisive will survive. However, destruction will surely come to those that do not heed this warning.

ᛁᛋ·ᛒᛇᚦ·ᛟᚠᛖᚱᛖᚫᛚᛞ·ᚢᚾᚷᛖᛗᛖᛏᚢᛗ·ᛋᛚᛁᛞᛟᚱ·ᚷᛚᛁᛋᚾᚫᚦ·ᚷᛚᚫᛖᛋᚻᛚ
ᚢᛏᚢᚱ·ᚷᛁᛗ·ᛗᚢᛗ·ᚷᛖᛚᛁᚲᚢᛋᛏ·ᚠᛚᛟᚱ·ᚠᛟᚱᛋᛏᛖ·ᚷᛖᚹᛟᚱᚢᚻ·
ᚠᚫᛖᚷᛖᚱ·ᚫᚾᛋᛇᚾᛖ·

Is byþ ofereald, ungemetum slidor, glisnaþ glæshluttur gim mum gelicust, flor forste geworuht, fæger ansyne.

Ice is very cold and immeasurably slippery;
it glistens as clear as glass and most like to gems;
it is a floor wrought by the frost, fair to look upon.

The Anglo-Saxon rune poem highlights the duality of ice. On the one hand, it describes the beauty of ice, in awe of its splendor. On the other hand, it represents the dangerous aspects of ice in a way that almost seems a fearful reverence. This duality is reminiscent of how fairies were regarded in fairy tales, otherworldly, beautiful, unpredictable, and incredibly dangerous. This is further reinforced by the line about ice that is clear as gems, this is reminiscent of fairy gold, beautiful to look at, but if you take it with you, it will just disappear.

Historic use in charms and amulets

Isa seems to have been used in several amulets to cool things down, literally and figuratively. The first amulet is a copper plate found in Sigtuna, Sweden. The inscription seems to deal with the literal coolness.

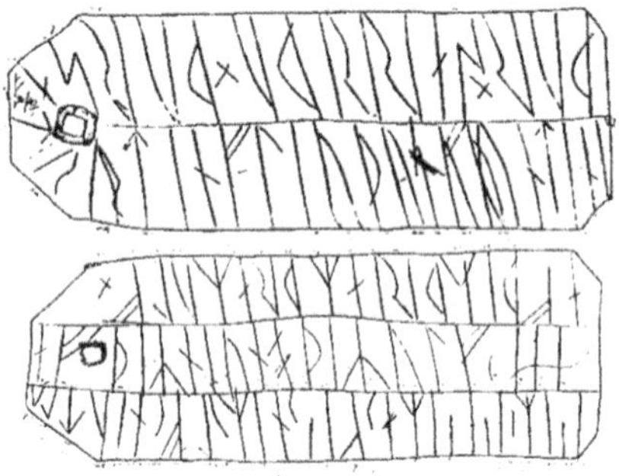

Figure 32: Sigtuna copperplate

U Fv1933;134

ᚦᚢᚱᛊ·ᛊᚨᚱᚱᛁᛞᚺᚢ·ᚦᚢᚱᛊᚨ·ᛞᚱᛟᛏᛏᛁᚾᚾ·ᚠᛚᛁᚢ·ᚦᚢ·ᚾᚢ·ᚠᚢᚾᛞᛁᚾᚾ·ᛖᛊ·ᚺᚨ
ᚠ·ᚦᚨᛖᚱ·ᚦᚱᛁᚨᚱ·ᚢᛚᚠᚱ·ᚺᚨᚠ·ᚦᚨᛖᚱ·ᚾᛁᚢ·ᚾᚨᚢᛞᚺᛁᚱ·ᚢᛚᚠᚱ·ᛁᛁᛁ·ᛁᛊᛁᚱ·ᚦᛁᛊ·ᛁᛊ
ᛁᚱ·ᚨᚢᚲᛁ·ᛊ·ᚢᚾᛁᚱᚢᛚᚠᚱ·ᚾᛁᚢᛏ·ᛚᛇᚠᛁᚨ·

Þurs särriðu, Þursa dröttinn! Flïu Þü nü! Fundinn es. Haf Þǽr Þriär, ülfr! Haf Þǽr nïu nauðir ülfr! Iii isir Þis isir auki s unir, ülfr. Niüt lyfia!

Troll of fevers, prince of the trolls, Fly now, you are found!
You get three tears, wolf! You get nine cravings, wolf!
III Ice With These Ice runes be satisfied Wolf, May the healing satisfy you (Eriksson & Zetterholm, 1933)

The Ogres (Thurs) and the wolf represent the malicious influences causing the fever. They are treated to three pangs (Thurisaz runes) to harm them, nine needs (Naudiz runes to constrain them), and three Isa runes to break the fever. The Ice runes are referenced three times (mark the repetition of the number three), once as a set of three times the rune Isa, and twice as the word 'isir' (Ice), so ice seems to be the core focus of the spell.

Since this spell specifically targets wound fever, the cold of Isa was likely meant to counteract the heat of fever and initiate healing.

We see Isa used again to cool things down on another coper amulet dating from the seventh century, found in a Gotlandic grave.

G 361

Figure 33: Gothlandic copper plate

ᚦᚢ·ᚢ· ᚦᚢᚱᚢᛊ·ᛁᛁᛁ·ᚺᚨᛏᚱ·ᚾᛖᛗ·

þu-u- þurus iii hatr nem

Thor Thor (isa)(isa)(isa) take hate. (Macleod & Bernard, 2006)

The second part of the charm is written upside down. The previous charm was meant to cool down the physical heat of a fever, but this one is intended to cool down the metaphorical heat of an argument. Interestingly, in rune magic, there is no real difference between the two.

Cultural relevance

In Hans Christian Anderson's: "the ice queen,"[45] a glass shard from an enchanted mirror made by trolls gets lodged into a boy's heart. At that moment, the boy's heart freezes over, and he can no longer love nor see the beauty in things except for ice crystals. The ice queen takes the boy away and is eventually saved by Gerda, the girl who was his closest childhood friend. She finds the boy in the ice palace of the ice queen, sitting on a lake of ice, trying to solve a puzzle the ice queen made for him.

When she finds him in this almost frozen state, the girl cries hot tears on the boy's chest, which melt his heart. It is a great story, and this summary does not do it justice. In this story, we find the otherworldliness of ice, its beauty, the way it temporarily stops everything, and its danger. We can infer that the shard of glass symbolizes a shard of ice. In ancient Scandinavia, glass was rare and did not become common until the Christian era. Therefore, the original myth is unlikely to have mentioned glass.

In fairy tales, ice-glass is often represented as a temporary state where beauty from the other world enters the realm of reality. For example, the glass coffin of snow white where she lay, magically suspended in time until her true love freed her. Or the glass slipper of Cinderella, the focus of the spell cast by her fairy godmother (the Fylgja, in Norse mythology) that temporarily gave her the appearance of a noblewoman.

The ice of winter is an in-between moment, like dusk or dawn. If the circle of the year can be symbolically seen as the circle of life, then spring is birth, summer is our prime, autumn is our slow decline, and winter is death. Death is the moment that we pass into the other unseen world until we are again reborn in spring. Ice is the unearthly moment between dying and rebirth.

---

[45] An originally Scandinavian folk tale.

Conclusion

Isa is the rune of ice, the force that suspends all growth for a few months and covers the world with wonder, beauty, and danger. Isa is the force that, against all common sense, allows you to walk on a river. The icy winter of Isa is steadier than the frozen hail of Hagalaz and its sudden storm, but that does not mean that it is safe or reliable.

In readings: Isa means that things are coming to a halt, the natural order is temporarily suspended, and it is at these moments it is crucial to watch your steps. This is also a moment of contemplation; no sustainable new projects can start in the ice of Isa, but that does make this a great moment to take stock and see where you want to go when the ice melts.

In combination with Sowlio (sun rune), this rune indicates that the time of standing still is coming to an end, and the sun is melting the ice. In combination with Algiz (elk rune), this might say that the frozen state you are in is necessary and keeping you safe. When drawn with Eihwaz (world tree rune), this rune represents Niffelheim, the realm of eternal ice hanging from the world tree.

In advice and counseling: Like in nature, where everything has its season, winter is necessary for every life. This is true not just for the winter following the autumn of our lifespan but for moments of introspection in our daily life. Burn-outs are on the rise in every job sector and even in schoolchildren. In our modern lives, we have learned that we no longer have to be controlled by winter. This allows us much greater flexibility, but it also steals from us the rest that winter brings. We will burn out if we don't let winter into our lives.

Don't try to force your way through, don't see your current situation as stagnation but as a moment of rest like a tree in winter. Blooms that sprout before the end of the frost will wilt away. Save your energy for the proper time.

In magic and ritual: As a rune of ice, Isa has many different applications in charms and spells. Isa can be chanted, made part of a charm in combination with Ansuz (Odin's rune) and Naudiz(destiny rune), or made into a bind rune with Berkana(birch rune) to help with healing magic to assist in bringing down a fever.

Isa can also be used in a bind rune with Mannaz (humankind rune) and placed under a doormat to cool down relationships, both the fires of passion and burning rage in the household.

Experiencing the runes

Into stillness: There are two types of meditation. The first type we have discovered in Wunjo(joy rune) relies on focusing more upon one single thought, object or point until the mind becomes a laser burning through the outer layers of reality, opening us up to more profound truths. The second type of meditation aims at slowly letting go of all thoughts and ego until only stillness remains. A gaping nothing, brimming with possibility like the Ginnungagap.

Take a comfortable position, with your spine as straight as possible, mimicking the Isa rune. Start by slowly breathing; for each breath in, take a count, and for each breath out repeat the same count (breath in one, breath out one, breath in two, breath out two, etc.). Do this until you reach the count of ten and then count down in the same manner back to zero.

After you reach zero, stop counting your breaths but keep focusing on them for as long as you want. Then as you feel relaxed and comfortable, let go of focusing on your breath. Try to let go of all your thoughts with the last breath out. New thoughts will flow in, but observe them and let them pass.

Try this meditation once a day for a week, set an alarm each day starting at least 5 minutes, and add a minute every day. Having an alarm will help give you a goal, and slowly lengthening it will help you increase your focus.

Finding tranquility: Take a day off, and leave behind your phone and all your electronics. Go swimming, go to an amusement park but most importantly, leave your home and all connections to your day-to-day life that give you stress behind. Being away and without electronics, you cannot affect the regular world. Enjoy this short respite in the other world.

Frost jewels: Depending on where you live, and the time of year, you might not always have an opportunity to experience the beauty of ice while studying this rune. To circumvent that, we will use some modern technology. First, collect some small flowers, violets, lilies of the vale, or daisies are good choices. Get an ice tray out and place a flower in each segment.

For the next step, double-boil a kettle of water. Let the water completely cool between boiling. This will allow for very clear ice. After letting the water cool down a second time, put the flowers in an ice tray, pour the water over the flowers then cover them with plastic. Put the tray, still covered, into the fridge. Wait a couple of hours and take out your results.

Figure 34: Snowflake

ᛃ

2.4 Jera - Year

Germanic	Gothic	Old English	Old Norse	Sound
Jera	Jér	Gér	Ár	J

Jera is the fourth rune of the second Ætt, and you can see that the English word year has its roots in Jera. Jera represents the turning of the seasons. The hail storms drift away, the ice melts, and we prepare to reap a plentiful bounty. It is time to harvest what we have sown with our efforts and no longer be dependent on the whims of the Norns.

The rune poems

Norwegian

ᚨᚱ·ᛖᚱ·ᚷᚢᛗᚾᚨ·ᚷᛟᛞᚺᛖ·ᚷᛖᛏ·ᛖᚲ·ᚨᛏ·ᛟᚱᚱ·ᚹᚨᚱ·ᚠᚱᛟᛞᚺᛖ·

Ár er gumna góðe; get ek at orr var Fróðe.

Plenty is a boon to men; I say that Fróði was generous.

The first line of the Norwegian rune poem immediately alludes to the most critical aspect of Jera. In modern-day society, most food is purchased in stores, but in the old days, food came in seasons. This is a rune of bounty and harvest.

The name Fróði mentioned in the second line has three possible interpretations. Fróði has been speculated to be one of the nicknames for Freyr. In the context of this poem, this makes sense, as Freyr is a God of fertility and plenty. In *Heimskringla,* Freyr falls in love with the Jötun maiden Gerðr, and at the end of the saga, they are to be wed in a place called Barri. The translation of Barri is contested, but one interpretation is grain island. This translation fits Freyr as a fertility God. The tradition of having ritual weddings or having sex in the farm fields to magically increase the fertility of the land was widespread in the Nordic regions.

Fróði is also the name of several Danish, mythical and historical kings. In the Old days, the king was more than just a figurehead or a holder of political power; the king was thought of as the literal representation of the kingdom he ruled. A strong and vital king would ensure a bountiful harvest, mild winters, and economic growth.

The burial places of beloved kings became places of worship, and the kings themself were treated as Alfar. There is a strong relationship between the Alfar and burial mounds. There are many myths throughout Europe about hapless shepherds or greedy thieves that enter a grave mound. The thief is usually quickly turned around by the supernatural forces that haunt the tomb, but the accidental wanderer often shares a night at the court before leaving. The most famous examples of this are those of Charlemagne and King Arthur. Both are said to sleep under a hill somewhere until the hour of their country's greatest need when they will rise again. The Fróði mentioned might be representing a deceased king.

In the Ynglinga saga, Snorri's story somewhat integrates these three interpretations. For the Christian Snorri, Freyr was not necessarily a God but a man. According to the Ynglinga saga, Odin and the Aesir came from Asia, and after many wars, Odin became king of Sweden. Njord inherited the crown after Odin, and Freyr, in turn, inherited the crown from his father, Njord. When Freyr took the throne, an unprecedented period of prosperity and peace began, called the Frode[46] period. After Freyr passed away, his sister Freya kept his death a secret, and for three years, while Freyr was embalmed in a grave mound, offers of gold, silver, and copper were made to him. According to Snorri, the Swedes kept bringing offerings to Freyr's grave mound, and he was worshiped as the "God of this world." After three years, the Swedes found out Freyr had passed away and insisted that he be kept embalmed and not cremated so that he could keep bringing prosperity to Sweden.

Icelandic

ᚨᚱ·ᛖᚱ·ᚷᚢᛗᚾᚨ·ᚷᛟᛞᚺᛁ·ᛟᚲ·ᚷᛟᛏᛏ·ᛊᚢᛗᚨᚱ·ᚨᛚᚷᚱᛟᛁᚾᚾ·ᚨᚲᚱ·ᚨᚾᚾᚢᛊ·
ᚨᛚᛚᚹᚨᛚᛞᚱ·

Ár er gumna góði ok gott sumar algróinn akr. annus allvaldr.

Plenty is a boon to men and good summer and thriving crops.

The Icelandic rune poem focuses again on the gift to men, that is, the harvest. It is also worth noting when Yera speaks of abundance concerning food, it is only positive, whereas in contrast, Fehu's abundance of gold is not so unambiguously positive. Plenty is simply a good summer and thriving crops.

---

[46] This is possibly etymologically related to the Norwegian Fróði, It is also the origin of the name Frodo that JRR Tolkien picked for his main character.

ᚷᛖᚱ·ᛒᛇ·ᚷᚢᛗᛖᚾᚨ·ᚺᛁᚺᛏ··ᛞᚺᛟᚾᚾᛖ·ᚷᛟᛞ·ᛚᚨᛖᛏᛖᚦ·ᚺᚨᛚᛁᚷ·ᚺᛖᛟᚠ
ᛟᚾᛖᛋ·ᚲᛇᚾᛁᚾᚷ·ᚺᚱᚢᛋᚨᚾ·ᛋᛇᛚᛚᚨᚾ·ᛒᛖᛟᚱᚺᛏᛖ·ᛒᛚᛖᛞᚨ·ᛒᛖᛟᚱᚾᚢᛗ
·ᛟᚾᛞ·ᛞᚺᛖᚨᚱᚠᚢᛗ·

Ger byþ gumena hiht, ðonne God læteþ, halig heofones cyning,
hrusan syllan beorhte bleda beornum ond ðearfum.

Summer is a joy to men, when God, the holy King of Heaven,
suffers the earth to bring forth shining fruits for rich and poor alike.

The Anglo-Saxon rune poem is somewhat Christianised, where God, the holy king of Heaven, might have been Freyr, Fróði, or even Odin. The sentiment that a good harvest is a boon is repeated in this rune poem as in the other two. In modern days Yera is sometimes taken as a rune of karma because of its cyclical nature and connection to harvest, reaping what you sow.

While this is an interesting connection, all three rune poems are clear that it is not one hundred percent our actions that determine the outcome of what we reap. Good harvest, shining fruit, and summer are boons given to us; with what we are given, we have to do our best.

Historic use in charms and amulets

In the early 19th century, a runic stone was found in the Swedish town of Stentoft. The stone dates to the fifth century and gives blessings to new farmers in the area in a fashion reminiscent of the Norwegian rune poem.

Figure 35: the stentoft standing stone

DR357

ᚾᛁᚢᚺᚨᛒᛟᚱᚢᛗᚱ·ᚾᛁᚢᚺᚨᚷᛖᛊᛏᚱᚢᛗᚱ·ᚺᚨᚦᚢᚹᛟᛚᚠᚨᚱ·ᚷᚨᚠ·ᛃ·ᚺᚨᚱᛁᚹᛟ
ᛚᚠᚨᚱ·ᛗᚨᚷᛁᚢᛊᚾᚢ·ᚺᛚᛖ·ᚺᛁᛞᛖᚱ·ᚱᚢᚾᛟ·ᚾᛟ·ᚠᛖᛚᚺᛖᚲᚨ·ᚺᛖᛞᛖᚱᚨ·ᚷᛁᚾᚾ
ᛟᚱᚢᚾᛟᚱ·ᚺᛖᚱᛗᚨᛚᚨᛊ·ᚨᛖᚱ·ᚨᛖᚱᚷᛁᚢ·ᚹᛖᛚᚨᛞᚢᛞᛊ·ᛊᚨ·ᚦᚨᛏ·ᛒᚱᛁᚢᛏᛏᛁ
ᛈ·

Niuhabörumr, niuhagestrumr Haþuwolfar gaf J. Hariwolfar magiusnu hlë. Hider rünö no felheka hedera, ginnoruünör. Hermaläs ær ærgiu; wëladüds sä þat briuttip.

To the new farmers, to the new guests, Hathuwolf gave J(Yera). Hariwolf protection to (your) descendants. A run of bright runes I commit here: Mighty runes. Protectionless (because of their) perversion; an insidious death to he who breaks this (Macleod & Bernard, 2006).

The name Hatuwolfar[47] is most likely ritual in nature, just as the similarly themed HariWolf[48] later on the stone. Hatuwolfar and

[47] Meaning warrior wolf.

[48] Meaning battle wolf.

Hariwolf are welcoming new farmers and new guests to the land. In all probability, they were either the Jarl of this region or Landvættir / Alfar, as they are implied to be able to protect not only this generation but those to come as well.

Whether it's the current Jarl or a supernatural entity being invoked, the end goal is the same, good harvest. Similarly to the Norwegian rune poem, we see that a good harvest is a gift given to the farmers by a greater political or spiritual power.

Cultural relevance

When we think of the Norse, most people think of Viking raids, plundering, and pillaging. However, much like their more southern European cousins, they were farmers in the Northern regions. Even those who went on the raids and gave the Vikings their now commonly used name would return home to farm.

The summer months would be the high point of the year, just before the hard toil of the harvest came and long before the semi-starvation of winter set in. This was a time of plenty when hunting and gathering came easy. The abundance of food and good weather allowed people to make social calls to neighbors and visit festivals.

The summer and autumn months also allowed traveling storytellers and artisans to peddle wares. These distractions were very welcome in a time before digital entertainment and made for a stark contrast with the isolation of the winter months.

This rune is the joy that summer brings and represents that golden moment once per year where you are full after a hungry winter when there are feasts instead of isolation and progress instead of slow entropy.

Conclusion

Yera is a rune that represents the year cycle but emphasizes the return to summer and harvest. As the year's wheel turns, you face the consequences of what you did before. A farmer that works hard both in spring and autumn and is frugal in winter is more likely to prosper. The people of the North were realists, and no amount of hard work could save you from unforeseen outside influences. In this rune, those outside influences are more often than not seen as benign, giving just that extra push to make it to another great summer

In readings: Yera means that things are moving along and coming to fruition. This is the movement up towards a bustling summer. You will leave the darkness and cold of the previous situation behind and breathe freely again. Now comes a time of greater freedom.

In combination with Fehu(cattle rune), for instance, this rune can indicate that your financial situation is either getting out of a slump or taking a turn for the better. The main message of Yera is that your financial situation is going to allow for more freedom.

In combination with Kenaz(torch rune), Yera is the end of sickness. The fever has been burned away, and feverish heat turns into the more gentle, pleasant warmth of a Scandinavian summer

In advice and counseling: Yera can signify transitional periods in one's life. This is a gentle reminder that all winters must end, and summer will come again. It invites you to an optimistic approach to life's problems and asks you to remember the cyclical nature of our existence. Life is a combination of joy and suffering.

In magic and ritual: Yera was used in the Stentoft standing stone as part of a conduit for the Jarl to channel his power to give a good harvest and good summer for the people moving there. Given the importance of a good harvest, it is very likely that this rune was used in multiple rituals and objects.

Today, this rune can be used during rites of passage where you move from one part of your life to another. This rune can be made into a bind rune with Ansuz (Odin's rune) and Sowilo (sun rune) to help with successful graduation and moving on to a successful career.

Experiencing the runes

Circle of growth: Experiencing the bounty that nature gives is easier than it might seem. Plant a little fruit-bearing plant indoors or outdoors, depending on the weather conditions and your garden. Strawberries and blueberries are both relatively low maintenances options. Make sure your little plant stays watered and fertilized (but take care not to overdo it) and see what you get in return for this minimal effort.

The harvest king: No matter our wit, perseverance, and hard work, luck will always remain a factor in our successes and failures. Make a charm to honor and thank the harvest king for the success in your life. You can use bind runes, charm symbols, and written statements. Place the charm somewhere central and make small offerings to it over the week. The precise runes and offerings you use depend on what your idea of the harvest king is. Is it the God Freyr, an ancient king, or the local Landvættir or Alfar? Try to find runes and offerings that fit your focus.

The great feast: Great feasts are still a part of many different cultures. America has a harvest festival in the form of Thanksgiving, and cultures worldwide celebrate the shortest day and the true king's return with a meal in many different names. Go for dinner with friends or see a movie or show to celebrate life.

ᛇ

2.5 Eihwaz – Yew Tree

Germanic	Gothic	Old English	Old Norse	Sound
Eihwaz	Eihwas	Eoh	ÁlWar	Y

Eihwaz is the fifth rune of the second Ætt and the middle point of the runic alphabet. Where Jera is a rune of the people and celebration, Eihwaz is a rune of Seidh[49] and introspection. Eihwaz is fittingly a rune of center points as it represents the world tree that connects the nine realms and stands as the center of the universe.

The rune poems

ᛇᚱ·ᛖᚱ·ᚹᛖᛏᚱᚷᚱᛟᚾᛊᛏᚱ·ᚹᛁᛞᚺᚨ·ᚹᚨᛖᚾᛏ·ᛖᚱ·ᛖᚱ·ᛒᚱᛖᚾᚾᚱ·ᚨᛏ·ᛊᚹᛁᛞᚺᚨ·

Norwegian

Ýr er vetrgrønstr viða vænt er, er brennr, at sviða.

Yew is ever green it is wont to crackle when it burns.

The first line is very straightforward. The yew tree is an evergreen, so it

[49] A form of Shamanistic magic associated with Odin and women, more on this in the chapter on Magic.

stays green even in the heart of winter. One of the kennings for Yggdrasil, the world tree, is vetrgrønstr viða (evergreen), the exact same wording used in this rune poem. Yggdrasil, in older translations,[50] is often described as an ash tree; however, this is likely a mistranslation because the ash tree is not an evergreen tree. This confusion originates from a kenning for the yew tree, *barraskr,* meaning needle ash.

Therefore, this rune represents not only yew trees in general but also the most essential tree in Nordic cosmology, Yggdrasil. The yew tree is also one of the longest-living trees in Europe, making it a likely candidate for the eternal Yggdrasil.

Yggdrasil's origin is unknown, and perhaps in the cyclical nature of Nordic mythology, it has always been there and always will be. Its mighty branches form the stage for all Nordic mythology, from the realms of Muspelheim and Niflheim to Ragnarök, where the ancient tree is burnt but not destroyed.

Yggdrasil's branches reach into the heavens, and its three roots plunge to depths unknown where they drink from sacred wells. All kinds of mythological creatures live in the tree. The name Yggdrasil translates to Odin's steed; this could have multiple meanings. In a shamanistic context, the bridge between worlds is often described as a tree reaching into the heavens. It could be that Yggdrasil is Odin's steed because it is the medium through which he travels the nine realms. This would make a certain amount of sense as the way Odin acquired knowledge is not in a scholarly way but instead in an ecstatic shamanistic way[51].

Another interpretation might be that Yggdrasil references Odin claiming the runes. The *Hávamál* describes Odin hanging himself for nine days and nine nights from the Yggdrasil while fasting. Fasting and physical hardships were used in shamanistic rituals to achieve a trance-

---

[50] And some modern ones as well.
[51] This form of magic is more similar to Sidh magic then to Galdr. this part of the mythic stories the runes were about to be discovered. More on this in the chapter on magic

like state. On the ninth day, Odin fell from Yggdrasil and gained insight into the mystery of the runes. No matter the interpretation, Yggdrasil or the Yew tree is a mystical bridge between realms

The second line is straightforward, the wood of the yew tree burns slowly with intense heat and is good as firewood. Also, the wood is rich in resin, which gives a pleasant smell and causes crackling when burnt.

Icelandic

ᛇᚱ᛫ᛖᚱ᛫ᛒᛖᚾᛞᚱ᛫ᛒᛟᚷᛁ᛫ᛟᚲ᛫ᛒᚱᛟᛏᚷᛃᚨᚱᚾᛏ᛫ᛃᚨᚱᚾ᛫ᛟᚲ᛫ᚠiᚠᚢ᛫ᚠᚨᚱᛒᚨ
ᚢᛏᛁ᛫ᚨᚱᚲᚢᛋ᛫ᛇᚾᚷᛚᛁᚾᚷᚱ᛫

Ýr er bendr bogi ok brotgjarnt járn ok fífu fárbauti. arcus ynglingr.

Yew is bent bow and brittle iron and giant of the arrow.

The yew tree is not native to Iceland, so that would mean it would be imported in the form of bows. Yew wood was the most popular for making bows because it combines remarkable strength with excellent elasticity.

The historical connection between the bow and the yew tree is reinforced mythologically in Grímmnismál. In this saga, Odin tells us one of the rare titbits of lore we have about Ullr. The exact nature of the God Ullr has been lost to us, and we know only about this God through kennings and side mentions in the sagas. We know that he was known for his skill in the bow and that his domain was Ydalir, the dale of yew trees.

Older Yew trees can grow so heavy that their trunk rips apart. Sometimes that is the end of the tree, and other times the tree lives on as two separate trees. The fact that such a hard tree can split itself probably earned it the nickname Brittle Iron. The last line is another kenning for the yew tree and links to the archery aspect of the yew.

ᛖᛟᚻ·ᛒᛇᚦ·ᚢᛏᚨᚾ·ᚢᚾᛋᛗᛖᚦᛖ·ᛏᚱᛖᛟᚹ·ᚻᛖᚨᚱᛞ·ᚻᚱᚢᛋᚨᚾ·ᚠᚨᛖᛋᛏ·ᚻ
ᛇᚱᛞᛖ·ᚠᛇᚱᛖᛋ·ᚹᛇᚱᛏᚱᚢᛗᚢᚾ·ᚢᚾᛞᛖᚱᚹᚱᛖᚦᛇᛞ·ᚹᛇᚾ·ᛟᚾ·ᛖᚦᛚᛖ·

Eoh byþ utan unsmeþe treow, heard hrusan fæst, hyrde fyres,
wyrtrumun underwreþyd, wyn on eþle.

The yew is a tree with rough bark, hard and fast in the earth,
supported by its roots, a guardian of flame and a joy upon an estate.

The yew tree's bark is a very distinct pattern but is not necessarily rougher than the average tree. The first line might be interpreted more along the lines of "don't judge a book by its cover," as the bark does not show the tree's many uses inside.

The second line is fitting for Yggdrasil and also for other yew trees. They can grow hundreds of years old and produce strong and resilient wood.

The positive burning qualities from the last line have already been covered. The joy on the estate has to do with the magical qualities ascribed to the Yew tree. Germany still has the saying "Vor den Eiben kann kein Zauber bleiben" or "No magic can last in front of the yew." This saying paints the yew tree as a very potent countercharm.

Figure 36: Bark of a yew

Historic use in charms and amulets

In the Dutch town of Britsum, in the province of Frisia, a small yew charm has been found dating from around the end of the fourth century.

Figure 37: photo from Fries Museum, Leeuwarden / Collection Koninklijk Fries Genootschap.

R III. 11

ᛒᚫᛖᚾ·ᛁ·ᚨ·ᛒᚺᛖᚱᛖᛏ·ᛞᚢᛞ·ᛚᛁᛞ·ᛁᚾ·ᛒᚫᛖᚱᚫᛖᛏ·ᛗᛖ

bæn i a beret dud / : LID / in bæræt me

It is inscribed with a mix of different styles of runes and Latin in an uncommon dialect. Because of the translation difficulties, this gives interpretations varying from: "Always carry this Yew, Strength is contained in it (Thorson, 1984)" to "this yew, you bring about, numbness go away (Thorson, 1984). "

A second charm is also found in the Netherlands in Westeremden, which suffers from some of the same problems. Several runes are unique and might or might not be bind runes.

Figure 38: Runestick, Found in Westeremden, ca. 800-900, Yewwood, 11,86 cm, Groninger Museum, gifted by A. van Deursen, photo: Marten de Leeuw

R III.13

ᛟᛈ·ᚺᛟᛖ·ᛗᚢ·ᚷᛁᚹᛖᛞᚨ·ᚨᛖᛗᛚᚢᚦ·ᛁᚹᛁ·ᛟᚲ·ᚢᛈᛞᚢᚾᚨ·ᛚᛖ·ᚹᛁᛗᛟᚠ·ᚨᛖᚺ·
ᚦᚢᛊᛖ·

op hœ mu givëda æmluÞ / iwi ok upduna / (a)le wimôv æh Þusë

A likely interpretation is: "luck stays at home; and at the yew may it grow on the hill; Wimœd has this (Kapteyn, 1937) ."

Because of the limited amount of data, we might never be able to translate inscriptions like these fully. However, a good takeaway from these charms is that the yew tree was important as a protective symbol.

Cultural relevance

The Yew tree is a potent symbol of life, death, and by extension, shamans[52] , who are the guardians, gatekeepers, and diplomats of the domain between.

The yew tree is found on graveyards throughout Northern Europe. Some of these trees are well over a thousand years old and outdated the Christian churches next to them. While Christianity spread throughout Europe, it often assimilated the holy places and customs of the pagans, and this is also true for the yew tree.

The relation to death is easy to explain. The tree is a symbol of protection against evil. Because of that, the yew tree in the graveyard could stop evil spirits, Drugar[53] , and necromancers. The yew tree is also a deadly poisonous tree. The seed and the needle contain a poison that can quickly kill a fully-grown human if ingested. Today the poison from the Yew tree is used in a diluted form as the basis for chemotherapy. It is not hard to see how the most poisonous tree in Europe is connected to death. The yew tree was not only planted on graveyards to symbolize death but also to symbolize eternity. It is incredibly long-lived and resistant to all weather conditions because of this, it was considered a symbol of eternity.

According to Dr. Kukowka, a German medical professor at the University of Greiz, on sweltering days, the melting resin of the yew trees release enough poison into the air around them to result in hallucinations if you sit underneath them. This might be one of the explanations as to why the tree is connected with traveling between worlds and ecstatic knowledge.

---

[52] Here used in its common meaning not the specific Siberian set of rituals. The closest equivalent in Nordic culture is Seidh.

[53] A type of revenant from Scandinavian Foklore that hunts the living.

Conclusion

Eihwaz represents the word tree Yggdrasil and all associations that come with it. In contrast to the monotheistic religions, where the central conflict is good versus evil, Norse mythology can be seen as a struggle between order versus chaos. Eihwaz is a symbol of that creative order, as the thing that holds the universe together, the structure within all things play out, and the one thing that endures from before creation until after Ragnarök.

In readings: Eihwaz as the world tree gives a powerful message of the connection between opposites. Depending on the question asked, that can be finding common ground with an enemy, finding a solution for an impossible problem from an unseen angle, or gaining a new perspective.

Combined with Ansuz (Odin's rune), this rune hints at a sacrifice that has to be paid for this glimpse into the new perspective, like Odin hanging from Yggdrasil. In combination with Ehwaz (horse rune), it talks of journeying the nine realms. If combined with Jera (year rune), it symbolizes the cycle of life and death in both runes. [54]

In advice and counseling: Eihwaz asks you about your boundaries. What boundaries keep you from what you want to do, and how can you overcome them? What boundaries do you need in your life to keep order?

Ultimately, all boundaries are conventions, but we put them up for a reason. Do not tear down walls before you understand their meaning but do not keep the wall up that keeps you, prisoner.

---

[54] All rune meanings are always relative to the question and the other runes around it. For Eihwaz in particular, it is interesting to really delve into the cosmology of the world tree as all kinds of interesting mythological connection might pop up.

In magic and rituals: Eihwaz is a good candidate for protective charms combined with Othala (ancestors rune). It can be used as a ward for your house, especially if carved on a piece of yew wood or a Yew tree. Eihwaz is also suitable for any charms or rituals involving setting boundaries or removing them to bring opposites together. Combine with Berkana (birch rune) to use in healing rituals.

Experiencing the runes

Riding the tree: Yggdrasill is Odin's horse. To hang from a tree for nine days and nights without food or drink is not a feat that we mortals can match. But we can emulate Odin's path on a smaller scale. Pick a tree that for you represents Yggdrasill and paint Eihwaz on this tree. Every day for nine days, sit under the tree and meditate once in the morning and once in the evening for at least five minutes, no excuses. See what comes to you on the ninth day.

Protecting the home: Make a bind rune with Eihwaz as its central rune. Use the chapter on stave runes to select a set of runes that are appropriate to your home situation, and take your time to design a personalized rune sigil. You can draw this sigil on a piece of paper, but if you have the means, inscribing it on a piece of yew wood would be even better.

The eternal: Yggdrasil stands forever as the single constant in the cyclical mythology of the Nordic people. Some of this solemn eternity can be experienced by visiting a graveyard. Depending on where you live, the cemeteries in your neighborhood might not have a yew tree but during a walk in a cemetery that reverend tranquillity can still be experienced

ᛈ

2.6 Pertho - Dice Cup

Germanic	Gothic	Old English	Old Norse	Sound
Pertho	Pairthra	Peordh	-	P

Pertho is the sixth rune of the second Ætt and is a rune of games, both those played on the table and those larger ones we play in life. It is a rune of skill but also a rune of chance. It does not matter how well you plan; sometimes, you must roll the dice and hope that luck is on your side. Pertho is one of four runes with only an Anglo-Saxon rune poem.

The rune poems

ᛈᛖᛟᚱᛞᚻ·ᛒᛇᚦ·ᛋᛇᛗᛒᛚᛖ·ᛈᛚᛖᚷᚨ·ᚨᚾᛞ·ᚻᛚᛖᚻᛏᛖᚱ·ᚹᛚᚨᚾᚲᚢᛗ·ᛟᚾ·ᛗᛁ
ᛞᛞᚢᛗ·ᛞᚻᚨᚱ·ᚹᛁᚷᚨᚾ·ᛋᛁᛏᛏᚨᚦ·ᛟᚾ·ᛒᛖᛟᚱᛋᛖᛚᛖ·ᛒᛚᛁᚦᛖ·ᚨᛖᛏᛋᛟᛗᚾᛖ·

Anglo-Saxon

Peorð byþ symble plega and hlehter wlancum [on middum], ðar wigan sittaþ on beorsele bliþe ætsomne

Chessman is a source of recreation and amusement to the great, where warriors sit blithely together in the banqueting hall.

The rune poem on its own is relatively straightforward. Chessman represents the games that warriors played in the feasting halls during their downtime. The Proto-Germanic name of this rune is Pertho, meaning dice cup. However, the old English word is Peordh, meaning chessman.

Both dice games and chess are mentioned in the sagas. In the Hervarar saga, a man called Gestumblindi[55] starts a riddle game. One of his riddles goes:

"What creature kills the cattle men have, and is iron-clad, without? Eight horns it has, but head it has none, and runs when run it may. "[56]

-Hervarar 8

Another riddle states:

" Who be the women who, weaponless, for their king kill each other? Every day the dark ones shield him, but the fair ones aye go forth."[57]

-Hervarar 19

In Northern Europe, both playing with dice and playing tafl [58] must have been widespread because otherwise, the riddles would have been unguessable.

Another sign of the importance of board games is the nine boasts of Jarl Rögnvald Kali Kolsson in the Orkeyinga saga. He speaks of the nine skills he has mastered, including knowledge of the runes, hunting,

---

[55] Odin in disguise.

[56] The answer here is a die. Killing the cattle is losing bets and of course a six sided dice has eight corners and is uncontrollable.

[57] This is a reference to tafl a viking age board game similar to chess.

[58] Rules for Tafl are printed later in this chapter.

archery, and board games. This shows that skill in board games was ranked among enviable and prestigious skills.

Skill in tafl was seen as training for skill in strategy. People of all ages have been buried with a tafl board and pieces. The game represents the Viking raiding style of war, where the attackers have an advantage at the beginning of the game but slowly lose this as their opponent has a chance to reposition.

Historic use in charms and amulets

Due to the limited number of runes archaeological finds, the Pertho rune has not been found in a magical context. That is not to say that nothing with relation to Pertho has been found. Many graves contained tafl boards and pieces or dice. Tafl itself has been depicted in several rune stones like the Ockelbo rune stone

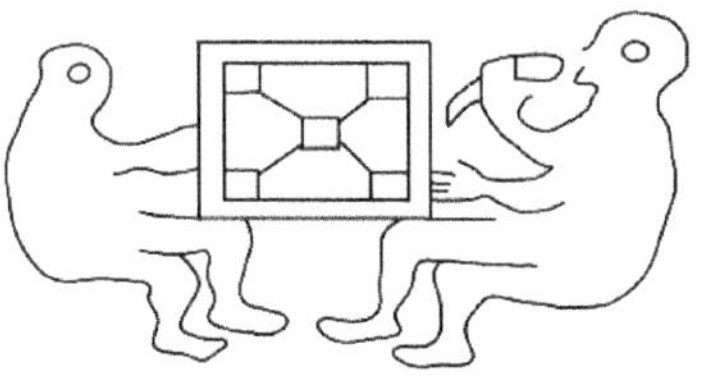

Figure 39: Drawing of two people playing Tafl on the Ockelbo Runestone

The game of Tafl has a mythological symbolic meaning. In Völuspá, Odin interrogates a Völva[59], and the complete history of the universe is told from Creation to Ragnarök. In stanza eight, the golden age of the Gods starts after the world's creation. According to the Völva, the Gods played tafl with golden pieces during this age. After Ragnarök, the remaining Gods find the golden pieces as a treasure of the last age. In this way, the game pieces are a framing device for the story. They also

---

[59] A female priest or magic user

represent times of peace that existed at the beginning of the universe and the peace that will return after Ragnarök.

Not only is tafl a symbol of peace but also a symbol of Öorlog, the universe's fundamental laws. While humanity is bound to certain rules, we can make choices within those rules. While we have no control over our opponent's choices, we can still anticipate their next move.
This is also true for the game of dice. While you might not know the exact outcome of your roll, the possible results are limited and, therefore, calculable.

Since the beginning, the Gods have been bound by Öorlog, by the universe's rules, and even after Ragnarök, they will be still.

Cultural relevance

The first mention of tafl was as early as 400 AD and was widely spread across the North of Europe. Boards have been found from Ireland to Ukraine. After the middle ages, the popularity of chess pushed tafl out to the more rural areas and finally replaced it completely.

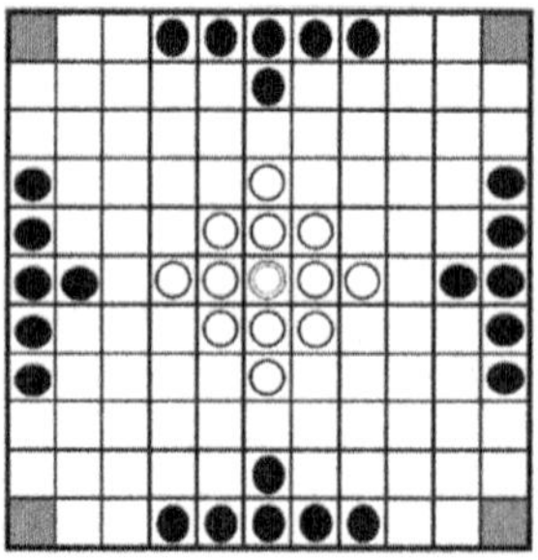

Figure 40: Diagram of a Tafl board

Even while tafl was popular throughout Europe, the rules seemed to differ from one area to the next, with a variable number of playing pieces and board size. The rules were commonly known but not written down, meaning that we can only guess the rules through archaeological data, using snippets from sagas and pieces found in graves.

Together these paint a picture, and below are the rules for a probable approximation of what a game of tafl would have played like.

1. All pieces move like the rook in chess. That is to say, they can move horizontally or vertically as many spaces as they want but can't jump over other pieces
2. The center square and the four corners are king's squares. Only the king (the large white piece) is allowed to end his move in a king's square. White wins if the king ends his movement in one of the corner king's squares. The king's squares count as an opposing piece for all other pieces, except that all pieces may move through (but not end) in the center square.
3. If any non-king piece is flanked on two opposite sides by an opposing piece, it is captured and removed from the board. Again a king's square counts as an opposing piece.
4. The king is captured if he is ever flanked on all four sides. If the king is captured, black wins. Even for the king, the king's squares count as opposing pieces.
5. The attackers get the first move.

Optional rules:

The game of tafl slightly favors the king's side. To balance things out, there are a couple of optional rules

I. Counting, The game is played twice, with both sides playing each side once. The two players then compare the number of turns it took for the king to escape if both players succeeded. The player who saved the king quickest won.
   If both players fail to save the king, the player who kept him alive the most turns wins. If only one player got the king to safety, that player wins.
II. Boasting, after both players have learned the flow of the game a little better, the boasting variant can be played. Here both

players boast how many moves they need to let the king escape. The players keep alternating lower boasts until one player thinks the other can't live up to his boast. The player who bid the lowest number of turns plays the king's side. If he needs more turns to let the king escape, he loses his boast on top of all the other win-and-lose conditions.

Conclusion

Pertho is a rune that shares some characteristics with the carefree attitude of Yera and the destiny of Naudiz and yet stands completely separate. Micro-cosmologically it is a game that both warriors and Gods played in times of peace, but it is also a teaching tool to teach about choice and consequence. Working under the rules and trying to win within the boundaries gives victory and defeat meaning and allows us to enjoy the game.

In readings: Pertho on its own is a rune of measured risks and working within the system. Where Naudiz (destiny rune) is a cold binding fate and Yera (year rune) is guaranteed success, Pertho is creating your own luck. On its own, this rune could signify that you influence the outcome as long as you play the game.

In combination with Tiwaz (justice rune), it means that you cannot just rely on justice to come to you but that you have to play within the rules to get the desired outcome. In combination with Fehu(cattle rune), wealth will come your way if you work smarter, not harder. This is not purely a gambling rune; it is a rune of joyously applying your wit and cunning to the system. While luck is a factor, it is not blind luck.

In advice and counseling: We have seen runes of choice and destiny before, but Pertho is unique because it focuses on the rules not as boundaries but as potential. Everybody has to follow the same rules (Öorlog), and to wish for things against these rules is setting yourself up for failure. But knowing the rules as they apply not just to you but to everyone gives you options to work with them and is the path to victory.

In magic and rituals: Pertho is an excellent central rune for any charm made to increase your success in an upcoming project. It can be combined with Ansuz (Odin's rune) to create a charm giving you the glib and quickness of mind to win an argument.

If you are planning to go on a road trip with no set destinations, Pertho could be coupled up with Ehwaz (horse rune) to create an exciting journey where new roads always open up for you.

Combined with Laguz (lake rune), it can create a spell for maximum flexibility where everything flows like water.

Experiencing the runes

Playing the game: Playing games around the fire was one of the favored pastimes of the Norse. In times of calm, it allowed a fun diversion and a battle of wits. This experience is about the joy and camaraderie that games bring. Board Games are now making a revival after some thought that video games would leave them in the dust. It is the social aspect that draws people in.

Find a board game shop in your area and pick out something that strikes your fancy. Make sure you know the rules, and invite your friends for a night of social gaming, drinks, and snacks.

Casting the lots: Pertho is also translated as the dice cup and fitting for how dice can change a person's fate; according to Tacitus, runes were sometimes cast from a cup. It is fitting to do a rune reading while studying Pertho's because it represents Öorlog. Before, we used the more straightforward method of drawing runes; here, the runes always have fixed positions that contextualize their meaning, but for this chapter, you will cast the runes. In a rune casting, are not only the runes separately important but also their relation to each other. More detailed instructions are in the chapter on divination.

Battle of wits: tafl was not only a fun pastime but also a training tool for keeping the mind sharp and developing tactical and spatial awareness. To be skilled at tafl was a sign of a great leader. The game of tafl is not easy to get these days, and crafting your version out of wood is not for everyone. A paper copy is easy to print. Find a partner to play tafl with you.

Figure 41: Playing Tafl

2.7 Algiz - Elk

Germanic	Gothic	Old English	Old Norse	Sound
Algiz	Algis	Eohl	-	Z

Algiz is the seventh rune of the second Ætt and is a rune of protection. The literal meaning of the rune is elk, and you can see the horn of the elk in the shape of the rune. The elk is well represented in the myths and the sagas. As a rune of protection, Algiz was a popular rune to use in charms and amulets. The Ægishjálmr is perhaps the most famous bind rune from Norse mythology; It is a bind rune composed of several Algiz runes. Because of this, we can still clearly picture what this rune means despite there only being a single Anglo-Saxon rune poem to interpret it.

Figure 42: Ægishjálmur

The rune poems

ᛖᛟᛚᚺ·ᛋᛖᚲᚷ·ᛖᚨᚱᛞ·ᚺᛟᛖᚠᚦ·ᛟᚠᛏᚢᛋᛏ·ᛟᚾ·ᚠᛖᚾᚾᛖ·ᚹᛖᚲᛖᛞᚺ·ᛟᚾ·ᚹ
ᚨᛏᚢᚱᛖ·ᚹᚢᚾᛞᚨᚦ·ᚷᚱᛁᛗᛗᛖ·ᛒᛚᛟᛞᛖ·ᛒᚱᛖᚾᛖᛞᚺ·ᛒᛖᛟᚱᚾᚨ·ᚷᛖᚺᚹᛇ
ᛚᚲᚾᛖ·ᛞᚺᛖ·ᚺᛁᛗ·ᚨᛖᚾᛁᚷᚾᛖ·ᛟᚾᚠᛖᚾᚷ·ᚷᛖᛞᛖᚦ·

Eolh-secg eard hæfþ oftust on fenne wexeð on wature, wundaþ grimme, blode breneð beorna gehwylcne ðe him ænigne onfeng gedeþ.

The Eohl sedge is mostly to be found in a marsh; it grows in the water and makes a ghastly wound, covering with blood every warrior who touches it.

Eohl-sedge is a further unspecified type of swamp plant, most likely a type of reed, as the coarse texture of a reed can cause cuts. However, the description seems extreme, "covering with blood every warrior who touches it" describes more severe wounds as reeds would typically cause. This has led to the theory that Eohl-sedge is also a kenning for either spears or swords, which is easy to imagine seeing the long straight stalks forming a spear wall around a lake.

Historic use in charms and rituals

The Ægishjálmr (awe helm) is the best-known of all the bind runes and charms. It was used as a protection symbol, described in several sagas, and found on various historical artifacts. The depictions of the Ægishjálmr are not uniform but vary in design, from very simple to elaborate.

The Ægishjálmr consists of at least four and often eight Algiz runes, but more is possible. The Algiz runes can be decorated with perpendicular lines, and sometimes a motif is made in the center.

Historically, other protection charms seem to follow the same structure. For instance, The Vegvisir, a charm found in the *Huld* manuscript, was used as protection against getting lost at sea. The basic structure stays the same, including the Algiz runes, but other shapes are added on top. [60]

In *Fafnismal*, the dragon Fafnir claims that he has no equal among men because he uses the Ægishjálmr to protect himself:

"The Ægishjálmr I wore to afright mankind, While guarding my gold I lay; Mightier seemed I than any man, For a fiercer never I found."- **Fáfnismál 16**

We see this power of the Ægishjálmr repeated in a spell appropriately named "There is a Simple Helm of Awe Working." The spell is included in the works of Jon Arnason, a writer, librarian, and museum director that lived in the nineteenth century. Following in the footsteps of the brothers Grimm, who had set it upon themselves to collect Germanic folktales, Jon Arnason gathered and published a great set of Icelandic folktales. The spell goes as follows:

---

[60] More information on how runic charms like this are constructed can be found in the chapters on Magic.

Make a helm of awe in lead, press the lead sign between the eyebrows, and speak the formula:

Ægishjálm er ég ber [I bear the helm of awe]
milli brúna mér! [between my brows!]
Thus a man could meet his enemies and be sure of victory.
- Galdramyndir[61]

It is important to note that the helm of awe was a helm in the metaphorical sense; it is applied to the head and protects its wearer.

The positioning of the Ægishjálmr on the brow is significant. Many cultures believed the third eye (located on the forehead at the pineal gland) to be spiritually significant. For the Hindus, it is where the Bindi (dot on the forehead) is placed, and in Jewish mythology, it is also the

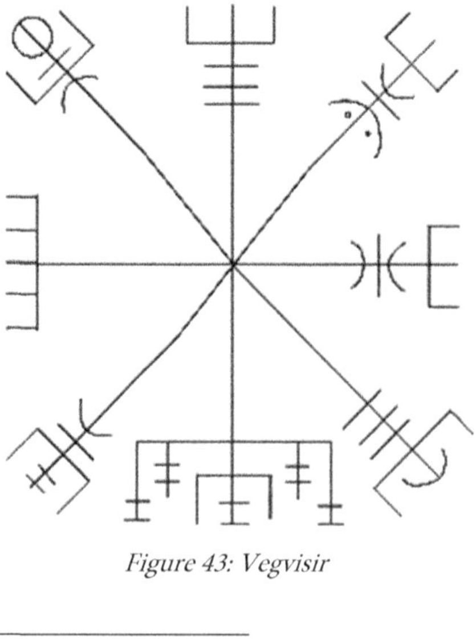

Figure 43: Vegvisir

---

[61] Árnason, J (1862). Íslenzkar Þjóðsögur Og Æfintýri. Leipzig, Germany: Museum of Folklore. Translation by Waggoner, B.

location where the Shem is added to a clay golem to give it life. Algiz was not only used in bind runes. We can also find it in a charm found in Lindholm, Denmark

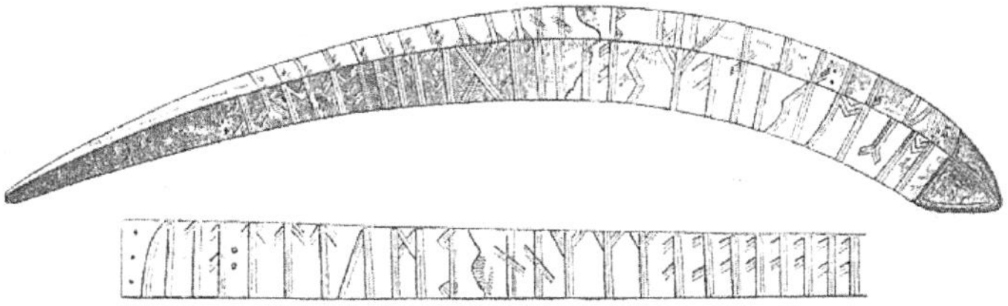

Figure 44:*The Lindholm amulet*

ᛖᚲ·ᛖᚱᛁᛚᚨᛉ·ᛊᚨᚹᛁᛚᚨᚷᚨᛉ·ᚺᚨ·ᛏᛖᚲᚨ·
ᚨᚨᚨᚨᚨᚨᚨᚨᛉᛉᛉᚾᚾᚾ·ᛒᛗᚢᛏᛏᛏ·ᚨᛚᚢ

DR 261

Ek Erilaz Sawilagaz ha teka.
Aaaaaaaazzznnn bmuttt alu

The first line gives the name of the runemaster that made and probably used this charm. The second line shows the familiar structure of calling on Odin with multiple Ansuz runes. In this case, the purpose of the charm is protection, represented by Algiz, and finally fixing it into destiny with three Naudiz runes (the Norn run). The charm ends with the word alu. A common charm word thought to give amulets more power.

Algiz represents the antler of an elk which was seen as synonymous with protection. People carried amulets with Algiz for protection, and sometimes real antlers were also carried around for protection. Antlers, as a sign of protection, seemed to have been widespread. During an excavation in Dublin, a piece of stag horn was found inscribed with the following runes:

IR 12

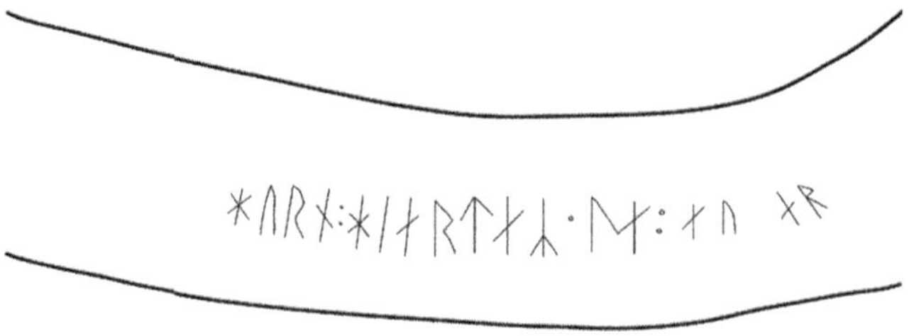

Figure 45: the Hart Horn Charm

ᚺᚢᚱᚾ·ᚺᛁᚨᚱᛏᚨᚱ·ᛚᚨ·ᚨᚢᛋᛋᚨᚱ·

Hurn hiartar, lá Aussar

Hart horn, Protection, Aussar (Macleod & Bernard, 2006)

Many runic artifacts have been found inscribed on antlers, but this one calls explicitly upon the hart's horn for protection for Aussar. From this example, we can infer that Alzig and the antlers it represents were considered magical sources of protection.

Cultural relevance

Tacitus, in his Germania, wrote about a Germanic tribe called the Nahanarvali. The Nahanavarli have a sacred grove presided over by a priestess, where they worship twin gods. It is heavily debated among scholars whether Tacitus wrote that the sacred grove was named Alcis or whether the twin Gods where called Alcis. Alcis translates to elk in the language of the tribe.

Tacitus links the twin Gods to their Roman equivalent, Pollux and Castor. The concept of twin Gods was a recurring theme in Nordic mythology, as seen in Freyr and Freya. One of the symbols associated with Freyr is the elk antlers because it is the weapon he uses to defend himself during the events of Ragnarök. Therefore, it is not unthinkable that the Twin Gods mentioned by Tacitus were not two brothers but Freyr and Freyr.

Another name for Algiz is Algis, meaning swan. In *Völundarkviða,* three Valkyries are weaving flax reminiscent of the three Norns of fate. Their swan-feathered cloaks hang next to them in the saga while they weave. The Valkyrie used swan cloaks to fly; from these swan cloaks, we get our modern-day interpretation of Valkyries with swan wings.

The Valkyries are part of the spirits of destiny called the Disir. All Disir are female and fall into various categories: Norns weavers of fate, Fylgia guardian spirits, and the Valkyrie choosers slain. Even though the roles are distinct within the Disir, they are sometimes vague and interchangeable. For example, a Disir might begin as a Valkyrie in the saga and become a Fylgia later. Although, The Valkyrie's primary task was bringing the worthy slain of the battlefield to the halls of Valhalla. Sometimes they would marry a hero or offer wise counsel. It is important to note that a swam maiden always bestows a measure of protection.

Conclusion

Above all else, Algiz is a rune of protection. It is a rune of the weapons we protect ourselves with, our armor to keep us safe, the walls around the settlement, and the spirits who watch over us. In our modern life, we are much safer than our ancestors were. We generally will not have to deal with disease, weather, famine, robbers, and raiding neighboring kingdoms. It is then understandable why this rune was one of the most used runes in charms.

In readings: In readings, Algiz is a comforting beacon of protection. Whatever your question, you are shielded. Depending on the question, Other runes can give a clue as to what is being protected or how.

For instance, combining Algiz with Othala (ancestors rune) could mean you can rely on your family for support. If found in a casting with Tiwaz (justice rune), this combination might signify that the law will keep you safe.

In advice and counseling: this rune is not only a rune of protection but also of safety. What makes your feel safe? What keeps you safe? Feeling safe is one of the most elementary human needs. Feeling unsafe at work, home, or on the street can cause significant psychological strain that manifests as physical problems. Running away is not the answer, but everybody needs a moment of respite.

In magic and rituals: On its own and in a bind rune, as with the Ægishjálmr, Algiz is the most helpful rune for protection.
The most useful combinations include Algiz with Raidho (wagon rune) for safe travels and Fehu (cattle rune) for financial stability.

Algiz can also be used in a ritual combination with Ehwaz (horse rune) to contact you Fylgja (guardian spirit), and those two runes combined with Eihwaz (yew tree rune) would create a good amulet for astral projection.

Experiencing the runes

The Elk: The shape of the rune itself is an antler. For an elk, the antler is not just his defense but his offense. The antler as an offensive weapon can also be seen in the story of Ragnarök, where Freyr uses an antler to defend himself against the fire giant Surtr. A good defense is not just hiding behind a shield but also striking back. The best way to experience this rune is by taking some martial arts or self-defense classes. Focus on the defense but also the counter-attack.

The Swan: Fylgja is etymologically related to the old English 'folgjan' and the Dutch 'volgen,' meaning to 'follow.' The Fylgja is a guardian spirit tied to fate and luck that follows a person from birth. They most often take the shape of an animal, symbolic of the person they are attached to, but in times of crisis, most often just before death, they also appear in human form. In the sagas, the Fylgja of a visitor would sometimes reveal themselves in the animal form before their arrival.

If you have not meditated before, it is better to start practicing meditation before trying to contact your Fylgja. If you have some proficiency, start your meditation as usual but use a bind rune of Ehwaz (horse rune) and Algiz as a focus. Try to keep the bind rune in your mind's eye. It helps to draw the rune and set it where you can easily see it so that the image gets reaffirmed if you open your eyes. Meditate until you start to visualize an animal; also note your feelings towards the animal.

Try this meditation regularly and write down your experiences after each; before your following meditation, read back through your notes and build a deeper connection. During readings, you can ask your Fylgja for guidance.

The shield wall: This rune's primary purpose is protection; the most visually interesting example is the Ægishjálmr. Use the Ægishjálmr as a basis to create your protective charm, for your car, for your house, for your family, or some other aspect of your life. Use the chapters on magic, specifically bind runes and rune codes, to create a personal charm.

ᛊ

2.8 Sowilo - Sun

Germanic	Gothic	Old English	Old Norse	Sound
Sowilo	Saugil	Sigil	Sol	S

Sowlio is the eighth and final rune of the second Ætt. This Ætt started with hardship and ice but ends with the blazing sun. The Sun is vital for all life and the energy source for our world. It dispels darkness and allows us to see. The Norseman used the sun as a compass to navigate. No wonder the Sun was worshiped and celebrated worldwide, and the Nordic people were no exception.

The rune poems

Norwegian

ᛟᛚ·ᛖᚱ·ᛚᚨᚾᛞᚨ·ᛚᛊᛟᛗᛖ·ᛚᚢᛏᛁ·ᛖᚲ·ᚺᛖᛚᚷᚢᛗ·ᛞᛟᛗᛖ·

Sól er landa ljóme lúti ek helgum dóme.

Sun is the light of the world. I bow to the divine decree.

The 'sun is the light of the world' is self-explanatory. Generally, most cultures distinguish between three lights, the stars, the moon, and the sun. The sun and the moon are often seen as a pair.

Ahmad Ibn Fadlan was a Muslim Explorer who wrote a travel journal of his encounters in Russia. From his journals, we know that part of the worshipping practice of the Rus-Viking traders was bowing down in front of Idols and poles. Therefore the 'bow' in the second line can represent divine judgment, but it can also mean literal sun worship.

ᛊᛟᛚ·ᛖᚱ·ᛊᚲᛇᛃᚨ·ᛊᚲᛃᛟᛚᛞᚱ·ᛟᚲ·ᛊᚲᛁᚾᚨᚾᛞᛁ·ᚱᛟᛞᚺᚢᛚᛚ·ᛟᚲ·ᛁᛊᚨ·ᚨᛚ
ᛞᚱᛏᚱᛖᚷᛁ·ᚱᛟᛏᚨ·ᛊᛁᚲᛚᛁᚾᚷᚱ·

Sól er skýja skjöldr ok skínandi röðull ok ísa aldrtregi. rota siklingr.[62]

Sun, Shield of the clouds and shining ray and destroyer of ice.

The sun and the moon are a set of twins called Sol and Mani. In Nordic mythology, the sun is female, and the moon is male, unlike most other mythology, where the reverse is true.

The first line in the Icelandic rune poem references Svalinn or his shield. According to myth, Svalinn rides in the chariot with Sol, carrying a giant shield to protect the world from the full brunt of Sol's power. In Grímnismál**,** Odin states that if the shield were not there, the land would burn, and the oceans would boil. This illustrates the natural balance in the sagas. Another example of natural balance can be seen in the stories about Thor. If Thor kills too many frost giants, this will lead to unbearable heat and drought in Midgard; if Thor kills too many fire giants, it will lead to harsh winters. Both Thor and Sol represent unfathomable potential; if full power were unleashed, it would be the end of the world.

[62] Rota Siklingr is not translated by B.Dickens but roughly translates to "turning wheel".

The second and third lines refer to the sun's two greatest gifts, light, and heat. Without light and heat, the world would end for the Nordic people, especially with their long dark winters.

According to Grímnismál, the moon is chased by a wolf called Skoll[63] and the sun by a wolf named Hati[64]. When the wolves finally catch the sun and the moon, it will be the start of the Fimbulvetr, the three years of winter, and the beginning of Ragnarök.

Figure 46: Skoll and Hati

---

[63] Betrayer.

[64] He who hates.

ᛋᛁᚷᛖᛚ·ᛋᛖᛗᚪᚾᚾᚢᛗ·ᛋᛇᛗᛒᛚᛖ·ᛒᛁᚦ·ᚩᚾ·ᚻᛁᚻᛏᛖ·ᛞᚻᚩᚾᚾᛖ·ᚻᛁ·ᚻᛁᚾᛖ·ᚠᛖᚱᛁᚪ
ᚦ·ᚩᚠᛖᚱ·ᚠᛁᛋᚳᛖᛋ·ᛒᛖᚦ·ᚩᚦ·ᚻ·ᛒᚱᛁᛗᚻᛖᚾᚷᛖᛋᛏ·ᛒᚱᛁᚾᚷᛖᚦ·ᛏᚩ·ᛚᚪᚾᛞᛖ·

Sigel semannum symble biþ on hihte, ðonne hi hine feriaþ ofer fisces beþ, oþ hi brimhengest bringeþ to lande.

The sun is ever a joy in the hopes of seafarers when they journey away over the fishes' bath, until the courser of the deep bears them to land.

The Anglo-Saxon poem focuses on the sun as a guiding star. Before the compass was invented in Europe, [65] sailors depended on the sun and the North Star to find their way across the open sea. Even after the invention of the compass, compasses were not always readily available so the sun and the north star remained the only guides.

Historic use in charms and rituals

In Sigrdrífumál, where Sigurd gets is taught about the runes by Brunhilde, the following verse is found:

Wave-runes learn, / if well thou wouldst shelter
The sail-steeds out on the sea;
On the stem shalt thou write, / and the steering blade,
And burn them into the oars;
Though high be the breakers, / and black the waves,
Thou shalt safe the harbor seek.
- Sigdrifumal 9

[65] The earliest mentions of compasses are from the late 12th century.

It is unclear what runes constitute the wave runes; they are never disclosed, but if the Anglo-Saxon rune poem is any indication, Sowilo is probably among them.

Another symbol associated with the sun is the solar wheel. This symbol is also strongly tied to Raidho as it represents the wheel of the chariot that pulls the sun. The symbol was used on runic charms to infuse the charm with more power. For a more in-depth look at the solar wheel, see the chapter Raidho

Cultural relevance

It cannot be stated enough how important the sun was for the Nordic people. In Alvismál, the dwarf Alvis and Thor are having a battle of wit; part of the exchange is as follows:

Thor spake:

"Answer me, Alvis! /thou knowest all,
Dwarf, of the doom of men:
What call they the sun, that all men see,
In each and every world?"

Alvis spake:
"Men call it 'Sun,' gods 'Orb of the Sun,'
'The Deceiver of Dvalin[66]' the dwarfs;
The giants 'The Ever-Bright,' elves 'Fair Wheel,'
'All-Glowing' the sons of the gods."
-Alvismál 15-16

---

[66] The word here translated as deceiver is 'Leika,' meaning play in Icelandic. This seems to be far removed from deceiving but you can imagine Dvalin as a plaything of the sun. Another translation is Dvalin's mockery this also fits the meaning of the sentence well.

Thor asks about natural phenomena, and we learn that the different races use different kennings. The dwarvish kenning is "The Deciever of Dvalin" for the sun. Dvalin is a dwarfish name that appears several times throughout the sagas in various circumstances. Dvalin is likely a typical dwarfish name. The Sun is Dvalin's deceiver or Dvalin's mockery because, like some trolls, the subterranean dwarfs are turned stone by the sun's light.

Ironically this was Thor's plan all along as he keeps Alvis talking for so long that the sun rises and Alvis turns to stone.

Conclusion

Sowilo is the blazing sun, strong and bright. It is a point to navigate by, a light to light guide you, and a fire to warm you from afar. The sun's power is vast and impersonal, shining down on the nine realms. Getting too close to the sun is to be overwhelmed by a force that is too great to handle.

In readings: By itself, Sowilo is a clear path to victory, a shiny beacon leading to success, and a bright light that burns away all the uncertainty.

Combined with Isa (ice rune) or Hagalaz (hail rune), it signifies that new forces are at work and burning the entropy away. Inertia is about to be kicked into motion. Combined with Raidho (wagon rune) or Yera (year rune), this might signify that you have reached or are about to reach the zenith. A comforting notion and, simultaneously, a warning as the wheel keeps turning.

In combination with Laguz (lake rune), it could indicate finding your way after being lost, or when combined with Dagaz (day rune), it signifies that the power of Sowilo is slowly going to manifest.

In advice and counseling: the victory rune lets you look back at your accomplishments. It does not matter who you are; you have accomplished many things. However, due to the nature of humanity, it can be hard to remember our success in life. It is easy to focus on our failures, but it is also important to remember our victories. Also, Sowilo

In magic and ritual: On its own, Sowilo is a powerful rune when you want to bring the blazing heat of victory to a situation or when you need a star to navigate by.

This rune can be combined with other runes in staves or bind runes to guide the effect. For instance, combined with Anzus (Odin's rune) and Tiwaz (justice rune), you could create a charm to lead people back to the right path.

reminds you to examine what motivates you: the star you navigate by and how you determine true north.

Experiencing the runes

Praise the sun: The sun was, in all likelihood, an object of worship in Nordic culture, as the Norwegian rune poem shows an object of reverence. Try bowing down to the sun on a sunny day and placing an offering in its honor.

True north: Sowilo is a rune of navigation. For this rune, go for a hike in nature and bring a compass. Try to find true north based on the direction of the sun. Use the compass to see if you are correct.

Blazing light: The sun is a blazing light, capable at the same time of giving life but also burning all that is into cinders. For this exercise, you will need ice, a cloth, and a large rock or hammer. Wrap the ice in the fabric and place them on the ground. Close your eyes and try to visualize the problems standing in your way as thé ice. Imagine the hammer or rock as a bolt of searing fire from the heavens and smash your problems. Afterward, let the ice flow away.

The third ætt

ᛏ

3.1 Tiwaz - Tyr

Germanic	Gothic	Old English	Old Norse	Sound
Tiwaz	Teiws	Tir	Tyr	T

Tiwaz is the first rune of the third Ætt, and the second rune directly representing a God. Tyr is a warrior God whose name translates to Divine Lord. Before Odin became the most important God in the Norse pantheon, it was believed that Tyr was the supreme God. Regardless Tyr was widely worshiped and featured prominently in several sagas. Like Tyr, Tiwaz represents justice, strength, and honor.

The rune poems

Norwegian

ᛏᛇᚱ᛫ᛖᚱ᛫ᚨᛖᛁᚾᛖᚾᛞᚱ᛫ᚨᛊᚨ᛫ᛟᛈᛏ᛫ᚹᚨᛖᚱᛞᚢᚱ᛫ᛊᛗᛁᛞᚢᚱ᛫ᛒᛚᚨᛊᚨ᛫

Týr er æinendr ása opt værðr smiðr blása.

Tyr is a one-handed god often has the smith to blow.

The Norwegian rune poem's first line references the most well-known story about Tyr, an adventure that leaves him permanently physically altered, as is often the case; the story starts with Loki. Loki has a relationship with the Giantess Angrboða, and they have three children; Hella the ruler of the dead, Jörmungandr the Midgard serpent (who will kill and be killed by Thor during Ragnarök) and the most fearsome of all, the wolf Fenrir, a wolf so huge his lower jaw scrapes the earth, and the upper jaw scrapes the heavens.

A Proficy revealed that Fenrir would become a dangerous enemy to the Gods and that he would devour Odin during the Ragnarök. Fenrir's strength and temperament were so fierce that none of the Gods, not even Thor, dared to face him. So a trick was devised; the Gods came with chains and dared Fenris, saying he would not be strong enough to break the bonds. Fenrir accepted the challenge but each chain the Gods brought, no matter how strong and thick, broke with ease under Fenrir's might. The final chain was named Gleipnir, made by the dwarfs from the sound of a cat's footsteps, the beard of a woman, the roots of a mountain, the breath of a fish, the sinew of a bear, and the spittle of a bird. This chain looked and felt like silk but was stronger than any iron chain.

As the Gods wanted to put Gleipnir on Fenrir, he became wary of trickery and demanded that one of the Gods would put his hand between his jaws as insurance. All the Gods refused this task except for Tyr, who took care of Fenrir when he was just a pup. When Fenrir could not break the chains, he roared to be let go, but the Gods refused. In his rage, Fenrir bit off Tyr's hand.

The Second line 'often has the smith' to blow, can have a couple of explanations. Smiths would have to pump the bellows and stoke the forge for Tyr to create weapons, armor, and shields. In Sigdrifumál, Brunhilde explains to Sigurðr that if you want to win a battle, you should engrave victory runes on your weapons and armor and call on Tyr twice. Weapons have been found in Germany with the Tiwaz rune engraved. This could indicate that the victory runes were Tiwaz.

Icelandic

ᛏᛇᚱ᛫ᛖᚱ᛫ᛖᛁᚾᚺᛖᚾᛞᚱ᛫ᚨᛊ᛫ᛟᚲ᛫ᚢᛚᚠᛊ ᛚᛖᛁᚠᚨᚱ᛫ᛟᚲ᛫ᚺᛟᚠᚨ᛫ᚺᛁᛚᛗᛁᚱ᛫ ᛗᚨᚱᛊ᛫ᛏᛁᚷᛁ

Týr er einhendr áss ok ulfs leifar ok hofa hilmir. Mars tiggi

God with one hand and leavings of the wolf and prince of temples.

The first and second parts in this rune poem are again a link to Tyr's most famous deed, the binding of the Fenris Wolf. Tyr has a clear role in the sagas as an individual God, but Divine Lord's name can be ambiguous. For example, Sig-Tyr (victory Lord) is a kenning for Odin, and Öku-Tyr (wagon-Lord) is a kenning for Thor.

However, because much of Norse lore is lost, we can only guess the significance of some Gods through the context clues left behind. This is especially true for Tyr. The Roman historian, Tacitus, tries to explain Norse Gods by comparing them to their roman equivalent. He portrays Tyr as the Roman God Mars (God of War), Odin he portrays as Hermes (God of many things including travel, trickery, and guiding the souls to the afterlife), Thor as Hercules (hero of great strength), and Freya as Isis (an Egyptian God of Magic and Nature who made her way into the Roman Pantheon).

Interestingly, when Tacitus visits a Norse temple, he identifies Tyr as the primary deity but observes that Odin receives more worship. He observes that Tyr and Thor receive animal sacrifice while Odin alone receives human sacrifice. This shows the remarkable paradox of Tyr being the primary God of the temple yet Odin being more important in worship. Similarly, a Friesian inscription is found on Hadrian's wall:

"*Mars- Thincsus*" or Mars of the Assembly [67]. This is a kenning marking Tyr as the God of assemblies. These roles of Tyr as the God of temples and assemblies could explain the third part of the Icelandic rune poem "Tyr the Prince of Temples."

ᛏᛁᚱ·ᛒᛁᚦᛏᚫᚳᚾᚫ·ᛋᚢᛗ·ᚻᛖᚫᛚᛞᛖᛞᚻ·ᛏᚱᛇᚹᚫ·ᚹᛖᛚ·ᚹᛁᚦ·ᚫᛖᚦᛖᛚᛁᚾᚷᚫᛋ·ᚫ·ᛒᛁᚦ.ᛟᚾ·
ᚫᛖᚱᛇᛚᛞᛖ·ᛟᚠᛖᚱ·ᚾᛁᚻᛏᚫ·ᚷᛖᚾᛁᛈᚢ·ᚾᚫᛖᚠᚱᛖ·ᛋᚹᛁᚳᚦ

Tir biþ tacna sum, healdeð trywa wel wiþ æþelingas; a biþ on ærylde ofer nihta genipu, næfre swiceþ.

Tir is a guiding star; well does it keep faith with princes;
it is ever on its course over the mists of night and never fails.

The Anglo-Saxon rune poem proposes an entirely different view. The guiding star likely represents the north star because it has been used throughout history as a beacon for navigation. The Anglo-Saxon rune poem compared Tyr to the north star because he is steadfast and reliable.

According to Tacitus, Tyr had priests that where responsible for the judgment and laws of the people. Therefore, another interpretation more figurative interpretation of the guiding star could be justice. Although the literal north star can be obscured by weather, the justice of Tyr was seen as a guiding light that will never fail.

---

[67] The Nordic use of the word Thing is the root of our current Things as an assembly of objects.

Historic use in charms and amulets

As touched upon in the analysis of the Norwegian rune poem, the Tyr rune was used for victory in battle. While teaching Sigurðr the secrets of the magic, in the Sigdrifumál saga, Brunhilde tells him:

Winning-runes learn, if thou longest to win,
And the runes on thy sword-hilt write;
Some on the furrow, and some on the flat,
And twice shalt thou call on Tyr.
- **Sigdrifumál 6**

In Gylfaginning, the then king of Sweden is challenged to a riddle game. In this riddle game, the king asks questions of his hosts. An excerpt of the exchange goes as follows:

Yet remains that one of the Æsir who is called Týr: he is most daring, and best in stoutness of heart, and he has much authority over victory in battle; it is good for men of valor to invoke him. It is a proverb, that he is Týr-valiant, who surpasses other men and does not waver. He is wise, so that it is also said, that he that is wisest is Týr-prudent.

- **Gylfaginning 25**

Nordic people believed that neither tactics nor strength of arms alone determined the winner in combat but also the favor of the Gods. In Combat Tyr, judged which side had the right to win.

Cultural relevance

In His Germania, Tacitus writes:

They choose their kings by birth, their generals for merit. These kings have not unlimited or arbitrary power, and the generals do more by example than by authority. If they are energetic, if they are conspicuous, if they fight in the front, they lead because they are admired. But to reprimand, to imprison, even to flog, is permitted to the priests alone, and that not as a punishment, or at the general's bidding, but, as it were, by the mandate of the god whom they believe to inspire the warrior.

- Germania Tacitus 7

In Gylfaginning, Tyr is seen as the God who inspires warriors. Even though Tacitus does not explicitly mention Tyr, the priests of Tyr, and Tyr, by extension, were responsible for judgments and law.

A form of law was called the 'hólmganga' or tiny island. A person who felt an injustice was done to him, his property, or his honor could challenge the other person to trial by combat. The challenger and the defendant would battle on a literal small island or a small staked-off area.

The accuser would be seen as in the right if the defendant did not show up. If the challenger did not show up, they would become an outcast. If both showed up and the challenger won, he would be seen as right in his claim; if the defendant had died during the challenge, the challenger had to pay half weregeld[68] to the defendant's family. If the defendant won, he would have been seen as right, and if the challenger was killed during the fight, the defended would not owe anything because he was falsely accused.

[68] A monetary fine

Different rules for weapons could be agreed on, and not all battles were to the death. These battles were seen as valid because the Norse people believed Tyr was a divine judge who would determine the outcome.

In the Landnámabók, it is described that each temple should have a metal oath ring. All legal oaths and agreements are sworn on to that ring invoking Freya, Njord, and a third unknown God called Almáttki ass. The oath reads:

I attest that I make an oath on the ring, a legal oath: May Frey and Njörd and the almáttki áss help me in this case as I prosecute or defend or bring witnesses or verdicts or judgments, as I know how to do most rightly or truly or procedurally correctly, and dispatch all legal pleadings which fall to me, while I am at the assembly.

- **Landnámabók,** (Lindow, 2001)

Considering what we know of the role of Tyr both in the temple and in law, it is likely that Almattki Ass is a kenning for Tyr.

Conclusion

Tiwaz, as the rune of Tyr, is a rune of divine justice, warriors, and self-sacrifice. While Tyr is not the strongest of the Aesir, he is the bravest. Tyr was the only one who dared to feed Fenrir when the God-devouring wolf was still a pup, and he sacrificed his hand to bind the wolf. In short, Tyr is the ideal image of the perfect noble warrior, brave, strong, self-sacrificing, and just.

In readings: First and foremost, this is a rune of Justice, but it can mean literal legal justice or figurative divine justice.

The more concise interpretation of Tiwaz in a reading can be gained from the surrounding runes. For example, Tiwaz, combined with Mannaz (humankind rune), leans towards social gatherings and how people should interact. Social cohesion and a code of conduct are essential.

In advice and counseling: Tiwaz asks you to be just and keep to your word. Treat your enemies with grace.

In magic and ritual: Tiwaz is a victory rune, which is how it can be used in magic and ritual. It can be inscribed on sports clothing or tools to ensure victory in sports. Tiwaz can also be combined in a bind rune to give a specific direction to the victory or to bring justice into a particular part of your life. In combination with Ehwaz (horse rune) and Algiz (elk rune), you can undertake a ritual of meditation to confront your inner wolf and bind him.

Experiencing the runes

Of the Thing: Tyr is the lord of the assembly and the prince of temples. Today our towns, villages, and cities are often so large that we lose the sense of connection to them. To get a feel of what an assembly must have been like, visit a local council meeting. Read up on the topics to be discussed, and try to see who are allies and enemies. Get a feel for how your community is run. Feel free to weigh in on any issue.

The left hand: We have all sworn oaths and made promises we did not keep. Tyr gave up his hand to pay for his betrayal of the Fenrir wolf. While working with this rune, come clean about a lie or make amends for a promise you broke to understand Tyr truly. This will hurt, and you might not be forgiven; it was true for Tyr. However, it is the just thing to do.

Victory: Tyr is also the God of victory, a name chanted before battle and a rune engraved on battle gear. The Nordic people believed their win was based not only on their actions during the war but also on the honor they had shown before that. While Odin takes from the battlefield those worthy for his army, he does not care what side they fought on. Tyr, however, will influence the battle's outcome in favor of the just.

Before a sports event, consider whether you have done the work and are worthy of this victory. Call out twice for Tyr if you believe you deserve it and ask for His judgment.

ᛒ

3.2 Berkana - Birch

Germanic	Gothic	Old English	Old Norse	Sound
Berkana	Baírkan	Beorc	Bjarkan	B

Berkana is the second rune of the third Ætt. The most literal interpretation of Berkana is the birch tree, a tree known for being fast-growing with bright green leaves and bright white skin. Mythologically speaking, you could almost say this a third rune is tied to a God, or more specifically, a Goddess, as this rune also represents the archetype of motherhood and nature. The name of this Goddess, probably a Vanir, is completely lost, with only the tiniest hints found in the rune poems and the customs relating to the birch tree[69].

The rune poems

ᛒᛃᚨᚱᚲᚨᚾ·ᛖᚱ·ᛚᚨᚢᚠᚷᚱᛟᚾᛊᛏᚱ·ᛚᛁᛗᚨ·ᛚᛟᚲᛁ·ᛒᚨᚱ·ᚠᛚᚨᛖᚱᛞᚺᚨ·ᛏᛁᛗᚨ·

Norwegian

Bjarkan er laufgrønstr líma Loki bar flærða tíma.

Birch has the greenest leaves of any shrub Loki was fortunate in his deceit.

[69] Freya is sometimes named mostly because she is the most prominent female Vanir.

The first line is reasonably straightforward; birch trees grow fast with bright green leaves. The Birch tree has the greenest of leaves is probably a reference to the belief that the birch tree is exceptionally fertile and full of healthy life force.

The second line is more enigmatic. There are plenty of tales where Loki is deceitful; however, none reference a birch tree. The best comparison is the story of Balder's death. Balder, the fairest and kindest of the Aesir, had a prophetic dream of being killed. Frigga, his mother, gets worried and demands that every living and non-living thing swear an oath that they will not harm Balder. However, because Frigga accidentally skips the mistletoe, so it does not swear the oath. This mistake does not go unnoticed by Loki.

Afterward, in Valhalla, the Gods make a sport of testing the invulnerability of Balder. Höðr, Baldur's brother, cannot participate because he is blind. Loki comes up to Höðr, offers to help him get in on the fun, and hands him a bow laden with a mistletoe arrow. When Höðr lets the arrow fly, it strikes Balder and kills him. Balder is not a warrior therefore, he is barred entry into Valhalla after death and instead is sent to Hel[70]. Eventually, Loki is punished for this crime and bound until Ragnarök.

The arrow that slew Balder was not a birch but a mistletoe. Loki has committed many deceits in his life, but the murder of Balder is undoubtedly the most significant because it irrevocably changes his standing among the Gods. Loki was indeed fortunate because Frigga went to extraordinary lengths to protect Balder.

---

[70] Not to be confused with Christian Hell.

ᛒᛃᚨᚱᚲᚨᚾ·ᛖᚱ·ᛚᚨᚢᚠᚷᚨᛏ·ᛚᛁᛗ·ᛟᚲ·ᛚᛁᛏᛁᛏ·ᛏᚱᛖ·ᛟᚲ·ᚢᚾᚷᛊᚨᛗᛚᛁᚷᚱ·ᚠᛁᛞᚢᚱ·ᚨᛒᛁᛖᛊ·ᚢᛞᚺᛚᚢᚾᚷᚱ

Icelandic

Bjarkan er laufgat lim ok lítit tré ok ungsamligr viðr. abies uðlungr.

Birch Leafy twig and little tree and fresh young shrub

The Icelandic rune poem paints the birch tree as a healthy sapling, emphasizing its youthful leaves and freshness. This is not surprising as the birch tree has a very high tolerance against the cold for a deciduous tree and did well in Scandinavia.

The birch tree has many applications, such as birch bark providing kindle, birch resin being used for tanning, and both its leaves and sap having medicinal properties. The most prominent application is that it can be used as an antiseptic to fight wound infection. Dirty cuts were a bigger problem in ancient than they are now.

ᛒᛖᛟᚱᚲ·ᛒᛇᚦ·ᛒᛚᛖᛞᚨ·ᛚᛖᚨᛊ·ᛒᛖᚱᛖᚦ·ᛖᚠᚾᛖ·ᛊᚹᚨ·ᛞᚺᛖᚨᚺ·ᛏᚨᚾᚨᛊ·ᛒᚢᛏᚨᚾ·ᛏᚢ
ᛞᛖᚱ·ᛒᛁᚦ·ᛟᚾ·ᛏᛖᛚᚷᚢᛗ·ᚹᛚᛁᛏᛁᚷ·ᚺᛖᚨᚺ·ᛟᚾ·ᚺᛖᛚᛗᛖ·ᚺᚱᛇᛊᛏᛖᛞ·ᚠᚨᛖᚷᛖᚱᛖ·ᚷᛖᛚ
ᛟᛞᛖᚾ·ᛚᛖᚨᚠᚢᛗ·ᛚᛇᚠᛏᛖ· ᚷᛖᛏᛖᚾᚷᛖ

Anglo-Saxon

Beorc byþ bleda leas, bereþ efne swa ðeah tanas butan tudder, biþ on telgum wlitig, heah on helme hrysted fægere, geloden leafum, lyfte getenge.

The birch bears no fruit; yet without seed it brings forth suckers, for it is generated from its leaves. Splendid are its branches and gloriously adorned its lofty crown which reaches to the skies.

The Anglo-Saxon rune poem focuses on another regenerative power of the birch tree. If you cut a branch off a birch tree and plant it, a new birch tree will grow.

Splendid are its branches is a reference to the unique white bark that a Birch tree possesses. Although birch trees have very shallow roots when surrounded by forest, they can grow to great heights.
Birch trees can grow so high that it may seem like they touch the sky from the ground.

Historic use in charms and amulets

In Sigdrifumál Brunhilde says:

Branch-runes learn, if a healer wouldst be,
And cure for wounds wouldst work;
On the bark shalt thou write, and on trees that be
With boughs to the eastward bent.
- Sigdrifumá 10

There are two tree runes in the Futhark Eihwaz, the yew tree, and Berkana, the birch tree. Since the yew tree is deadly poisonous, the branch rune referred to in this stanza is likely Berkana.
An alternative theory is that branch runes are a reference to runes that are carved into branches.

Carving runes into branches was not an uncommon practice. When Freyr sends his assistant to fetch the Giant maiden Gerd, the assistant cannot convince her to come. He only gets her to go with him by carving Thurisaz three times into a branch and telling her that he will only lift the curse if she agrees to come with him.

The Birch rune interpretation says that branch runes are what you must learn if you want to heal although branch runes are a general form of rune magic, it seems like they have many other applications, not only healing. Due to this, Brunhilda is most likely referring to Berkana when she mentions branch runes.

Cultural relevance

The birch tree plays a role in many different rituals throughout Northern Europe. In Scandinavia and Scotland, houses are decorated with birch twigs on midsummer to bring fertility into the home. The maypole is traditionally made from a birch tree and would be erected when the first bright green leaves opened on the birch trees.

In Germany, the custom of Maibaum Pflanzen still exists. Maibaum Pflanzen is a ritual in which a birch tree is planted secretly in someone's garden the night they are about to start something new. For example, this could be a wedding, a new job, a relationship, or a child. The next day the planter would come over and water the birch tree. This ritual represents symbioses where the growth and hardiness of the birch tree are linked to the development and hardiness of the new undertaking.

Conclusion

Berkana is not just the rune of the Birch but the rune of the archetypical mother nature. It is a new beginning; it shelters us and brings healing and comfort.

In readings: Berkana represents healing, natural growth, and regeneration. What this means differs depending on the question being asked. In sickness, it means recovery, for an undertaking, it might mean slow and steady growth, and when referring to a person, it signifies a nurturing individual, if not a literal mother.

When combined with other runes, more clarity can be gained. Berkana, in combination with Othala (ancestors rune), shifts the meaning firmly toward the caring role of the family. In combination with Kenaz (torch rune), the meaning would lean more toward healing because Kenaz is also linked to fever. With Ansuz (Odin's rune), the rune of the all-father and the mother lead more towards guardianship.

In advice and counseling: In some ways, Berkana is a rune of counseling, listening, and helping. This rune asks you to look at what nurtures you, what gives you strength. No man or woman is an island; we all have people who nurtured us, to whom we have a debt that can never be repaid, only paid forwards. How do you feel toward these people?

In magic and ritual: *Branch-runes learn, / if a healer wouldst be.* First and foremost, this is a rune of healing when used in charms. Inscribing a rune charm containing Berkana on a birch tree would be a traditional way of using this rune. Alternatively, we see in Sigdrifumál that runes were sometimes scratched into wood and then filled into food or drink; the Berkana rune etched onto a piece of birch wood would be perfect for this.

Be sure that the birch wood is untreated and contains no other contaminants before you do this, and always just a hint of filing.

Experiencing the runes

The mother: Berkana is the rune of a Mother Goddess whose exact identity is now lost like so much of Norse mythology. Often the tales of grand adventure are the stories that we remember, but the quiet support behind the hero is forgotten. Although we know almost nothing about the Landvættir, the spirits of the land, they were called on as often or even more than the Æsir. The Landvættir were called to do many more everyday tasks like save travel and good soup.
These are so common, fundamental, and natural that they are often not mentioned, and very little written about them.

To fully understand Berkana, you must first reflect on your parents. In what way did they support you? In what way are they still supporting you? And in extension, who else is helping you now? What do these people mean to you?

The healer: Berkana is a healer's rune. Modern medicine has made some giant leaps since the time of the Vikings age, so the way we deal with disease and injury has changed. While some new medical developments take years to understand, familiarizing yourself with basic first aid is still a good idea.

While studying this rune is a good time to ensure your first aid kit is still sufficient or if you do not have one to get your own. If it is possible, it is also never a bad idea to start a first aid course.

Growth: Berkana relates not only to the health and nurturing of humans but to the general well-being of all things in nature. While studying Berkana take some time to work on a garden or if that is not possible, bring some potted plants into the house.

Figure 47: Fylgja floating through a birch forest

ᛖ

3.3 Ehwaz - Horse

Germanic	Gothic	Old English	Old Norse	Sound
Ehwaz	Aíhws	Eh	-	E

Ehwaz is the third rune of the third Ætt, and its literal translation is horse. The horse was an essential and valued animal in Scandinavia. Nordic horses were not the giant armored cavalry of the french knights but were used for farming and trade. Regarding travel, Ehwaz is similar to Raidho (wagon rune), but a horse is more than just a tool; it is a companion.

The rune poems

ᛖᚺ·ᛒᛇᚦ·ᚠᛟᚱ·ᛖᛟᚱᛚᚢᛗ·ᚨᛖᚦᛖᛚᛁᚾᚷᚨ·ᚹᛇᚾ··ᚺᛟᚱᛊ·ᚺᛟᚠᚢᛗ·ᚹᛚᚨᚾᚲ·ᛞᚺᛞᚺæᚱ·
ᚺᛁᛗ·ᚺᚨᛖᛚᛖᚦ·ᛇᛗᛒᛖ·ᚹᛖᛚᛖᚷᛖ·ᛟᚾ·ᚹᛁᚲᚷᚢᛗ·ᚹᚱᛁᚲᛚᚨᚦ·ᛊᛈᚱᚨᛖᚲᛖ·ᚨᚾᛞ·ᛒᛁᚦ·ᚢᚾ
ᛊᛏᛇᛚᛚᚢᛗ ᚨᛖᚠᚱᛖ·ᚠᚱᛟᚠᚢᚱ.

Anglo-Saxon

Eh byþ for eorlum æþelinga wyn, hors hofum wlanc, ðær him hæleþ ymbe welege on wicgum wrixlaþ spræce and biþ unstyllum æfre frofur.

The horse is a joy to princes in the presence of warriors. A steed in the pride of its hoofs, when rich men on horseback bandy words about it; and it is ever a source of comfort to the restless.

Unfortunately, we only have one rune poem about Ehwaz, which means the information is limited. This poem makes it clear that horses were respected. Horses were not an ordinary commodity among the Norse people; only the most influential people could afford them. In the sagas, horses are rarely mentioned unless ridden by a king or Odin, a sentiment echoed in the first line of the Anglo-Saxon rune poem.

In the *Hávamál* Odin advices:

Washed and fed / to the council fare,
But care not too much for thy clothes;
Let none be ashamed / of his shoes and hose, Less still of the steed he rides
-Havamal 61

A steed symbolizes fortune and power, no matter how shabby the horse might be. However, the power of the horse is not just a status symbol. The horse can symbolize comfort to the restless, fast travel to far-off destinations, making the journey much more enjoyable.

Figure 48: Sleipnir

Historic use in charms and amulets

Several amulets and standing stones have been found inscribed with variations on the word Ehwaz and drawings of horses.
The stone of Roes is a large slab of sandstone found in Gotland. It contains the drawing of a horse together with the inscription:

ᛁᚢ᛫ᛏᚺᛁᚾ᛫ᚢᛞᛞᛉ᛫ᚱᚨᚲ

KJ102 *iu thin uddz rak*

Udd pushed this horse
(Krause, Runen, 1970).

Figure 49: the stone of Roes

The difficulty with this standing stone is determining the significance of Udd's carving and deciphering its meaning. A horse is drawn on the rune stone. Is this the horse that Udd pushed into the rock? Did Udd travel to this land on horseback? Or is there some other significance? Udd did take special care to create a bind rune for his name.

In Denmark, a small golden pendant was found called the Lekkende Bracteate. The pendant is engraved on one side, depicting a man on a horse. On the right is a stylized swastika, a common religious and magical symbol in the Viking age. The Germans later appropriated the symbol incorrectly in the second world war. On the right side, Ansuz (Odin's rune) and Ehwaz are visible.

IK 291

Figure 50: the Lekkende Bractaete

This leads to the theory among scholars that Lekkende Bractaete is dedicated to Odin's horse Sleipnir. Alternatively, the amulet could be referring to the divine nature of horses.

In Skåne, Sweden, a wealth of similar golden pendants have been found.

IK 352

Figure 51: the Scane Tirup-heide Skane Bractaete

ᛖᚺᚹᚢ

Ehwu ; Horse

In the pendant below, we see a horse being depicted again. Although the Lekkende Bracteate might have been a specific reference to Sleipnir, this pendant is a charm about a regular horse. This Pendant does not give any other clues as to its magical meaning

ᛖ·ᛖᛚᛁᛚ

Figure 52: the Skane Bracteate

e elil

Ehwaz to the horse (Krause, Runen, 1970)

The ehwaz is written again on this pendant but this time joined by horse spelled out into a bind rune. These pendants exemplify how the word horse represented some religious or magical significance.

Outside of archaeological finds, the magic power of the horse appears in three Sagas. When Egil, a famous runemaster, has to flee Norway after falling into an argument with the king. Egil leaves a níðstang (curse pole) and leaves behind a curse on Norway until King Eric and his queen Gunnhilda are banished.

And when all was ready for sailing, Egil went up into the island. He took in his hand a hazel-pole, and went to a rocky eminence that looked inward to the mainland. Then he took a horse's head and fixed it on the pole. After that, in solemn form of curse, he thus spake: 'Here set I up a curse-pole, and this curse I turn on king Eric and queen Gunnhilda. (Here he turned the horse's head landwards.) This curse I turn also on the guardian-spirits who dwell in this land, that they may all wander astray, nor reach or find their home till they have driven out of the land king Eric and Gunnhilda.'

This spoken, he planted the pole down in a rift of the rock, and let it stand there. The horse's head he turned inwards to the mainland; but on the pole he cut runes, expressing the whole form of curse.

- **Egil's saga 60**

The focal point of the curse is a horse's head that stands on top of a rune-inscribed staff. The curse is to banish the guardian spirits of the land.

A similar curse is found in the lesser-known Vatnsdæla saga. Finnbogi and Jökul are set to meet in Holmgang (a ritual trial by combat). When Finnbogi does not show up, Jökul places a níðstang in front of Finnbogi's house. This time the runic staff is topped with a carved human skull set in the breast of a dead mare.

The last example is a tale from the Flateyjarbók about a family where the grandmother wraps a horse's penis in linen and herbs. Each night the horse penis was brought out and prayed over. This practice continued until Olaf, king of Iceland, converted them all to Christianity.

A pattern begins to emerge in these examples if you consider the old Nordic saying: *marr er manns fylgja. (*The horse is man's Guardian spirit.)

The Fylgja is the Norse word for the idea that each person is born with a guardian spirit or familiar. The Fylgja represents a person's life force, their ability to affect destiny, and defend against the supernatural.

Mostly, Fylgja would take the shape of an animal fitting with the person they were attached to. This could be because the animal represented traits of the person it is connected to, like a fox for cunning, or simply because the animal is abundant at the location of the person's birth.

The literal meaning of Fylgja is following or follower, but in the sagas, a Fylgja is known to arrive ahead of the person it is attached to. For example, In the Hávarðar saga, Ísfirðings has a dream of 18 attacking wolves led by one vixen. This dream signified that 18 warriors and a sorceress were on their way and that their spiritual force or intent had already started the attack.

If a person's Fylgja were repelled or defeated, that would leave a person spiritually vulnerable. If the Fylgja of a person was chased off before a fight, that person had no chance of winning when they arrived; if the Fylgja were killed, that person would also die.

The Fylgja could also take human form to give advice. In Norse mythology, there are two names for the spirits tied to a person's destiny; one is Fylgja, who appears in human or animal form, and Hamingja, who always appears human. It is assumed that these are two names for the same thing because they never appear in the same saga. Hamingja means luck, this should not be understood as luck of the moment but more as the advantages one has in life.

When the Fylgja dies, so does the owner, but the reverse is not true. A person can leave his Fylgja to watch over a single person or his family after his death. A person can even send their Fylgja to guard a person while they are still alive. This comes with its risks as it leaves the sender vulnerable.

If we consider that Fylgja are often represented by horses, the curses performed by Egil and Jökul become clearer. The dead horse represents the Fylgja, and the curse pole is meant to either harm the Fylgja through sympathetic magic or scare it away. Either way, the curse's target is left open for ill fortune.

The ritual surrounding the horse penis becomes a ritual of appreciation of the Fylgja of that family. The pendants can then be understood as charms creating a stronger connection between a person and their Fylgja. Roes's rune stone can be understood as "Udd brought his spirit here." Udd likely intended to send his Fylgja to look over that land after his death.

Cultural relevance

The Scandinavian horse was short, stout, and bred to survive the harsh climate. Unlike the French knights' giant cavalry horse, the Scandinavian horse was not a dedicated war horse.

The Scandinavian horse was a jack of all trades used for travel, war, and architecture. The horse was a precious possession. Even owning a horse was a status symbol, as seen in the *Hávamál.*

Washed and fed / to the council fare,
But care not too much for thy clothes;
Let none be ashamed / of his shoes and hose,
Less still of the steed he rides,
-Hávamál ***61***

A horse is more than just a tool, however. A horse is an ally or companion.

Conclusion

Ehwaz represents the symbiotic relationship between humanity and the forces in the spiritual realm. In a way, Ehwaz is the opposite of Thurisaz (troll rune). While Thurisaz represents chaotic, destructive forces, Ehwaz represents the benevolent forces working with humanity's interests.

In readings: As previously seen with other runes, the Norse people believed our ability to forge our destiny was limited. They believed that outside forces always limited free will. On its own, this rune represents the external influences that benefit you. This can refer to people, organizations, or powers that were anthropomorphized in Nordic culture, like justice.

The other runes drawn in this question can clarify what you are supposed to be cooperating with. For example, with Mannaz (humankind rune), it means cooperation with your community. Othala (ancestor's rune) means the same but working together with your family.Besides working together, Ehwaz and Raidho (wagon rune) would emphases the travel aspect of the horse rune.

In advice and counseling: The advice that Ehwaz gives is that of symbioses. It is important to note here that there is a difference between symbioses and cooperation. In cooperation, you are both striving for the same goal, but in symbiosis, you might aim for different purposes but need to help each other succeed. Remember that you need them just as they need you, even though your goals might differ.

In magic and ritual:_ Ehwaz is the rune of the Fylgja, which can be used in meditations, charms, or to commune with your Fylgja. In that same vein, it can be used as a charm to ask for your Fylgja's protection. For instance, in combination with Algiz (elk rune) or in combination with Eihwaz (yew tree rune), ask your Fylgja to protect you during Shamanistic journeys.

Experiencing the runes

The Horse: One of the best ways to experience the meaning of this rune is to ride a horse. Horses are no longer as prevalent as in the old days, but most cities still have a riding school where it is possible to take a lesson in horse riding. A horse is a large and imposing beast, and it is natural to feel reverence toward the horse. Soon you will notice that a rapport will build between you and the horse. A horse is not like a car you control but a symbiotic relationship where the horse trusts your lead.

The offerings to the Fylgja: As the first line of defense against the supernatural forces of the world, your most devoted guardian deserves some gratitude. Make an altar using the Ehwaz rune to represent your Fylgja and potentially other runes depending on the bond you are trying to create or the situation you are giving thanks for. Traditional offerings include flowers, honey, mead, grains, or meat.

Riding the tree: One of the traditional uses of the guardian spirit is as a protector during shamanistic travel between worlds.

Below is a guided meditation you can record and then play back to yourself during meditation. The goal is to travel towards the world tree with your Fylgja. There is no traveling between the nine realms in this meditation, but if you want to, you can use the same meditation as a start. If you know the shape of your Fylgja, you can also edit the meditation to reflect that.

"*Close your eyes and breath deep*

You are standing on a sunny dirt road; the sky is clear, with hardly a cloud in the sky. To your left and right, flowing grasslands stretch out and in front of you is a gentle slope taking the path to the top of a hill. The temperature is pleasant, and you decide to take a walk.

As you walk in the sun gently up the hill, you feel a nice breeze on your skin and hear the birds chirp in the distance.

As you reach the crest of the hill, you see a forest before you; the path gently curves into the woods and then disappears from sight. The chirping of birds is more pronounced now, and in the distance, you hear the soft murmur of a river.

As you make your way down towards the forest, you notice that the vegetation to the left and the right of the path is starting to become thicker. First, it is only small plants and shrubbery, but as you approach the forest, the vegetation becomes taller and wilder, and without being able to tell precisely when it happens, you are in the woods.

The air here is cool and welcoming, and the singing of birds is now all around you. As you look up, the sunlight shines through the leaves, streaming light to the forest floor. You keep walking through this beautiful forest.

You hear a soft rustling in the forest to your right, and when you look, you notice your Fylgja walking parallel to you some distance away. Sometimes in the shape of an animal, sometimes in the form of a person. You nod in acknowledgment; no words are needed now.

The two of you keep walking, and as you keep walking, the forest grows denser and denser around you. The river that first murmured in the distance now sounds much closer; your Fylgja is slowly walking closer and closer to you and just a little bit ahead of you.

As you turn another bend, you arrive at the river, and there is a bridge across the river. Your Fyglia beckons you to cross. You follow your Fylgjia.

On the other side, the forest is darker still, and the chirping of birds is silenced. Your Fylgia shines out with a faint inner light that gives you peace. The two of you walk for a while in this otherworldly forest. Then as you turn the bend again, a clearing in the woods becomes visible. In the middle of this clearing stands an enormous tree. So vast that you can not see its top, so vast that to walk around it would be to walk around eternity, but at the same time, it is a regular tree.

The Fylgja looks at you; you know you can ask it any question, and it will answer you to the best of its ability.

----Take some pause here for questions ----

As you have asked your questions and received your answers, the two of you return back home again. You make your way to the bridge and cross it back to the other side of the river. Here, the forest is brighter again, and you hear the birds singing.

As you walk back to where you began, your fylgja retreats into the forest. Always close but not on the same path as you. The trees become less dense, and before you know it, you again walk out of the forest, making the ascent to the top of the hill.

The wind gently rustles the golden field to your left and right, and you are back where you began your journey.

Take a deep breath and open your eyes."

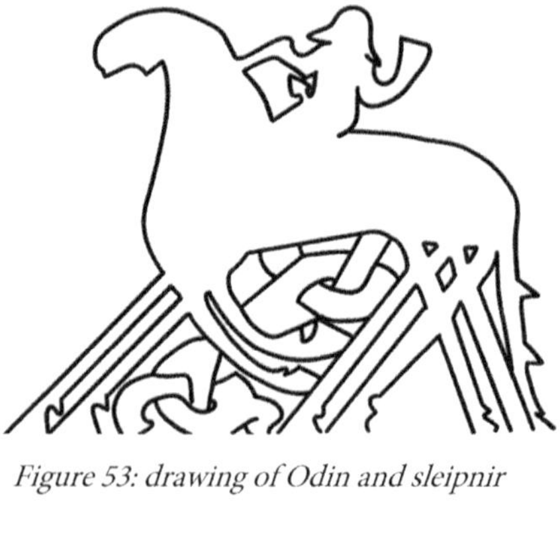

Figure 53: drawing of Odin and sleipnir

ᛗ

3.4 Mannaz - Humankind

Germanic	Gothic	Old English	Old Norse	Sound
Mannaz	Manna	Mann	Madhr	M

Mannaz is the fourth rune of the third Ætt. In a time when the world was more hostile and unpredictable, Mannaz is the rune that represents humanity. It represents more than just humankind; it is a rune of community, the bonds that bind us, and in a broader sense, the bonds that all humankind shares. Mannaz can be seen by those living in Midgard as civilization's safe haven. All things outside Midgard were known as Utgard, the outer realm where strange things lurk.

The rune poems

Norwegian

ᛗᚨᛞᚺᚱ·ᛖᚱ·ᛗᛟᛚᛞᚨᚱ·ᚨᚢᚲᛁ·ᛗᛁᚲᛁᛚ·ᛖᚱ·ᚷᚱᚨᛖᛁᛈ·ᚨ·ᚺᚨᚢᚲᛁ.

Maðr er moldar auki mikil er græip á hauki.

Man is an augmentation of the dust great is the claw of the hawk.

The first line can be interpreted as a man being created from the earth and rising from humble beginnings. This interpretation will sound familiar to those growing up where the Abrahamic religions are dominant. However, the Norse did not believe humanity was created from dust; it is more likely that Christianity already influenced this poem. In Norse Mythology, Odin, Hœnir, and Lodur[71] created the first man and woman at the same time out of trees. Odin gave them *önd* (breath, spirit, essence), Hœnir gave them *óð* (thought, inspiration), and Lodur gave them *lá* (there is no definitive translation, but it's translated as life or vitality).

The second line that references the talons of the hawk is also enigmatic. Although the hawk is not often named in the sagas, Odin and Freya can travel as a bird of prey. If the rune poem refers to this, then the hawk's talons represent the gods' might. However, it is unclear if Odin and Freya transform into a Hawk, a falcon, or an eagle. Either way, it is perhaps a warning telling humanity that although they enrich the earth, they are not as mighty as the Gods.

The second and final time a hawk is mentioned is the hawk Veðrfölnir which sits between the eyes of an unnamed giant eagle perched on the top of Yggdrasil. The role of Veðrfölnir is unknown. One theory[72] is that Veðrfölnir might symbolize the wisdom or knowledge of the eagle in the same vein as Huginn and Muninn do for Odin. If it is the case that the hawk represents wisdom in Norse mythology, then it would be logical to assume that the claw of the hawk means humanity's gift of wisdom. Another option is that Veðrfölnir symbolizes the divine. In the cosmology of the world tree, the Eagle sits at the top, and Veðrfölnir sits on top of the eagle, making him geographically the highest thing in the universe. In this interpretation of Veðrfölnir, we would again see the claw as the divine, literally above humanity.

---

[71] According to *Völuspá* 17. According to *Gylfaginning* it was Odin Vili and Ve that gave life to mankind. It is not specified in *Gylfaginning* who gives what gift.

[72] By professor John Lindow.

ᛗᚨᛞᚺᚱ·ᛖᚱ·ᛗᚨᚾᛊ·ᚷᚨᛗᚨᚾ·ᛟᚲ·ᛗᛟᛚᛞᚨᚱ·ᚨᚢᚲᛁ·ᛟᚲ·ᛊᚲᛁᛈᚨ·ᛊᚲᚱᛖᛇᛏᛁᚱ·ᚺᛟᛗᛟ·ᛗᛁ
ᛚᛞᛁᚾᚷᚱ·

Maðr er manns gaman ok moldar auki ok skipa skreytir. homo mildingr.

Man Delight of man and augmentation of the earth and adorner of ships.

The Icelandic rune poem starts with the uplifting statement; man is the delight of man. This sentiment is echoed in stanza 47 of the *Hávamál*:

Young was I once, / and wandered alone,
And nought of the road I knew;
Rich did I feel / when a comrade I found,
For man is man's delight.
-Hávamál 47

In modern life, we cannot always see the other people responsible for our food, houses, and other commodities we use. Because of this, it is easy to forget that they are there and how much we need other people.

For the Nordic people, this was not the case. Your neighbor was your ally against the unrelenting forces of Utgard; other people meant safety, entertainment, and civilization. Isolation, on the other hand, meant death.

The second line again places humanity as an augmentation of the earth. In the context of humanity being a delight, we might assume that humanity is an improvement to the world.

The last line can be seen as a specific addition to this poem from the Icelandic people. The inhabitants from Iceland came there by boat, so ships were integral to their way of life.

ᛗᚫᚾ᛫ᛒᚣᚦ᛫ᛟᚾ᛫ᛗᚣᚱᚷᚦᛖ᛫ᚻᛁᛋ᛫ᛗᚫᚷᚫᚾ᛫ᛚᛖᛟᚠ᛫ᛋᚳᛖᚫᛚ᛫ᚦᛖᚫᚻ᛫ᚫᚾᚱᚫ᛫ᚷᛖᚻᚹᚣᛚᚳ᛫ᛟ
ᛞᚻᚱᚢᛗ᛫
ᛋᚹᛁᚳᚫᚾ᛫ᚠᛟᚱᛞᚻᚢᛗ᛫ᛞᚱᛁᚻᛏᛖᚾ᛫ᚹᚣᛚᛖ᛫ᛞᛟᛗᛖ᛫ᛋᛁᚾᛖ᛫ᚦᚫᛖᛏ᛫ᛖᚫᚱᛗᛖ᛫ᚠᛚᚫᛖᛋᚳ᛫ᛖᛟ
ᚱᚦᚫᚾ ᛫ᛒᛖᛏᚫᛖᚳᚫᚾ᛫

Man byþ on myrgþe his magan leof sceal þeah anra gehwylc oðrum swican, forðum drihten wyle dome sine þæt earme flæsc eorþan betæcan.

Anglo-Saxon

The joyous man is dear to his kinsmen; yet every man is doomed to fail his fellow, since the Lord by his decree will commit the vile carrion to the earth.

The Anglo-Saxon rune poem starts with the same optimism as the Icelandic one, highlighting the happiness community can bring. It ends with the inevitable mortality of humanity. The Lord in this Christianised version of the rune poem is Yahweh, and The vile carrion is a reference to the bible verse (1 Thess. iv.1.)

"O what an honour is it, that our bodies (falling more vile than carrion) should. Thus arise in glory, like unto the body of the Son of God!"

This poem warns us not to rely too heavily on our fellow man because he is of the earth, unlike the Lord, who is greater and divine. The Lord in pagan times would be Odin. As a God of death, the choicer of the slain, and a deciding factor in the outcome of wars, Odin would fit the role of one who decrees the time of death.

Historic use in charms and amulets

There are no surviving charms or amulets that use Mannaz other than phonetically. Perhaps this means that community was seen as so fundamental that there was no need to work it into charms or curses.

Cultural relevance

Examining how Nordic people perceived the components of humanity and their place in the universe is important.

In the western world, it is commonly believed that humans are made up of two parts, a body and a soul. The Norse had a more complex view than the Christians, consisting of more than two aspects. Unfortunately, there is no definitive list of classifications, but combining various sources can summate the parts of the spiritual anatomy.

The spiritual anatomy:

The Lic / Lyke: This represents the physical aspect of a person, their body. This is also the root of the word Lich. The Lich is a type of revenant, a reanimated body lacking any of the spiritual parts of a human. In Dutch, the term "lijk" (pronounced lɛik) still means lifeless body.

Önd/ ǣþm(athem): This represents breath, or in this context, life. Breath is the force that animates the Lic. The Dutch word for breath is 'adem' which etymologically originates from 'athem'. The moment a person dies, their ǣþm leaves them. This idea is still seen in the saying "dying breath or last breath." In Dutch, dying is sometimes described with the euphemism, "je laatste adem uitblazen" or exhaling the final breath.

Hamr / Hama: This represents the shape of a person. As the Lic constitutes the base materials a body is made out of, the Hamr is the shape that a person can have. Someone's Hamr changes throughout their life. More than just the physical aspect, the Hamr is how someone is perceived. Some magicians or other gifted individuals have the ability to alter their Hamr at will and take the perceived appearance of animals.

The Hiw: Similar or perhaps synonymous with the Hamr, the hiw is a person's shape outside their Lic or body. We see this in the Yngling saga, where the feats of Odin are described. Among Odin's power is:

"Odin could transform his shape: his body would lie as if dead, or asleep; but then he would be in shape of a fish, or worm, or bird, or beast, and be off in a twinkling to distant lands upon his own or other people's business."
-Yngling saga 7

This traveling aspect that travels outside of the body is called the hiw. This is similar to the modern concept of astral travel.

The Óð / Ferþ: represents thoughts and inspiration, similar to the modern concept of the soul. The Anglo-Saxon word Ferþ can also be translated as the heart or the core. The óð itself is divided again into two parts. Huginn and Muninn, or thought and memory also the names of the two ravens that Odin uses to gather information around the world. In Grímnimál, it is said.

O'er Mithgarth Hugin / and Munin both
Each day set forth to fly;
For Hugin I fear / lest he come not home,
But for Munin my care is more.
- Grímnismál 7

Odin is saying that he cares more for his memories than his reasoning. A sentiment that many might agree with.

We already know that Odin is capable of traveling outside of his body. The metaphysics of this process is never fully explained. The óð takes the form of the Hiw, leaving the Lic and Hamr behind.

The three classes

Nordic society was split into three classes. Thralls (enslaved people), Karls (freemen), and Jarls (lords). Mythological this distinction starts in the Rígsþula. In Rígsþula, a wanderer called Ríg (king)[73] visits three couples; he lies between each couple for a night, and without fail, nine months later, a child is born. The first couple lives in a shabby hut and are called Ái and Edda (great grandfather and great grandmother); they give birth to Þræll (enslaved person). The second couple lives on a farm and are called Afi and Amma (grandfather and grandmother); nine months later, they have a child named Karl (freeman). Lastly, Rig visits a great house where Faðir and Móðir (father and mother) live; nine months later, they have a child called Jarl (noble or chieftain).

The grandchildren of the couples visited by Ríg form the three social classes in Nordic culture. Unlike what this story might suggest, the role someone was born with is not necessary for life; social mobility, both up and down, was common.

The enslaved people were bound to service and were property in all regards. To injure an enslaved person had the same penalty as damaging property. Enslaved people were kidnapped during raids, born from a mother who was enslaved or someone who became an enslaved person (temporary or long-term) to pay off a debt.
They lived in housing provided by their masters and worked land they did not own. An enslaved person could be freed by their master, or they could buy their freedom.

A Karl was allowed to own land and to vote on the Thing (meetings). They also had protection under the law. Karls lived together in small communities of a few buildings with strong family ties. Not all were farmers; all forms of trade were represented.

---

[73] Rig is sometimes identified as Heimdall because in the Völuspá he is described as the kinsmen of mankind. The wandering persona however also fits Odin and as the all-Father he is also a likely candidate.

Lastly, the Jarl, this is a local leader who also held some religious authority. The Jarl was the community leader because he was the richest and had the most followers. But a Karl could surpass the riches of the Jarl through raiding or other means, and if that Karl would also gain a strong following, he could replace the Jarl.

Community

These communities lived together in close interdependence but also with strong social ties. Tacitus describes it as follows:

No people are more addicted to social entertainments, or more liberal in the exercise of hospitality. To refuse any person whatever admittance under their roof, is accounted flagitious. . . . No one makes a distinction with respect to the rights of hospitality, between a stranger and an acquaintance. The departing guest is presented with whatever he may ask for; and with the same freedom a boon is desired in return. They are pleased with presents; but think no obligation incurred when they give or receive.

-Germania 21

Conclusion

Mannaz represents humanity, individual humans, and the ties between communities and the self. As such, the meaning of this rune seems very broad, but that is only from the modern individualistic point of view. A single person is defined by the family that came before them and the community they live in. The rare examples of children growing up in the forest show us that what we perceive as humanity is learned, not born into us. Biologically, we are human from the moment we are born, but in all ways that count, we become human through our family and community.

In readings: Depending on the question, Mannaz can reference the self or community you are a part of. Remember that for the Nordic people, these two were closely related, so it is not so much you or them but more your relation towards the community or the community towards you.

Different runes clarify what ties Mannaz is referring to. For example, in combination with Berkana (birch rune), it could indicate the relationship with the mother, or in combination with Thurisaz(troll rune), it could mean your relationship with those forces working against you.

In combination with Ansuz (Odin's rune), the message points towards humanity's relationship to the Gods or, depending on the question, the gift of Önd that Odin gave the first humans.

In advice and counseling: Mannaz references how we perceive ourselves and how others see us. According to the Nordic culture, the body (lych), the consciousness (óð), and the perceived shape (hamr). How we see ourselves or others see us is mutable, not just a component of the flesh. Accepting this gives both a measure of responsibility and freedom.

In magic and ritual: In magic and ritual, the Mannaz rune can represent the self or a community you are part of. In that way, it can be incorporated into a fetch as the focus of acts of sympathetic magic. As discussed in the chapter about Ehwaz (horse rune), Mannaz and Ehwaz combine as a symbol of symbioses between the human soul and its Fylgja.

Experiencing the runes

Finding the Hamr: We all have our concept of who we are. Nordic wisdom says our idea of self is not complete. This makes sense, If you meet someone for the first time, you might introduce yourself with your name, but you are not your name; there are many others with the same name. You might introduce yourself as a teacher, a soldier, a pagan, or an artist; these are not who you are. Although they might be helpful identifiers, they are your Hamr (shape), not your óð, your consciousness.

In this exercise, you will try to get a clear understanding of the Hamr that you wear. Perhaps later you can identify if this Hamr fits you well.

Use a recording device and for 1 minute, repeat the following statement and fill in the blanks with statements you feel are true for you.

I am .....

For example:
I am a man

I am confident

I am ...

If you are in a good flow, you can keep going after the minute is up. Listen to your recordings and ask yourself how you feel about what you said. Does it capture who you are? What defines you most, and what defines you least?

Shapeshifting: Now that you know who you are, you can think of who you could be. In the Norse myths, the berserkers were warriors devoted to Odin who, through ritual and magic, worked themselves into a frenzy, taking on the aspects of bears and wolves, increasing their prowess in battle.

For this exercise, think of an aspect not incorporated into your Hamr and try to incorporate it for a day. This can be an animal aspect or something like being funny, confident, and sly. Start the day calling upon an animal or a God that embodies this aspect you wish to incorporate into your Hamr; bring an offering. Then head into your day and dress appropriately. At the end of the day, take stock. Did you feel different? Were you treated differently?

Forging community: The most common application of Mannaz is that of society. To help those less fortunate because no one can carry the world alone and because you know you might be in a position where you need help one day.

Join a volunteering project, help in a soup kitchen, a big brother/sister program, or another program in your neighbourhood. Become a part of making your community better.

Figure 54: gathering

ᛚ

3.5 Laguz - Lake

Germanic	Gothic	Old English	Old Norse	Sound
Laguz	Lagus	Lagu	Lögr	L

Laguz is the fifth rune of the third Ætt, and with it, we enter the final half of the final Ætt. Laguz is an enigmatic rune. There is a good amount of information about the rune in charms, magic, sagas, and rune poems. There seem to be two very different interpretations of this rune, a masculine and a feminine one. Laguz is a historically powerful rune used in many rituals and charms

The rune poems

ᚷᚱ᛫ᛖᚱ᛫ᚠᚨᛖᛚᚱ᛫ᛟᚱ᛫ᚠᛃᚨᛚᛖ᛫ᚠᛟᛊ᛫ᛖᚾ᛫ᚷᚢᛚ᛫ᛖᚱᛟ᛫ᚾᛟᛊᛖᚱ᛫

Norwegian

Lǫgr er, fællr ór fjalle foss en gull ero nosser.

A waterfall is a River which falls from a mountain-side but ornaments are of gold.

The first thing that stands out in this poem and the other poems is that Laguz is not described as a tranquil lake. Laguz is a moving force of water, unstoppable in its power. The combination of the first and the second line brings to mind the story of the dwarf Andvari[74].

Andvari was a gifted craftsman and was capable of creating magical items; his prized possession was a ring he made called Andvaranaut[75]. This ring had the power to bring great riches to its owner.

Andvari also had the power to turn into a pike fish, and he used that form to hide his hoarded wealth at the bottom of a great waterfall. Loki plans to steal the treasure to pay weregild[76] for the dwarf Ótr, who he accidentally murdered. To steal this treasure, Loki first takes Ran's magical net, which allows him to capture Andvari and steal his treasure. Andvari escapes into the mountains, but before he does, he curses the treasure so that everybody who owns it dies.

This leads to the events of the Volsung saga, where the treasure brings nothing but misfortune to anybody possessing it. According to the Nibelungenlied, Hagen von Tronje gains possession of the treasure after killing Siegfried. He throws the treasure into the river Rhine; by doing this, he is safe from the curse. The implication seems to be that magical treasure is not meant for mortal hands, and under the water is where it belongs, in Ran's domain.

ᛚᛟᚷᚱ·ᛖᚱ·ᚠᛖᛚᚨᚾᛞᚨ·ᚠᚨᛏᚾ·ᛟᚲ·ᚠᛁᛞᚢᚱ·ᚲᛖᛏᛁᛚ·ᛟᚲ·ᚷᛚᛟᛗᚢᚾᚷᚱ·ᚷᚱᚢᚾᛞ·ᛚᚨᚲᚢᛊ
·ᛚᛟᚠᛞᚺᚢᚾᚷᚱ·

Icelandic

Lögr er vellanda vatn ok viðr ketill ok glömmungr grund. lacus lofðungr.

Water Eddying stream and broad geyser and land of the fish.

In the Icelandic poem, like the Norwegian poem, Laguz is described as

[74] Meaning the careful one.

[75] Meaning Andvari's gift.

[76] A fine for committing murder paid to the family of the victim.

water in motion, the eddying stream, the geysers that Iceland is famous for because of its volcanic nature, and the land of the fish as a kenning for the ocean.

The white water river, the geyser erupting from the ground, and the unpredictable ocean. All three of these are potent images of water. The word "vellande" is in this poem translated with eddying, but it also means boiling. "vell" is used in Icelandic poetry as a word for gold. It is possible that the poet composing the Icelandic rune poem picked this word for that double meaning tying it back to the Norwegian rune poem.

ᚨᛖᛋᚲ᛫ᛒᛁᚦ᛫ᛟᚠᛖᚱᚺᛖᚨᚺ᛫ᛖᛚᛞᚢᛗ᛫ᛞᛇᚱᛖ᛫ᛋᛏᛁᚦ᛫ᛟᚾ᛫ᛋᛏᚨᚦᚢᛚᛖ᛫ᛋᛏᛖᛞᛖ᛫ᚱᛁᚺᛏᛖ᛫ᚺ
ᛇᛚᛏ᛫ᛞᚺᛖᚨᚺ᛫ᚺᛁᛗ᛫ᚠᛖᛟᚺᛏᚨᚾ᛫ᛟᚾ᛫ᚠᛁᚱᚨᛋ᛫ᛗᛟᚾᛁᚷᛖ᛫

Anglo-Saxon

Æsc biþ oferheah, eldum dyre stiþ on staþule, stede rihte hylt, ðeah him feohtan on firas monige.

The ocean seems interminable to men, if they venture on the rolling bark and the waves of the sea terrify them
and the courser of the deep heed not its bridle.

Lastly, the Anglo-Saxon poem is about men and women who have ventured far across the seas from Scandinavia to Britain. It shows both the awe and terror the sea can represent.

The trip would take only a few days, but during that time, you would be stuck on a small boat with nothing to see but water in all directions, no wonder the sea seemed interminable. The rolling bark is a kenning for the waves. According to Norse mythology, the waves are anthropomorphized as the nine Nine Daughters of Ægir and Ran[77]. Each of the nine daughters has a kenning for a wave as their name.

30. Helgi bade higher / hoist the sails,
Nor did the ships'-folk / shun the waves,
Though dreadfully / did Ægir's daughters
Seek the steeds / of the sea to sink.
- Helgakviða Hundingsbana I 30

These nine daughters were seen as antagonists, forever trying to destroy ships and drown sailors. The sea was a terrifying place, and if you fell in during a storm, little could be done.

In the last sentence of the rune poem, "courser" means a swift horse and is a kenning for the ship. The Bridle is traditionally a way to steer your horse, but the waves and currents make it so that the boat is no longer under your control.

One thing that all three poems have in common is that the mysterious water is feminine. Although it is unclear why the water is feminine, there is a recurring theme of femininity associated with psychopomps in Norse mythology; the only afterlife that does not belong to a feminine God is Odin's hall. In the sea, Ran and her daughters house the dead; half of the slain warriors go to Freya, and the other dead go to Hella's hall. Besides that, the dead are collected by the Valkyrie, Your life and death are decided by the Norns, and you are guided through your life by a Fylgja. Also, woman priestesses would oversee the rituals surrounding death. There was within Nordic culture a powerful link between life, death, fate, and femininity.

[77] Ægir and Ran are sea Gods that does not belong to the Asir but are Jotun.

Historic use in charms and amulets

Laguz is used in several charms and amulets as an empowering symbol. This means that the rune Laguz was added to a charm, spell, or amulet to imbue it with greater power. There are several empowering words and symbols, but Laguz is the only rune used as such[78].

One such example is the Bülach fibula.

KJ 165

Figure 55: the Bülach Fibula

ᚠᚱᛁᚠᚱᛁᛞᛁᛚ·ᛚᛁᛞ·ᛞᚢ·ᚠᚢᛞ·ᚠ·ᛏ·ᛗᛁᚲ·ᛚ·ᛚ

Frifridil lid du fud f t mik L L

[your] Frifridil [who] has the member - You [who] [has] the vulva, receive me into you L L! (Klingenberg, 1976)

This is a direct love spell where the inclusion of the Laguz rune gives the statement of intent power.

[78] You can read more on this in the chapter in Magic

Another example is a small gold pendant found in Sweden.

IK 181

Figure 56: the Svarteborg medallion

ᛊᛁᚷᚨᚾᛞᚢᛉ·ᛚ

Ssiganduz L

Siganduz L(eek)

This charm is even simpler, just a name and an empowering symbol. The pendant was probably worn as a personal lucky charm.

There are more examples like this, and it would seem to make the uses of Laguz in magic reasonably straightforward. There is, however, some debate if the ᛚ in these charms represents Laguz (lake) or Laukaz (leek). The Leek is a vegetable with magical significance in Nordic culture. Voluspa stanza four says it is the first plant to grow after the universe was created. In the lay of Gudrun, Sigurd is described as a leek among the grass, and swords in poetry are described with the kenning: "wounding leek." The humble leek was held in high esteem.

In the chapter on Fehu, we already observed laukaz used as an empowering rune, carved on a meat cleaver uncovered in a grave from the 4th-century Fløksand, Norway. The following inscription can be found:

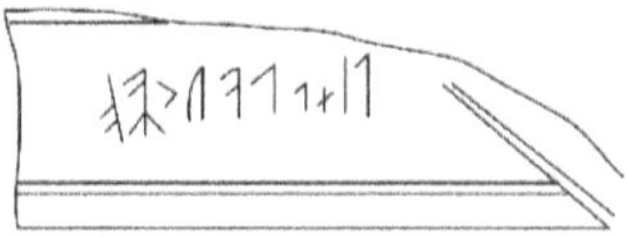

Figure 57: Floksand meatcleaver

ᛚᛁᚾᚨ· ᛚᚨᚢᚲᚨᛉ· ᚠ
Lïna, Laukaz, F(ehu)
Linnen, Leek, Cattle / wealth (Antonson, 1975)

The leek is also used in a spell against poison.

Thou shalt bless the draught
And danger escape
And cast a leek in the cup;
For so I know
Thou shalt never see
Thy mead with evil mixed.
- **Sigdrifumál 9**

In the Oldfs Saga from the Flateyjarbok, there is a story about a family who worships the severed penis of a horse as a totem. The horse's penis totem is wrapped in leeks.

We might never know whether the ᛚ rune stands for Laukus (leek) or Laguz (lake) in an individual charm or spell. However, their use is practically the same. The ᛚ rune is used to moderate the flow of positive and negative spiritual power. In the case of the Bülach fibula's spell it lets the magic flow. In the case of the counter-curse from Sigdrifumál, it washes the curse away.

Cultural relevance

Figure 58: Ran

Even in the ordinary sense, the significance of water for the Nordic people cannot be overstated. The rivers were and still are nature's highways for hauling goods, and the open sea was a route to endless possibilities.

Besides, the oceans and rivers were essential in fishing as fish was a common food source. In this way, water is a supporting nurturing force.

Water held more than a mundane meaning; the oceans, lakes, and rivers had mysteries in their deep unfathomable depths.

Three separate Goddess represents the sea, the rivers, and the lakes. Rán represents the oceans, Sága represents the rivers and waterfalls, and Nerthus represents the Lakes[79].

---

[79] The sea is also represented by two Gods, Njörðr God of fishing and sailing and Aegir, a Jotun whose name means sea.

Kennings for the sea include Rán's land and Rán's road; when describing a stormy sea, the kenning, Rán's mouth is used.

In Skáldskaparmal, for example, Ran is named:

"Then the Æsir became aware that Rán had that net wherein she was wont to catch all men who go upon the sea"

- Skáldskaparmal 33

Rán is a chaotic force that can bring sailors to their doom. She gives birth to nine daughters representing nine different storm waves.

Besides the references to Rán drowning sailors, several references indicate that Rán governed the realm of the drowned dead.

In "Friðþjófs saga hins frœkna," we see an example of this. The hero Friðþjófr and his men are stuck in a storm and fear for their lives. Friðþjófr then divides the gold and treasure aboard their ship among the men. The treasure will assure that they all will all look resplendent when arriving in Rán's hall and their allotted place in the afterlife.

Nerthus, the Goddes of the lakes, is only described by Tacitus. The most interesting part of his description is a yearly ritual involving Nerthus.

In an island of the ocean there is a sacred grove, and within it a consecrated chariot, covered over with a garment. Only one priest is permitted to touch it. He can perceive the presence of the goddess in this sacred recess, and walks by her side with the utmost reverence as she is drawn along by heifers.

Afterwards the car, the vestments, and, if you like to believe it, the divinity herself, are purified in a secret lake. Slaves perform the rite, who are instantly swallowed up by its waters. Hence arises a mysterious terror and a pious ignorance concerning the nature of that which is seen only by men doomed to die."

-Tacitus 40

The idea that another world lies under the surface of lakes and oceans is a common belief in Pagan Europe. According to Celtic folklore, the Tuatha Dé Danann[80] live in a world under the waves.

In the tale, Frau Holle, an old Germanic fairytale written down by the Brothers Grimm, a maiden falls into a well and ends up in a magical otherworld. It seems that throughout Europe, it was believed that the water could hide entire worlds beneath its surface.

Figure 59: The Goddess in the boat

---

[80] A mythical race that lived in Ireland according to myth and then relocated to the land under the waves called Tír fo Thuinn .

Conclusion

Laguz is a complicated rune. On the one hand, the rune poems are associated with water, lakes, and waves, represented by Nerthus, Ran, and her nine daughters. In that regard, Laguz is represented by feminine deities.

On the other hand, the Laguz rune is commonly used in charms to add potency. When used in this way, it symbolizes a leek. The Leek, with its phallic shape, suggests a more masculine energy. This idea is validated by the fact that a Leek was used as wrapping for a horse's penis in the Oldfs Saga, giving this rune a more phallic meaning.

However, if we step back from the gender interpretations that surround it is clear that the rune represents the threshold between this world and the unknowable otherworld. For the stories about Rán and Nerthus, only those who are doomed to die can fully experience the Goddess and their realm. This is also true for many Celtic and Germanic fairy tales. Those who pass the threshold into the other realm can never truly return.

Behind Laguz is not the realm of the Gods but a realm behind even the Aesir, their domain. Odin, the All-Father, had to go through extremes to gain knowledge from the other-world. To gain access to the well of Mimir, Odin had to sacrifice an eye; to gain the power of the runes, Odin had to offer himself by hanging from Yggdrasil, stabbing and starving himself. The secrets of the other-world are so powerful that even the All-Father cannot easily access them.

The mysteries that Laguz hides are not meant for the mortal world. The gifts stolen or granted from this other world, like the treasure in the Volsunga saga or King Arthur's sword, must be returned to that other world or become a curse.

In that regard, Laguz can also be seen as a threshold between life and death. A bridge between that place we all come from and that we must all return to. Both the feminine and the phallic symbolism would fit this interpretation. It would also explain why Laguz would be such a familiar charm rune, as it could act as a gateway between the mundane and magical worlds.

In readings: Laguz represents unknowable forces beyond our control and understanding. This rune is an indication that those forces are at work, gifts being given are only borrowed.

In combination with Fehu (cattle rune), this rune could be a reference to the Landvættir or the Alfar, the beings that live in the cracks between reality and reveal themself only on the threshold moments, like dusk and dawn, sleeping and waking, birth and death. In combination with Eihwaz (yew tree rune), this is a rune of that final threshold; life is a gift from that other world, and one day must return to it.

In advice and counseling: Laguz represents those things you cannot control in your life. Accept that not all things can be controlled, and let go.

In magic and ritual: Historically, Laguz was used to enhance other charms and spells. If Laguz is the threshold between the mundane and the magical world, it makes sense that incorporating this design into your magic work will allow some of the supernatural worlds into your work. As a threshold rune, Laguz is also a likely candidate for rituals involving contacting the death in combination with Eihwaz (yew tree rune) and protective runes like Algiz (elk rune). However, be careful when working with Laguz, as even Odin is not above the powers of the other-world.

Experiencing the runes

Fairy Tales: While studying this rune, it is a wonderful moment to read up on the other world in fairy tales. Look for a book on Celtic or Germanic fairy tales in your local library. By reading the stories about the fairies and the heroes that visit their realm, you can better understand the fear and awe the other-world represents.

Through the looking glass: Using the runes for divination is the book's subject and a likely method used in the Nordic culture. The runes come from the other-world where Odin found them and brought them back at significant personal cost.
Studying Laguz is an excellent moment to try another reading now that we are getting close to the end of this book. Try one of the more advanced readings from the chapter on divination.

The flow of power: As the Laguz rune is used to power amulets and charms, studying this chapter is an excellent moment to try making a charm using the Laguz rune. (See the chapter on magic for more information on making charms.)

3.6 Ingwaz - Ing

Germanic	Gothic	Old English	Old Norse	Sound
Ingwaz	Engus	Ing	Ing	Ng

Ingwaz is the sixth rune of the third Ætt, representing wealth in potential, a seed waiting for the right season to grow. Ingwaz comes from the older name Yngvi for the God Freyr, the God of bounty and harvest. In a way, Ingwaz shares some characteristics with the first rune from the first Ætt, Fehu (cattle rune). Although Fehu is realized wealth and gives us a warning not to be too greedy with our wealth, Ingwaz is a seed of potential wealth and prosperity.

The rune poems

ᛁᛜ·ᚹᚨᛖᛊ·ᚨᛖᚱᛖᛊᛏ·ᛗᛁᛞ·ᛖᚨᛊᛏ·ᛞᛖᚾᚢᛗ·ᚷᛖᛊᛖᚹᛖᚾ·ᛊᛖᚲᚷᚢᚾ·ᛟᚦ·ᚺᛖ·ᛊᛁᛞᚺᚨᚾ·
ᛖᛊᛏ·ᛟᚠᛖᚱ·ᚹᚨᛖᚷ·ᚷᛖᚹᚨᛏ·ᚹᚨᛖᚾ·ᚨᛖᚠᛏᛖᚱ·ᚱᚨᚾ·ᛞᚺᚢᛊ·ᚺᛖᚨᚱᛞᛁᚾᚷᚨᛊ·ᛞᚺᛟᚾᛖ·
ᚺᚨᛖᛚᛖ·ᚾᛖᛗᛞᚢᚾ·

Anglo-Saxon

Ing wæs ærest mid East-Denum gesewen secgun, oþ he siððan est
ofer wæg gewat; wæn æfter ran ðus Heardingas ðone hæle nemdun.

Ing was first seen by men among the East-Danes, till, followed by his chariot, he departed eastwards over the waves.
So the Heardingas named the hero.

For Ingwaz, we only have the Anglo-Saxon rune poem. The rune poem starts with a mention of Ing; in this context, this is the God Freyr. Ing or Yngvi might be the actual name of Freyr as Freyr translates to Lord and is more of an honorific than a name. The East-Danes are the Anglo-Saxon name for the Geats, a people that lived in Sweden.
The kenning Éast-Den or East Dane is also used for the Geats in the Epic poem of Beowulf, as well as the kenning Ingwine or friend of Ing. Tacitus uses Ingvaeones also meaning friends of Ing for the area covering the north of the Netherlands, Northern Germany, Denmark, and Scandinavia.

The oldest dynasty of kings in Sweden were called the Yngling because they were believed to be descended from Yngvi. The chariot in the second line of the rune poem is a reference to the *Ögmundar þáttr dytts,* a saga where a statue of Freyr is driven around in a chariot.

The departing and heroic story of the Heardingas is unfortunately lost to us. There is no clear historical indication of who the Heardingas were or what mighty deeds Freyr accomplished to become their hero.

Figure 60: Freyr

Historic use in charms and amulets

Not many artifacts have been found with the Ingwaz rune used as a magical charm. However, in Wijnaldum, the Netherlands, a small amulet made from a horn was found with the following inscription:

Figure 61: The Wijnaldum piece

ᚾᚷᛉᛁᚾᚷᚢᛉᚾᚷᛉ
Ngzinguzngz

The runes above are Frisian Futhork, ngz Inguz ngz; the central Inguz is probably a Frisian spelling of Ingwaz, similar to the Gothic spelling Enguz. NGZ (ing) is repeated twice, once before and once after Inguz.

NgZ is simply a shorthand spelling for the God Ingwaz. This allows his name to be placed three times onto the charm. Three being a magic number would have increased the potential of the charm.

It shows the importance of Ingwaz as a God. Possibly even going so far as replacing Odin with Freyr to evoke magical rituals.

Cultural relevance

The name Yngvi after which Ingwaz is named, shows up several times throughout the Eddas and the sagas. Yngvi first appears in the list of dwarfs; in Volspula stanza sixteen. The dwarfs are named in couples, and Yngvi is coupled with Alf.

The naming of Yngvi in a list of Dwarfs[81] can be explained. Dwarfs, especially in the Eddas, do not share any specific characteristics. Only later on do dwarfs become short and bearded. Until then, dwarfs might have been a classification of lesser divine beings. This idea is reinforced by other names in the list of dwarf names, such as Gandalf, meaning Elf of the wand. The name Alf that Ygnvi is compelled with

Not just the diminutive bearded smiths are included in this list. The pairing of Yngvi and Alf is a logical one if we look at the Grímnismál:

Ydalir call they / the place where Ull
A hall for himself hath set;
And Alfheim the gods / to Freyr once gave
As a tooth-gift in ancient times.
- Grímnismál 5

A tooth gift is given when the baby shows its first tooth. In the time before our current level of medical knowledge, babies were often not named or celebrated at birth because the chances that they would not live past a month old were high.

This stanza shows that Freyr is the lord of Alfheim, the realm of the Alfar or elves. Freyr is not of the Aesir but a member of the second family of Gods called the Vanir. This might be why Freyr was

---

[81] *dvergr*

included in the list of dwarfs.

However, the name Freyr also appears in the Ynglinga saga:

Freyr was called by another name, Yngvi; and this name Yngvi was considered long after in his race as a name of honour, so that his descendants have since been called Ynglinger.
-Ynglinga saga 11

In the Ynglinga saga, Snorri believes that the stories of the Northern Gods originated in Asia. Snorri was a Christian and tried to make the Norse myths work within Christianity; he explained the Aesir as heroes who were mistaken for Gods because of their great deeds. Snorri reasons Odin's worshippers mistake him for a God because of his great success as a warlord.

Although there is no historical evidence, Snorri writes that Odin arrives in Scandinavia and passes the crown to Njord, who, in turn, passes the crown to his son Freyr. This shows that even from Snorri's Christian standpoint, Freyr was still a significant figure within Norse culture, even a millennium after Tacitus wrote about him.

In the *Ynglingatal*, a poem by Þjóðólfr of Hvinir, a skald from the late ninth century, the then-ruling royal family of Sweden is described as descending from Yngvi. Sigurd, who shares this bloodline, is also described as a descendant of Yngvi in the Reginsmál.

"Here shall I foster / the fearless prince,
Now Yngvi's heir / to us is come;
The noblest hero / beneath the sun,
The threads of his fate / all lands enfold."

- Reginsmál 14

This connection between the mythical kings and Yngvi or Freyr shows his importance among the Gods. Freyr is next to Odin and Thor, one of the most important deities in the Nordic pantheon. The earliest written source we have of Freyr comes from *Adam von*

Bremen, a German historian who lived between 1050 and 1090. He is most famous for his book *Gesta Hammaburgensis Ecclesiae Pontificum* (*Deeds of Bishops of the Hamburg Church*). While not a reliable narrator because of his apparent attachment to the church, Adam does give an interesting description of a pagan temple in Upsala

In this temple, entirely decked out in gold, the people worship the statues of three gods in such wise that the mightiest of them, Thor, occupies a throne in the middle of the chamber; Woden and Frikko have places on either side. The significance of these gods is as follows: Thor, they say, presides over the air, which governs the thunder and lightning, the winds and rains, fair weather and crops. The other, Woden—that is, the Furious—carries on war and imparts to man strength against his enemies. The third is Frikko, who bestows peace and pleasure on mortals. His likeness, too, they fashion with an immense phallus (Tschan, 2002).

- Gesta Hammaburgensis 26,

Frikko is another name for Freyr. In the Ynglinga Saga, Snorri confirms the connection between peace, pleasure, and Freyr. In Snorri's version of events, Freyr is not a God but a mortal.

When it became known to the Swedes that Frey was dead, and yet peace and good seasons continued, they believed that it must be so as long as Frey remained in Sweden; and therefore they would not burn his remains, but called him the god of this world, and afterwards offered continually blood-sacrifices to him, principally for peace and good seasons.

-Ynglinga saga 13

There is no other mention in the sagas or stories about the size of Freyr's phallus; statues have been found with exaggerated phalluses but without other identifying marks linking them to Freyr. As a fertility God, it is not unlikely that phallic symbols were part of Freyr's iconography.

In Völsa þáttr, the story is told of king Olaf who visits a family who worships the penis of a horse. Jarls and other more educated people would have had Odin, the God of war and wisdom, as their primary God. On the other hand, farmers had little to do with war and more with working the land. It is not unlikely that Thor and Freyr had a very strong following among the common folk, and this story is an example of Vanir worship. We have lost most of the evidence of Vanir worship because farmers were less likely to have elaborate stones engraved or amulets made out of precious metals.

Conclusion

The lines between the Vanir and the Aesir are blurry at best. The lines between the Gods and the Jötunn are not at all clear. If anything can be said about what divides the Vanir and the Aesir, then it is that the Aesir seem more focused on civilization, knowledge, poetry, marriage, justice, and innovation, whereas the Vanir are more focused on nature, growth, sex, fertility, death, forests and lakes. If Ansuz is the rune of Odin and, by extension, the Aesir, then Ingwaz is the rune of Freyr and, therefore Vanir.

The shape of the rune is that of a seed; similarly, this is a rune of potential. It is a rune of mythical powers that work towards growth.

If we accept that Yngvi is the proper name of Freyr, it is a testament to his popularity that he became known as Lord. Ingwaz has a lot in common with Yera (year rune), but whereas Yera focuses on the natural cycles and the results, Ingwaz is the power that brings forth the bounty of Freyr and the Alfar he rules.

In readings: In readings, the meaning of Ingwaz is strongly dependent on the question asked. Like the God, this rune represents Ingwaz as a multifaceted rune. If the question asked relates to a person, Ingwaz points to a masculine presence full of vitality and abundance, just like Yngvi. If the question is more growth-related, this rune represents a wealth of potential ready to be unleashed. However, unlike the primal chaos forces of the rune Uruz, this force is controlled and conscious.

The other runes drawn will show how that abundance will grow. Ingwaz combined with Fehu (cattle rune) or Yera (year rune) represents tremendous financial growth. Ingwaz, combined with Mannaz(humankind rune), is an abundance of powerful, strong, and celebratory community.

In advice and counseling: This rune advises you to live in your strength. Inside all of us is the same potential and lust for life that Freyr represents. This rune reminds you that, like a seed, there might be moments in our life where we lie in wait to flourish, but this is not our goal. We sometimes get comfortable waiting, but now is the time to shake loose and blossom.

In magic and ritual: As seen in the Wijnaldum charm, Ingwaz can be used to contact the God Yngvi and draw on his powers. In that same way, Ingwaz can be used on altars to represent Freyr in his aspect as the Lord of Nature.

Combined with other runes, you can create a direct flow of primal energy. In the Wijnaldum charm, it was paired with Algiz (elk rune) to create a protective amulet. Yera (year rune) would make an excellent combination for invoicing plenty. Combined, Year, Ingwaz, and Wunjo (joy rune) accentuate Yngvi as the bringer of joy to men. The same can be done with Fehu to focus on Yngvi as the bringer of prosperity.

Experiencing the runes

The Hero's Journey: Yngvi is as multifaceted as Odin. To the Heardingas, we are told he was seen as a hero. The lines between the Gods and heroes sometimes become blurred as the hero's deeds become more legendary as he starts to bleed into the archetype of the hero.

The Anthropologist Joseph Campbell proposed that all mythic and modern heroes follow a similar heroic journey. A pattern that starts with an unusual birth leads the hero into an otherworldly adventure from which he returns victorious but forever touched by the other world.

This cycle can be found in ancient myths and modern movies alike. To better understand the mythic cycle, take the schematic of the hero's journey and see if you can apply it to a favorite movie or book. I would also urge you to read *The hero with a thousand faces* by Joseph Campbell.

Meeting the horned God: The phallic God, with his horns, is a familiar figure throughout European myth. Freyr, wielding an antler during the events of Ragnarök, depicted with an enormous phallus, is the Scandinavian incarnation of this archetype. The horned God represents nature's virility and growth in all his manifestations. To feel this aspect of the Ingwaz rune, take a walk outside in spring or early summer. Try to feel the wild energy of a forest if you can. Feel how all plants and animals try to grow and reproduce, taking up as much room as possible. This is not a moment of balance but of expansion.

Planting your seeds: Just as a seed needs nurturing and fertile ground to grow, so do ideas. This exercise is twofold; first, take a project you have been running around within your head this can be a big project, and write it down, including a to-do list. Secondly, plant a couple of seeds of your choice in a flower pot marked with the Ingwaz and Fehu runes.

Place your to-do list next to the potted plant. Each time you water your plant, check your to-do list and see if things can be done now to get your project moving. Observe how both your project and your plant blossom.

ᛟ

3.7 Othala - Heritage

Germanic	Gothic	Old English	Old Norse	Sound
Othala	Othal	Éthel	Ódhal	O

Othala is the seventh rune of the third Ætt and the penultimate rune in our Journey. Othala is a rune of ancestral property and family. The word Othala splits up into 'ot' and 'halla.' Ot means old; the Dutch word 'oud,' pronounced oat, is etymologically connected. The word 'halla' comes from hall, similar to the suffix halla in Valhalla, where 'val' means slain, making Valhalla the hall of the slain and Othala the hall of the ancestors.

The rune poems

ᛖᚦᛖᛚ·ᛒᛇᚦ·ᛟᚠᛖᚱᛚᛖᛟᚠ·ᚫᛖᚷᚻᚹᛇᛚᚳᚢᛗ·ᛗᛖᚾ·ᚷᛁᚠ·ᚻᛖ·ᛗᛟᛏ·ᛞᚻᚫᛖᚱ·ᚱᛁᚻᛏᛖᛋ·ᚫ
ᚾᛞ·ᚷᛖᚱᛇᛋᛖᚾᚪ ᛟᚾ· ᛒᚱᚢᚳᚪᚾ·ᛟᚾ·ᛒᛟᛚᛞᛖ·ᛒᛚᛖᚪᛞᚢᛗ·ᛟᚠᛏᚪᛋᛏ·

Anglo-Saxon

Eþel byþ oferleof æghwylcum men, gif he mot ðær rihtes and gerysena on brucan on bolde bleadum oftast.

An estate is very dear to every man, if he can enjoy there in his house whatever is right and proper in constant prosperity.

Owning a piece of land with a house on it is a dream that many people share, and few things are nicer than having a part of the world that you can call home.

The Nordic relation to home was a complex one, as these passages from the *Hávamál* show:

Wits must he have / who wanders wide,
But all is easy at home;
At the witless man / the wise shall wink
When among such men he sits.
-Hávamál 5

Forth shall one go, / nor stay as a guest
In a single spot forever;
Love becomes loathing / if long one sits
By the hearth in another's home.
-Hávamál 35

Better a house, / though a hut it be,
A man is master at home;
A pair of goats / and a patched-up roof
Are better far than begging.
-Hávamál 36

Though glad at home, / and merry with guests,
A man shall be wary and wise;
The sage and shrewd, / wide wisdom seeking,
Must see that his speech be fair;
A fool is he named / who nought can say,
For such is the way of the witless.
-Hávamál 103

For the Nordic people, the house and the ancestral lands were an anchor, a place to return to and enjoy. However, staying home your entire life would leave you foolish in the ways of the world and weak in character. The house is a safe space and, in some ways, a sacred space but not the whole world.

Historic use in charms and amulets

No known amulets or runestones exist where Othala is used outside its phonetic use. However, the concept of ancestry is loaded with symbolism and ritual significance. Even though the idea of hearth and home is rarely mentioned, ancestor worship was prevalent in Nordic culture.

In *Gesta Hammaburgensis Ecclesiae Pontificum* (*Deeds of Bishops of the Hamburg Church*), Adam von Bremen writes that the Swedes make Gods out of men and worship them. Man becoming Gods is a theme repeated in Snorri's stories about Freyr as a mortal king. There is more evidence that the Swedes worshiped their deceased kings from the saga surrounding King Olaf Geirstaðaálfr.

In the saga, King Olaf Geirstaðaálfr has a vision of his impending death. After receiving this vision, he instructs his people on how to prepare for the proper burial. King Olaf warns his followers not to worship him, or he shall become a Troll. There is a bad harvest within a year after his burial, and the people, against Olaf's wishes, start bringing offerings to his burial mount. Because of this worship, Olaf became an Elf and earned the title to his name, Alfar.

The reason Olaf does not want people worshipping him is not that he does not believe in pagan superstitions but because he believes it will turn him into a supernatural entity. What we can tell for sure is that, even in the Christian age, ancestor worship was practiced and seen as effective.

Generally, all that is left to us are the stories of kings and heroes. Since the Norse people believed that kings shared a spiritual bond with the land, they ruled only kings could become spiritual protectors of the land after their death. It is not a massive leap that if a good king caused the land to be fertile in life, he could also do so in death.

However, it is not difficult to imagine that what happens to kings can also occur on a family level. The belief that the ancestors were still watching over the land that they owned, that they raised their children on, and that they worked their whole life on.

Cultural relevance

The ties between the ancestors and the living are not limited to their returning as guardian spirits. The beliefs about the afterlife were complex and even, at times, contradictory.

The most commonly known afterlife is Valhalla, the home of Odin and his bodyguards, the Einherjar[82]. Those who die in battle and are shown to possess exceptional bravery and skill are selected by the Valkyrie and taken to Valhalla, where they will practice their skill until the final days, and they join the final battle at the side of Odin.

The ninth is Folkvang, / where Freyja decrees
Who shall have seats in the hall;
The half of the dead / each day does she choose,
And half does Othin have.
- Grímnismál 14

In Grímnismál, Snorri writes that half of the warriors that die in battle go to the hall of Freya, but not all warriors go to Valhalla. Thus,

---

[82] Translates to "Those that were once Fighting"

contrary to popular belief, Odin's hall is not the only destination for warriors.

Because the stories of kings, heroes, and brave warriors are the most exciting, they are the ones that reach us from across the centuries. Although most Norse people were farmers, heroic combat was far from the number one cause of death. The glamour of heroes is an enduring one.

There are several options for different afterlifes within the body of Nordic mythology. The most well-known place for non-warriors is Hel. Hel should not be confused with the Christian concept of Hell, which borrowed its name from Norse mythology. The word Hel means hidden or covert place. It is difficult to understand what Hel meant for the Nordic people because all stories we have are filtered through a Christian lens. In Gylfaginning, king Gylfi of Sweden is unknowingly tricked into a riddle game with the Gods. He is asked what Odin's most extraordinary feat is:

"The greatest of all is this: that he made man, and gave him the spirit, which shall live and never perish, though the flesh-frame rot to mould, or burn to ashes; and all men shall live, such as are just in action, and be with himself in the place called Gimlé. But evil men go to Hel and thence down to the Niffelheiml; and that is down in the ninth world."

-Gylfaginning 3

Gimle is a golden-roofed building, likely another name for Valhalla. Snorri makes a point of saying that Gimle survives after Ragnarök, which is probably due to Christian influence. Hel is described here as the place where evil men go, so the classical heaven & hell dichotomy is at play here. Heaven is where the righteous and the brave go, and the wicked, in this case almost everybody, go to Hell.

However, the truth about Hel must have been much more complicated. From the Gylfaginning stanza 49, we learn that Baldr, one of the sons of Odin, went to Hel after his death. Baldr is far from an evil man, and in stanza 12 of the same text, he is described as:

"The second son of Odin is Baldr, and good things are to be said of him. He is best, and all praise him; he is so fair of feature, and so bright, that light shines from him. A certain herb is so white that it is likened to Baldr's brow; of all grasses it is whitest, and by it thou mayest judge his fairness, both in hair and in body. He is the wisest of the Æsir, and the fairest-spoken and most gracious; and that quality attends him, that none may gainsay his judgments.

He dwells in the place called Breidablik, which is in heaven; in that place may nothing unclean be, even as is said here:

Breidablik 't is called, / where Baldr has A hall made for himself: In that land / where I know lie Fewest baneful runes."

- Gylfaginning 12

There are many stories describing pleasant places within Hel. For the Nordic people, Hel was just a place you went to after death.

In Grímnismál, we read about the actual place where evil men go after they die:

I saw there wading / through rivers wild
Treacherous men / and murderers too,
And workers of ill / with the wives of men;
There *Níðhöggr sucked / the blood of the slain,*
And the wolf tore men; / would you know yet more?
- Grímnismál 39

Níðhöggr is a dragon that lives in Niffelheim, at the bottom of Yggdrasil. Niffelheim is a place of freezing rivers, ice, and cold death. In this frozen realm, the traitors, murderers, and oath breakers go to be tortured by the monstrous dragon, Níðhöggr.

Many ideas are put forth throughout the sagas about what happens after death. The warriors might join Odin or Freya as their bodyguards. Other people, depending on how they lived, go to Hel or Níðhöggr and at the same time, some people might become Alfar, Landvættir, or Draugr.

Conclusion

Othala is a rune of history. Each generation that has come before was necessary to get us to where we are today. In the Nordic culture, there is a real active connection to our ancestors and their influence on our lives. The living are, in turn, expected to pay our respects to those that came before.

In some ways, this rune is similar to Mannaz (humankind rune) as it is also a rune of community. Although in this instance, the community is defined by blood, not proximity. It is the rune of the gifts we receive from the past and those we will pass down to future generations.

In readings: Unsurprisingly, this rune represents family when drawn in a reading. Depending on the question, that might be your children, parents, extended relatives, or even someone becoming family.

If paired with Fehu (cattle rune), Othala refers to more material gifts passed down from our ancestors, be it land or other inheritances. Coupled with Ansuz (Odin's rune), Othala becomes a rune of ancestral wisdom.

Othala can also mean actual living family. For instance, when drawn with Berkana (birch rune), it points toward a female family member, either a mother or grandmother.

In advice and counseling: In today's world, when our food comes from the store and our pension comes from the state, we sometimes imagine ourselves as self-sufficient. However, our ancestors knew that no one is entirely self-sufficient. We rely on our parents from birth; as children, we are helpless. Afterward, we rely on the community when we can't care for ourselves.

In magic and ritual: In magic and ritual, this rune can be used to call upon the ancestors. Combining Othala with Algiz (elk rune) can be used as a charm to protect the family home. A charm containing both Ansuz (Odin's rune) and Othala can be used to call upon the ancestors' wisdom. Othala can also be used on altars to call upon the ancestors and bring offerings.

Experiencing the runes

Tracing your roots: Today, with the internet, it is easier to dig deeper into your family history. We often know little about our ancestors beyond our grandparents, and learning their stories can bring perspective. Try to figure out who your ancestors were and their strengths and flaws. You can get this information from your family or public records. These days there is also the option of DNA tests where you can see even further back in the past to get a general idea of your ancestors' travels.

Nature versus nurture: A long-standing debate is what defines us. Is it our social interactions after birth or the gifts passed down to us by our parents at birth? Whether by nature or nurture, our existence is due to our ancestors.

Make a list with your ten defining traits and try to figure out what is nature and nurture.

Family gathering: While studying this rune, it is also an excellent time to spend some extra time with family. Not all study is academic, and nothing exemplifies the spirit of this rune more than spending time, laughing, working, and learning with family.

ᛞ

3.8 Dagaz – Day

Germanic	Gothic	Old English	Old Norse	Sound
Dagaz	Dags	**Dæg**	Dagr	D

Dagaz is final rune of the Elder Futhark. Dagaz is a rune of new beginnings and the positive side of life. Dagaz has similarities with Yera (year rune) in many ways but bears a stronger sense of duality. It is a fitting final rune, representing transcending from old to new.

The rune poems

Anglo-Saxon

ᛞᚨᛖᚷ·ᛒᛇᚦ·ᛞᚱᛁᚻᛏᚾᛖᛋ·ᛋᛟᚾᛞ·ᛞᛖᛟᚱᛖ·ᛗᚨᚾᚾᚢᛗ·ᛗᚨᛖᚱᛖ·ᛗᛖᛏᛟᛞᛖᛋ·ᛚᛖᛟᚻᛏ·
ᛗᛇᚱᚷ ᚦ ᚨᚾᛞ·ᛏᛟᚻᛁᚻᛏ·ᛖᚨᛞᚷᚢᛗ·ᚨᚾᛞ·ᛖᚨᚱᛗᚢᛗ·ᛖᚨᛚᛚᚢᛗ·ᛒᚱᛁᚳᛖ·

Dæg byþ drihtnes sond, deore mannum, mære metodes leoht, myrgþ and tohiht eadgum and earmum, eallum brice.

Day, the glorious light of the Creator, is sent by the Lord;
it is beloved of men, a source of hope and happiness to rich and poor,
and of service to all.

The Anglo-Saxon rune poem has strong Christianised tones as the Nordic creation myth does not have a creator in the same way the monotheistic religions do. Initially, the rune poem probably spoke about the God of day named Dagr. Dagr translates to day. Dagr is of the Aesir, but his Mother, who is the night, is a Jötun.

"Nörfi or Narfi is the name of a giant that dwelt in Jötunheim: he had a daughter called Night; she was swarthy and dark, as befitted her race. She was given to the man named Naglfari; their son was Audr. Afterward she was wedded to him that was called Annarr; Jörd was their daughter. Last of all Dayspring had her, and he was of the race of the Æsir; their son was Day: he was radiant and fair after his father. Then Allfather took Night, and Day her son, and gave to them two horses and two chariots, and sent them up into the heavens, to ride round about the earth every two half-days. Night rides before with the horse named Frosty-Mane, and on each morning he bedews the earth with the foam from his bit. The horse that Day has is called Sheen-Mane, and he illumines all the air and the earth from his mane."

- **Gylfaginning 10**

This excerpt shows two critical elements about the Nordic people's view of day and night. The night is the mother of the day; for the Nordic cultures, the next day starts at nightfall.

Another important takeaway is that the night is a Jötun, a force of chaos and hunger, while the day is an Aesir, a force of order and creation. This makes sense as the night is cold, dark, and hard to navigate, and the nights can run long in the north. On the other hand, the sun brings light, safety, and warmth that can be enjoyed regardless of social status.

Historic use in charms and amulets

As a single rune, Dagaz is used as part of a runic inscription on a rock face near Inglestad, Sweden. All other runes are younger futhark runes except de Dagaz rune, signifying its importance in this charm.

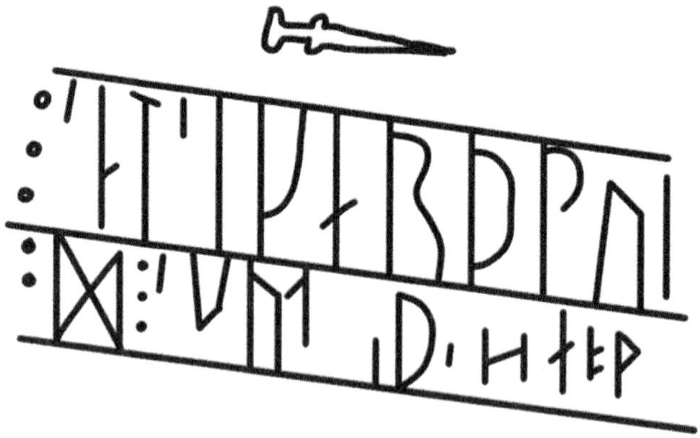

Figure 62: The Ingelstad runestone

Sôlsi gerði sól. D(agr) skút aí þ(ett)a hjó

Sôlsi made the sun. Dagr cut this on the cliff-face (Samnordic Rune Text database, 1993).

Beneath this inscription is a carving of a sun, and above it is a sword presumably revering to the words "sun" and "cut." Because Dagaz is the only rune from the Elder Futhark in the inscription, it is seen as the focus of the charm. It can be interpreted as a call for a new day with a bright sun or, more concisely, a good fresh start.

In the opening stanzas of the Sigrdrifumal, the Valkyrie Brunhilda wakes up and offers a prayer to the day and the Gods. These stanzas are remarkable as they are the only surviving direct prayer to Norse Gods:

Hail, day!
Hail, sons of day!
And night and her
daughter now!
Look on us here
with loving eyes,
That waiting we victory win
Hail to the gods!
Ye goddesses, hail,
And all the generous earth!
Give to us wisdom
and goodly speech,
And healing hands, life-long.

- **Sigrdrifumal 2-3**

The importance of the day as a powerful entity and influence in life can be seen in this prayer. Even before the Gods are honored, the day and night are honored. The Gods in the Poem are asked for wisdom, eloquence, and health, but the day and the night are asked for victory in life. This prayer shows the strong positive association of Dagaz, the new day or dawn.

Cultural relevance

The day and night are easy to differentiate. The time of day is much harder to define, especially in the north, where the length of a day and night varies dramatically.

To be able to tell the time, the Nordic people used a system of Daymarks. If you live close to the equator, the sun will be at the same location in the sky regardless of the time of year. If you live high up north, the sun will be much higher in the sky in summer and lower in winter.

Regardless of the sun's path, if you are standing at a specific spot, the sun will always be over the same point on the horizon at the same time of day. For example, standing in front of your house, you would always see the sun above a mountain top at midday. Sometimes the sun would be higher and other times lower but consistently above the same mountain top.

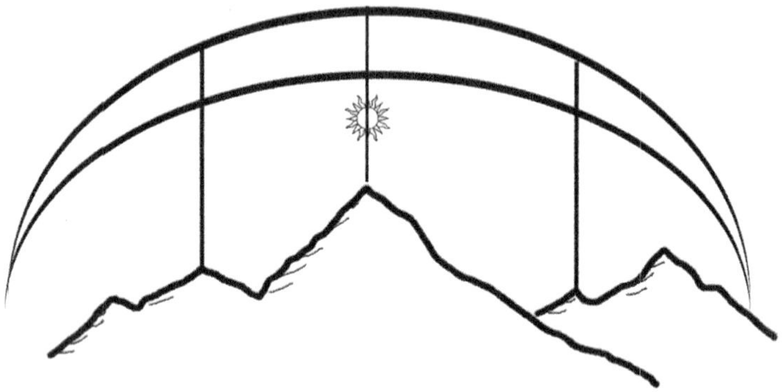

Figure 63: Diagram of landmarks

This leads to several mountains in Scandinavia, including the word middag (midday) in their name, like the Middagstind and Middagskollane in Norway. Not only mountains but any landmark at the horizon could be used for this. Of course, each landmark is only usable from the point of view of a single town.

The day would be split up into eight parts, called an Ætt or *eight,* just like the rune rows. The evening marks, especially the midnight mark, would only be used high north where the sun does not set in the summer months. Using this system, the day cycle could easily be tracked with reasonable accuracy.

Conclusion

Dagaz is a rune of new beginnings. The light of order and growth following the dark chaos of the night. This is true for the spring coming after a long winter and the break of the day after a long night.

According to Nordic mythology, the Ragnarök starts with the Fimbulvetr, the long winter, and the long winter begins with a day without dawn. Dagaz, the new dawn is life, rebirth, and new beginnings. Helheim, the land of the dead, is located in Niffelheim, a land of eternal ice where the sun does not shine and hope is lost.

Dagaz is similar to Sowilo (sun rune); they are runes of light and warmth in a world where dark and cold are the greatest enemy. But where Sowilo is a guiding star and a decisive victory, Dagaz is inevitable, it is the dawn that breaks every night, it is the promise that after the darkness comes a new beginning.

In readings: Dagaz is a generally positive rune in any reading. It shows us a new start is coming or that what you have been waiting for is about to begin. This can represent a new opportunity, a new job offer, or an end to a negative period in your life.

Combined with runes of ice like Hagalaz (hail rune) or Isa (ice rune), it means that what has been holding you back is finally melting. Combined with Yera (year rune), it can indicate that the work you have been putting in will pay off.

In advice and counseling: A new day is arriving. The night represents chaos and the day represents order. Dagaz does not mean that all your problems are automatically solved but that you can find a moment of stability, a ledge to catch your breath.

In magic and ritual: Dagaz is the rune of a new day, the rune of a new day, and can be used in charms to help new beginnings. Combined with Algiz (elk rune), it can focus on protection against darkness in your life.

Experiencing the runes

Daybreak: Dagaz is the rune of daybreak and victory of light over darkness. It is a powerful experience. Depending on where you live, and the time of year, it is always possible to find a moment to watch the sunrise. Pick a time that works in your schedule and wake up well before dawn. The best location to watch a sunrise is from an elevated position or on a large expanse, so it pays to plan.

Safe harbor: Dagaz ends the night with all its dangers and guides you home to the safety of the day. With this rune, you can reflect on where you feel safe.

Set up a room or space to be entirely your personal space. This does not have to be a big space or even in your home. Decorate the space to your taste, hang pictures, put down plants, place statues or add books that represent you. Make the area feel like yours.

Completion: With Dagaz, you have completed the Elder Futhark, and this is fitting as Dagaz is a rune of completion and new beginnings, the closing of the cycle and the opening of the new one.

It is good to mark the occasions when you finish a project. This does not have to be a significant thing, but it is good for motivation to reward yourself. Have a nice meal or treat or give yourself a small gift next time you feel you have completed a project.

Magic

Introduction to Magic

The old Norse for magic is Galdr and translates to chanting or singing. The most notable user of Galdr in Norse mythology is Odin, who in *Baldurs Draumar 3* is called Galdrafǫðr: "the father of Galdr."

In the *Hávamál,* Odin speaks of eighteen songs he knows and describes their magical effects.

The songs I know / that king's wives know not,
Nor men that are sons of men;
The first is called help, / and help it can bring thee
In sorrow and pain and sickness.
-Hávamál 147

Even though they are called songs, it becomes clear from the text that this type of magic goes beyond the spoken word. For example, in the twelfth song, Odin talks about writing and coloring runes to speak to a dead man.

A twelfth, I know, / if high on a tree
I see a hanged man swing;
So do I write / and color the runes
That forth he fares,
And to me talks.
-Hávamál 158

The writing of runes played an important role within Galdr, and because written magic endures in a way that spoken magic does not, this is also the type of magic we have the most sources for.

In the sagas, other Gods and heroes use runes in their magic. Skirnir inscribes Thurisaz runes into a tree to curse the Giantess Gerd, and Brunhilde teaches Sigurd runes to use in healing.

Besides the magic called Galdr, there was also the magic called Seiðr. This practice mostly disappeared after the Christianisation of Scandinavia and was mainly referred to as black magic or witchcraft in later works.

In the Ynglinga saga, it is said that Freya taught the Aesir about Seiðr and that the magic originates with the Vanir. Seiðr appears to have been a Shamanistic practice focused on divination, fate, life, and death. Like the Norns, a practitioner of Seiðr called a Völva could see the future and weave new futures. The völva was also important in the rituals surrounding birth and funerals.

Seiðr magic was considered "ergi" or unmanly and was predominantly a woman's domain. However, there are several examples of men practicing Seiðr, the most notable being Odin, who learned the magic from Freya.

In Lokasenna, Loki bursts into a party of the Gods and insults all the Gods in order, using Flyting verse. He accuses Odin of ergi because he practiced Seiðr and took the shape of a seeress. Odin does not refute this; he replies that Loki is also guilty of shapeshifting into a woman. Because Odin reacts with indifference, we can see the pursuit of magical knowledge is more important to him than traditional gender roles.

These chapters will focus on Galdr in historical artifacts, how these artifacts here used and how these artifacts were constructed.

Writing with the runes

First and foremost, the runes are a system for writing; this is the purpose that they were used for most of their history. Many charms are simply statements of intent, written down in runes using symbols or formulaic language to give the charm strength. The Norseman enjoyed solving codes and riddles as entertainment; some have made it into magical amulets.

Runic Grammar

The runes were used in several forms across the centuries, throughout a vast area of the world, and without uniform consensus of their grammar. When referring to the runic script, we refer to the most common patterns, but for each rule, there are exceptions. Keep this in mind when making your designs, and if you feel it is better to ignore one or more of the rules written down here, there was probably a Viking who felt the same way.

A common question is: "Do I have to write in Icelandic / Norse if I want to write in the runes?." It is perfectly acceptable to use the runes in your native language. The Germanic, Russian, Icelandic, Scandinavian, Saxon, and Frisian people used their language to write in the runes, and we can do the same.

Four important things to remember are:

I. Phonetics

The runes are used phonetically, meaning that you write what you hear when writing with the runes. Book, for example, would become buk (ᛒᚢᚲ), not book (ᛒᛟᛟᚲ) because BUK sounds more like book than BOOK does.

II.Spacing

Words are separated by an · or : or x or, in rare cases, another symbol instead of a space.

ᛞᚨᛗᚷ·ᛒᛇᚦ·ᛞᚱᛁᚾᛏᚾᛗᛊ

III. Irregular shapes

A rune is sometimes mirrored over the vertical axis to emphasize a text segment. For example, in the Fløksand meat cleaver, we can see that some runes are reversed.

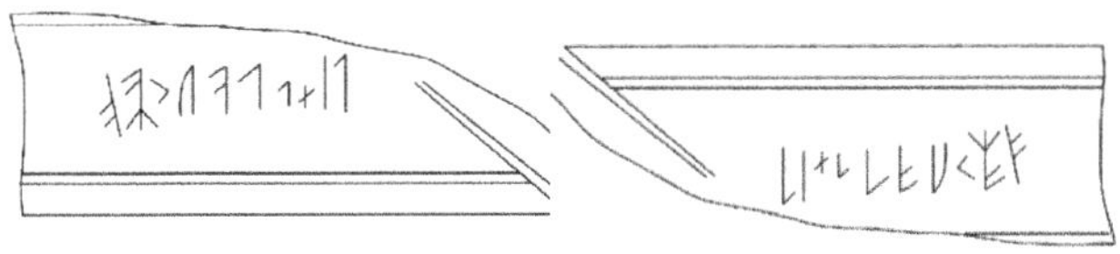

IV. Bind Runes

Another way of creating emphasis or, in some cases saving space was the bind rune (*bandrún)*. A bind rune is formed by connecting two or more runes with shared lines. Historically, bind runes were most often used phonetically, and combinations of more than two runes were exceptionally rare.

For instance, Luck written in runes would become:

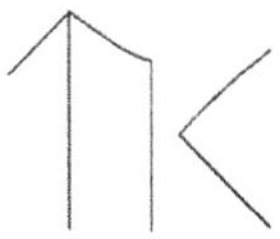

First, Luck is brought back to the phonetic LUK. Using a bind rune, the first two letters can be joined together as LU emphasizing the word and possibly saving space. The most famous non-magical bind rune is the Bluetooth logo. Bluetooth is named after a Danish king called Harald Blatand or Harald Bluetooth. Harald earned his name from the vast amounts of blueberries he liked to eat. The Bluetooth logo is a bind rune of the Danish Younger futhark letters H and B.

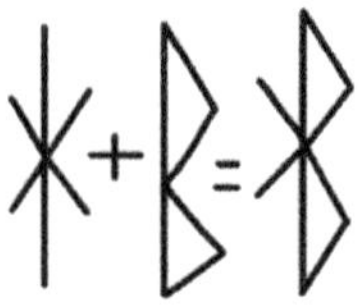

In Modern heathenism, bind runes are often used to combine the esoteric meaning of two runes. Bind runes made of more than two runes are no exception, and the results are often stunningly intricate and artistic symbols.

The bind rune below is created to help win a court case where justice is on your side. It combines Tiwaz (justice rune), Eihwaz (protection rune), and Ansuz (both for Odin and for eloquence)

In a bind rune, several runes can overlap across several lines. For example, for a successful family outing, the bind rune could look as follows:

Wunjo (joy) Othala (family) Gebo (Gift) Algiz (protection)

Alternatively, all runes can be linked in order, each rune sharing one line with the previous rune. Below is an example where Fehu is spelled out using runes sharing their lines. Note how the first rune was flipped to create room.

You can combine all three above techniques to create your bind runes. Feel free to make them as artistic or elaborate as you want.

Lonnruner

Besides a phonetic sound or an esoteric meaning, each rune also has a numeric value. This value is based on the runes Ætt and location in the Ætt.

For example, Yera is 2.4 because it is the fourth rune in the second Ætt. These numeric values were used to create codes called "Lønnruner" or secret runes. These codes are not complicated to decipher if you know where they are, but they can be hidden in plain sight. Lønnruner were primarily used for regular communication, but examples of amulets with Lønnruner have been found. There are two general types of Lønnruner. The first encodes each rune into a single symbol.

The most simple example of these Lønnruner are the tree or branch runes:

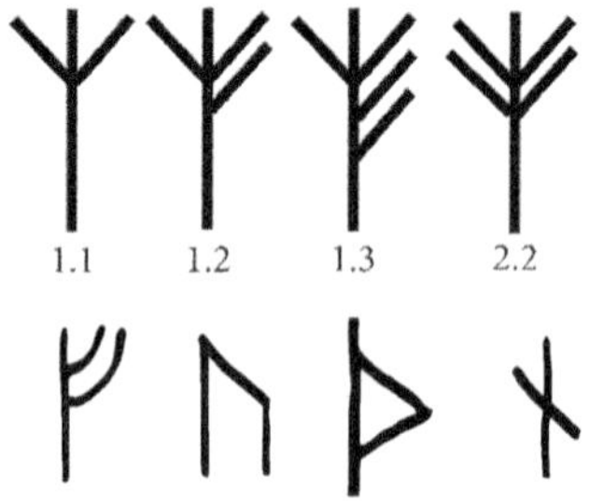

The number of branches on the left represents the Ætt, and the number on the right represents the location in the Ætt, for example. Yera would be two lines on the left-hand side and four on the right-hand side. There are endless variations for encoding runes this way.

For example, the stone of Rök uses a similar method but based on the Eihwaz rune instead of the Algiz rune and pairs them up.

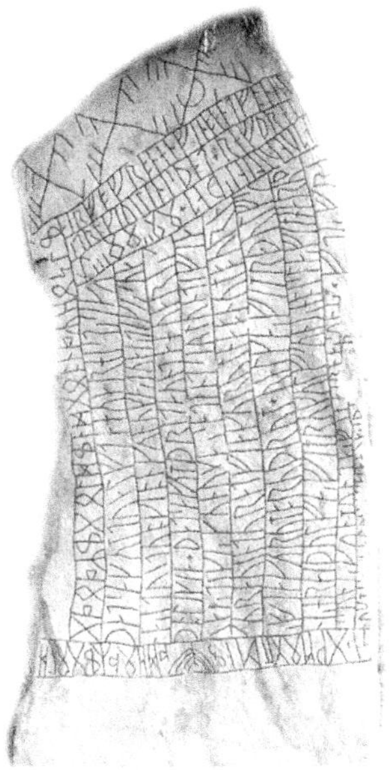

Figure 64: Stone of Rök (ög 136)

Here the top number of lines represents the Ætt, and the bottom number of lines represents the location in the Ætt. So the cross in the example below represents Hagalaz (2.1), the first rune in the second Ætt, and isa (2.3), the third rune in the second Ætt.

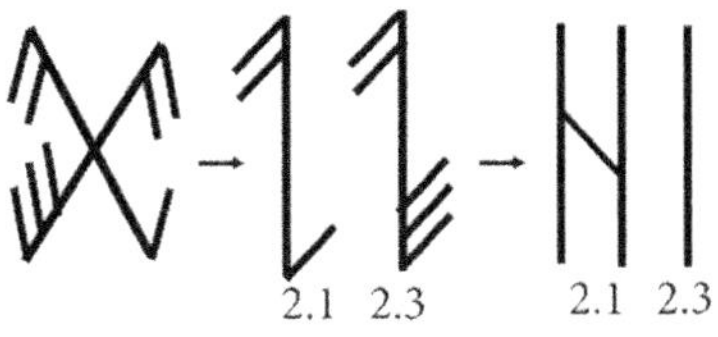

One of the most creative uses of this method of Lønnruner are the beard runes found in Berger, Norway

Figure 65: drawing of the Bergen beard runes

The beard hairs left of the nose represent the Ætt, and the beard hairs on the right represent the rune in that Ætt.

The second method of "Lønnruner" uses repetitions to encode the runes. The simplest examples of this are known as ice runes:

The number of long lines in a group represents the Ætt; the number of short lines in a group represents the rune's location. The above example starts with one long line followed by one short line; this gives us the first rune, 1.1 Fehu. Following the same structure, we get 3.3 Ehwaz, 2.1 Hagalaz, and 1.2 Uruz. As a whole, the lines read FEHU

The rök stone shown earlier contains both types of "Lønnruner." As it used Eiwaz for single symbol encoding, it also uses Eiwaz for multiple symbol encoding. Eihwaz is being flipped with the mirrored Eihwaz groups representing the Ætt and the regular Eihwaz groups representing the location in the Ætt.

Writing Fehu would look like the rune line above. One mirrored rune followed by one regular rune 1.1 is F. Three mirrored runes followed by three regular runes is 3.3 E. Following the whole line, in the same way we did with the ice runes, we get FEHU.

Cipher

Besides using "Lønnruner," the ancient nordic people are known for their love of ciphers and riddles. Runic texts have been discovered written in what is commonly known now as the Caesar Cipher. The Caesar Cipher is a method of encoding information where each letter is replaced with the letter that sits on an agreed number of places further down the alphabet or, in this case, the Futhark.

F	U	Th	A	R	K	G	W	H	N	I	J	Y	P	Z	S	T	B	E	M	L	ng	D	o
D	O	F	U	Th	A	R	K	G	W	H	N	I	J	Y	P	Z	S	T	B	E	M	L	Ng

Using the Ceasar Cipher with a shift of two, FEHU would become DTGO. This Cipher can be made more complicated by shifting within each Ætt or even shifting a different amount for each Ætt.

Many more ciphers were used, but one more is important to mention. A message in runes that had appeared to be gibberish at first until it was later discovered that each rune was used to represent the third letter in the full name of the rune. For example, Fehu would describe the H sound, Uruz would stay a U sound, Thurisaz would become an R sounds, and so forth.

Magic formulas

When talking about rune magic, the greatest amount of sources come with written magic. The written word has a permanence that the spoken word does not have. Written magic covers all the rune stones, amulets, enchanted items, and books. It also covers power symbols, charms, words, bind runes, sigils, and written invocations, as any piece of written magic contains at least one and often multiple of these forms of magic.

While there is no definitive formal guide on how runic magic was practiced, there are several elements that repeat:

1. Charm words & power symbols: these symbols on their own have no known meaning but are added to magic items, presumably to enhance their power or to activate them
2. A statement of intent: this can be a written sentence, a word, or a combination of runes. This shows the purpose of the charm.
3. The name of the person who cut the runes: It is uncertain if this was done to link the rune caster to the item so that the rune caster's will could work through it or if it was more a form of advertisement for future clients.
4. The object that the charm is written on: perhaps to connect the magic to the object.

Not each object has all four elements, but most will have at least two.

Charm words & symbols

Charm words and power symbols are words and symbols that appear on a wide selection of religious and magical artifacts but don't seem to have any connection to the artifact's purpose. A good example of a charm word is Leek. As described in the chapter on Laguz the word Leek is inscribed on several charms not explicitly dealing with this particularly long member of the onion family. Leek, instead, is used to give power to the magic of the charm.

Charm words:

Lauk: meaning leek is a widespread charm word that is sometimes abbreviated with just the L rune.

Alu: There is no definitive translation for *Alu* as it is only used in charms and never in a sentence. It is sometimes translated as Blessing, magic, or dedication, but there might not be a direct translation; it may have been only a charm word.

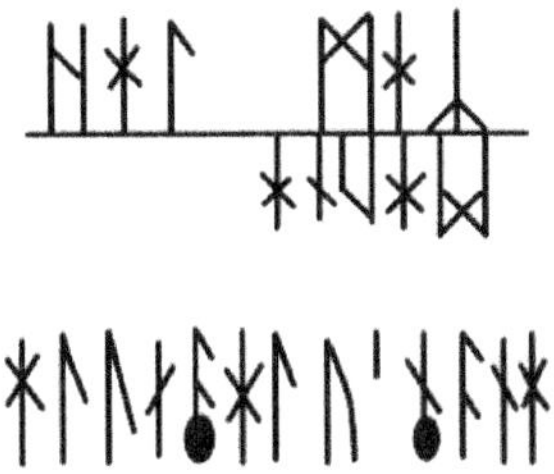

DKJ 40

Figure 66: The Setre Comb runes

Hail mar mauna Alu Nanna Alu Nanna

Hail maid of maids. Alu nanna alu nanna (Macleod & Bernard, 2006)

Nanna is the wife of Baldur in the sagas; After Baldur dies, she throws herself on his funeral pier to join him in Hel. The comb calls upon her and asks for her blessing using *Alu.* The devotion shown by Nanna to her husband Balder makes it likely that this was a love charm.

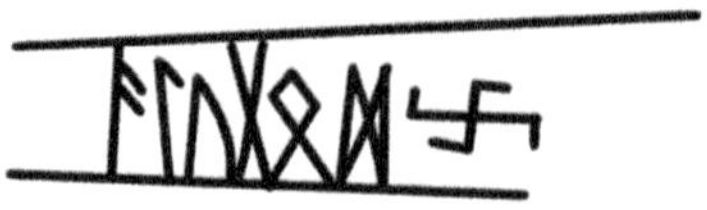

DR EM85;123

Figure 67: runes on the Værløse Fibula

ᚨᛚᚢᚷᛟᛞ 卐

Alu God 卐

The second example contains only *Alu,* followed by God and a swastika. Swastikas are one of the oldest symbols used by humanity, dating back at least 5000 years, and can be found all over Asia, Europa, Africa, and the Americas. The Swastika was used in all different cultures to symbolize good fortune or divinity. On runic artifacts, the Swastika was used as a power symbol to increase the charm's potency, similar to the power word *Alu.* Because of its terrible use in Nazi Germany and its connection to the Third Reich, it's better to use other power symbols on your charms.

The purpose of this charm is not completely clear because it only contains *Alu,* the word God and a Swastika. It is most probably a devotional or luck charm.

Futhark: The runes are seen as gifts of Odin and possessing a certain magic. It is no surprise then that just writing down the futhark is seen as magical. This charm word comes in 4 variations.

- Just the word Futhark
- Just the first Ætt
- The entire Futhark, including all three Ætts
- Just the first three letters, Futh. A side note here is that Futh is the old Scandinavian word for vagina

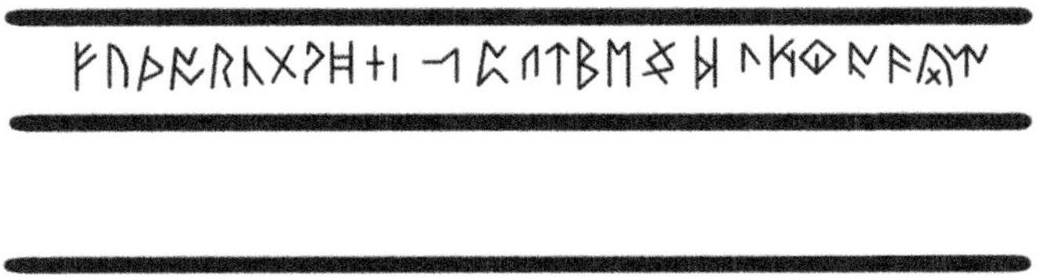

Figure 68: The Seax of Beagnoth

ᚠᚢᚦᚩᚱᚳᚷᚹᚻᚾᛁᛄᛇᛈᛉᛋᛏᛒᛖᛝᛞᛚᛗᛟᚪᚫᚣᛠ ᛒᛠᚷᚾᚩᚦ

fuþorcgwhnijïpxstbeŋdlmœaæyea Beagnoþ

Several runic alphabets are changing around the order and shape of the runes and, in some cases adding extra runes. The oldest runic alphabet, the Elder Futhark, is used in this book, but the Seax of Beagnoth uses the Anglo-Saxon Futhorc. The Name Futhorc, just like the name Futhark, is derived from the first letters of the alphabet.

The Charm on the sword contains two parts, the runic alphabet, and the name Beagnoth. The name on the blade might be the name of the person who made the charm or the owner of the charm. Putting the owner's name on the sword connects the power of the charm to the owner. If the name is the creator, it connects the charm with their power.

Alliteration: In fairy tales and movies, spells and enchantments are often set in rhyme. This structure lends a certain formality to the spell; it helps to give the feeling that something extraordinary is happening. While the Norse branch of magic does employ rhyme, they more often use alliteration. As a charm word or symbol, non-sense alliteration is used on this rune stick found in Narsaq, Greenland.

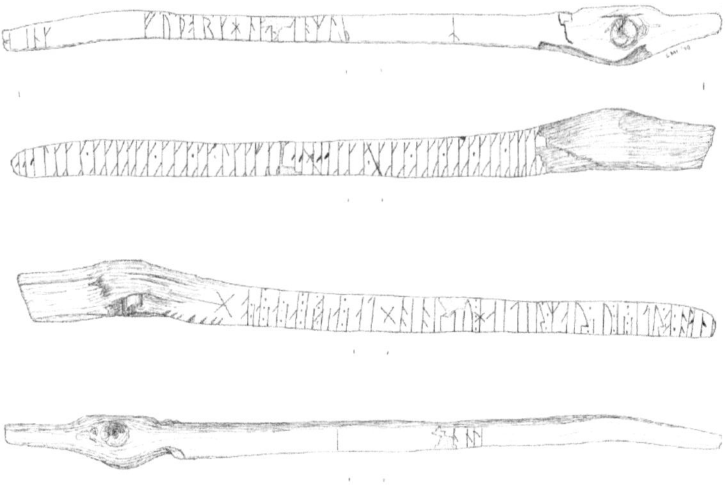

Figure 69: the four sides of the Narsaq stick

Hvat sá sá, er í sá sá? Sik sá sá, er í sá sá.

What did he see who looked into the tub? He saw himself, he who looked into the tub (Knirk, 1994).

Ansuz & Naudiz chain:

On the Sigtuna copper disk [U AST1;166], it is written: “I speak three Thurs and nine needs Ansuz, Lord of the sanctuary I call on you.” This combination of Naudiz and Ansuz combined with a third rune is a typical formula on runic artifacts.

The Ansuz rune represents Odin, and the Naudiz rune represents fate. Combining these two seems to ask Odin to bind your desired effect into destiny. In the example of the Sigtuna Copperdisk, the third rune was

Thurisaz representing trolls. The Sigtuna Copperdisk was then probably a curse.

Below is the Lindholm Amulet, another example of the same structure. Here the Ansuz and naudiz rune row includes Algiz runes making this a protection charm.

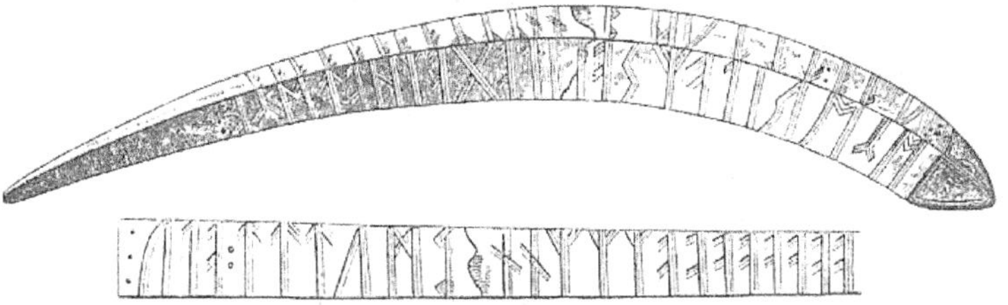

Figure 70: The Lindholm amulet,

ᛖᚲ·ᛖᚱᛁᛚᚨᛉ·ᛊᚨᚹᛁᛚᚨᚷᚨᛉ·ᚺᚨᛏᛖᚲᚨ·
ᚨᚨᚨᚨᚨᚨᚨᚨᛉᛉᛉᚾᚾᚾ·ᛒᛗᚢᛏᛏᛏ·ᚨᛚᚢ

Ek Erilaz Sawilagaz hateka aaaaaaaazzznnn bmuttt alu

Symbols:

Symbols are even more elusive than charm words. We can still imagine a meaning or grammar for the charm words, but not for symbols. These markings are used on magical objects in line with the text in the same way charm words are used and in the style of decorations.

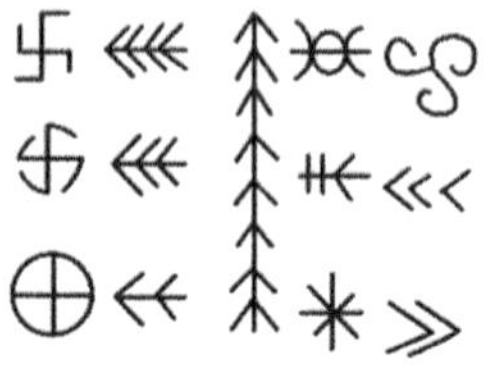

Besides these common symbols, many Nordic grimoires feature unique runic symbols used for specific spells. Unfortunately, there is no information on how these symbols were initially designed.[83] These often came with specific rituals to empower them.

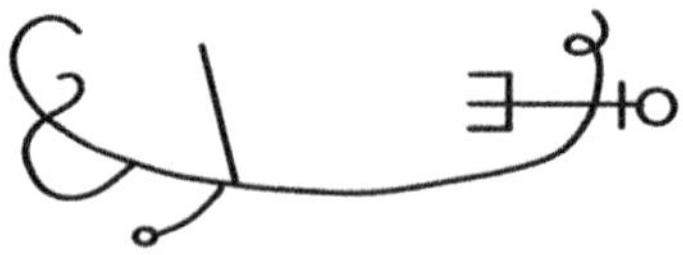

To make enemies afraid

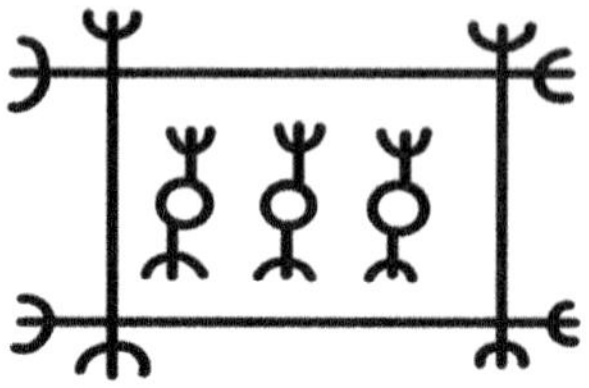

To break any lock

[83] Stephan Flowers Galdrbok has a very extensive collection of these magical symbols

Statement of intent

If the charm words and symbols are designed to give life and power to an enchantment, then the statement of intent is there to provide it with purpose and direction. All the rules concerning writing in runes still apply. Both Lønnruner and bind runes can be used in concert with regular runes. However, Creating a charm has some specific formulaic quirks of its own.

There is no single authority on runic magic; all these formulaic approaches have been used to create charms, and some have combined multiple formulas.

Runic meaning:

The simplest form of a statement of intent is based on the runic meaning, as with the earlier example of the Fløksand meat-cleaver

II KJ137 II

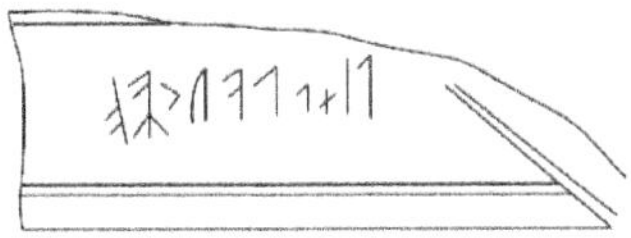

ᛚᛁᚾᚨ·ᛚᚨᚢᚲᚨᛉ·ᚠ
Lïna, Laukaz, F(ehu)
Linnen, Leek, Cattle / wealth
(Antonson, 1975)

On this Cleaver, Linen and Leek charm words are used to empower the rune Fehu. The goal of this charm is then to bring wealth to the household. Using a rune in this way can be written as a single rune, or the rune name can be written entirely as with the Pendant from Ølst Denmark or rendered in Lønnruner.

IK 13

Figure 71: The Ølst bracteate

ᚺᚨᚷ·ᚨᛚᚢ

Hag(ala), alu

Hail dedication (Macleod & Bernard, 2006)

Multiple runes might also be used for their esoteric meaning in one amulet, or those runes may be combined into a single bind rune

Rune staves:

Rune staves are similar to bind runes but more complex. In rune staves, the runemaster has greater freedom to create the amulet. Rune staves, in a way, can be seen as runic calligraphy where readability comes second to beauty. Because rune staves also include encoding, it becomes almost impossible to translate back from historical sources. Instead, this book will give an example of how one is created from the bottom up, returning to Fehu.

The rune stave at its core will be made up of the runes spelling out FEHU [ᚠᛖᚺᚢ].

The runes are placed vertically across a line that will become the backbone of the stave

The runes are then embellished for a more aesthetic result

The result would be this finished FEHU rune stave

This process allows for a lot of creativity. The above example uses all the runes in their original orientation and perfectly in line.
Here is an example of how the rune stave would look if we play with the position of the runes in relation to the central stave:

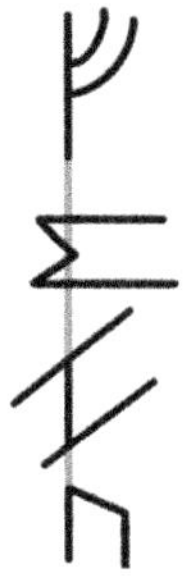

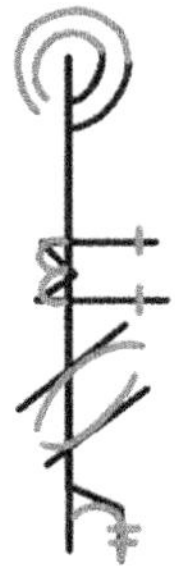

There is a lot to experiment with. In both examples, a straight line was used to create the core of the stave, but there is no reason not to use a curved line, a square, or a spiral; feel free to experiment

Sympathetic inscriptions:

Sympathetic magic is perhaps the most common type of magic used worldwide. It is throwing a coin into a well to get greater riches, a small act that symbolically relates to a more significant result. In modern western magic systems, this is sometimes called the microcosmic and macrocosmic, leading to the famous phrase "as above, so below."

The runes are good examples of sympathetic magic, as each rune is a small representation calling upon mythic archetypes.

DR 261

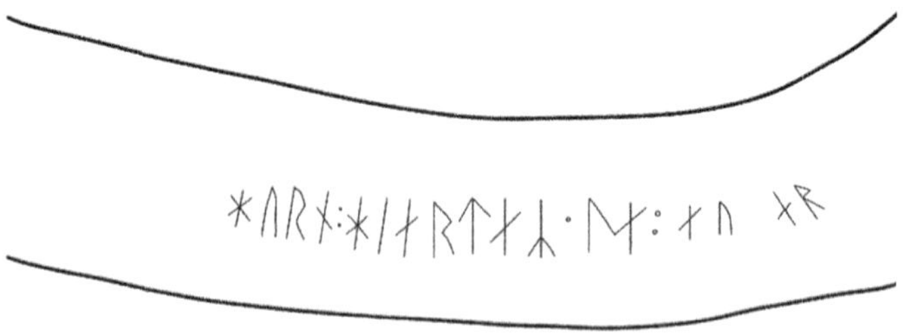

Figure 72: The Hart Horn Charm

ᚺᚢᚱᚾ·ᚺᛁᚨᚱᛏᚨᚱ·ᛚᚨ·ᚨᚢᛊᛊᚨᚱ·

Hurn hiartar, lá Aussar

Hart horn, Protection, Ausar (Macleod & Bernard, 2006)

The charm mentioned earlier in the chapter on Algiz was found in Dublin and has a non-runic form of sympathetic magic.
Harts Horn calls upon the protection by writing down the word

protection after it. Sympathetic magic can be used in many ways. A small piece of gold or a small precious gem might be used in a charm to call upon greater wealth, or a tiny bit of water might be poured out over crops at the end of a ritual intended to bring rain.

Narrative inscription:

A narrative charm is a form of sympathetic magic based on a myth. Where a typical example of sympathetic magic is a drop of water, a golden coin, or a rune to link the desired effect, a narrative inscription uses a fragment of myth.

Figure 73: Thor fighting Jörmungandr

A story about Thor beating a foe or Odin outwitting an opponent might empower you to do the same. For example, a small copper plate was found in South Kvinneby on the Swedish island of Öland Öl inscribed With the following message:

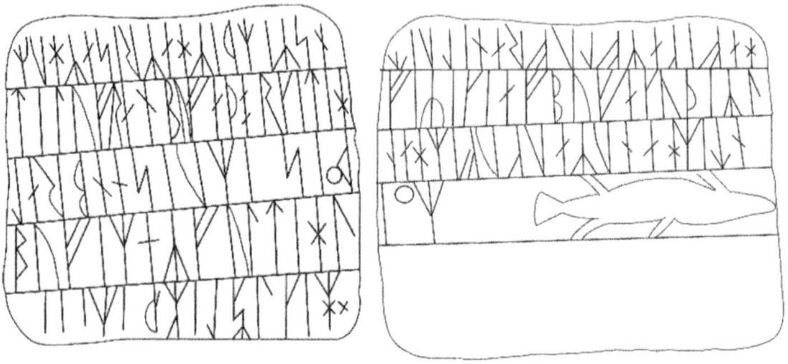

Figure 74: The Kvinneby pendant front and back

H(æ̃)ʀ'k ī kūri (ī)ms undiʀ guþi,(æ)ʀ ber'k Būfi mǣʀ fūlt ī hūþ
es þǣʀ vīs in brā alt illu frān Būfa! Þōrr gǣti hans mēʀ þæm hamri
(e)s Ām hyʀ! Haf ekka, Ām! Flȳ frān, illvētt! Fæʀ ækki af Būfa;
guþ eʀu undiʀ hānum auk yfiʀ hānum.

I cower herein, under the god of soot; I, Būfi, carry a festering sore in my skin you know where the glistening one is keep evil from Būfi! May Thor guard him with the hammer with which he strikes Āmr. May you have the affliction, Āmr! Be gone, evil being! The affliction leaves Būfi, there are gods below him and above him. (Louis-Jensen, Södra Kvinneby, 2005)

In this case, the story tells about Thor's fishing trip, where he almost caught the Midgard Serpent. While Thor was fishing with the giant Hymir, Thor managed to hook the Midgard Serpent. The Giant Hymir was terrified and cut the line before Thor could engage with his ancient foe. As the serpent sank back to the bottom of the ocean, Thor threw his hammer after the serpent, but he could not hit it. Part of the magic of

Thor's hammer is returning to his hand after he has thrown it. After Thor missed the serpent, it returned to his hand from the sea.

In this example, Bofi calls upon Thor's protection, not only by directly asking for it but by describing another instance where Thor fought great evil.

Another example is a silver belt buckle found near Pforzen in the Alps:

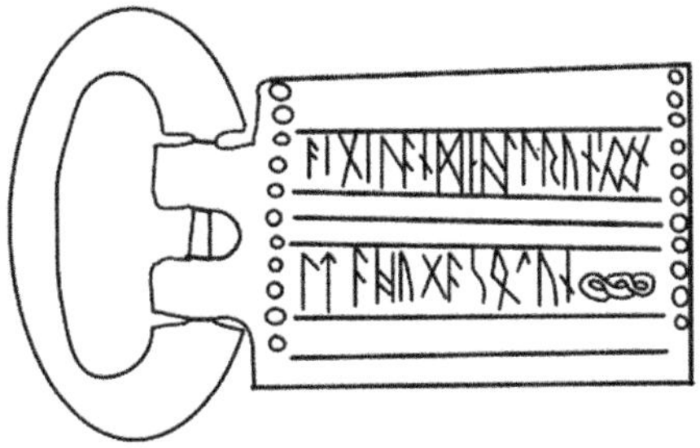

KJ 165

Figure 75: The Pforzen belt buckle

Aigil andi Ailrun elahhun gassokkun

Agil and Ailrun search for an elk (Macleod & Bernard, 2006)

A lot of things are going on in these two lines.

Ai|gil **An**|di **Ail**|r*ün*
El|ah|hu Ga|sök|*kun*

The first sentence uses alliteration, both sentences use six syllables, and both end on the same two runes, *Un.* These are poetic techniques, but poetry and magic are closely intertwined in Nordic mythology

The sentence itself is from a now-forgotten saga or poem, and the intention of the charm seems to have been to increase the wearer's prowess in the hunt without knowing the whole story; however, it cannot be said with certainty.

Leading inscription:

A leading inscription is a sentence stating the reality the rune caster wishes to bring forth. The example below is a love charm that was found in Swiss near Bülach; it uses a combination of charm words (the L for laukaz) and a leading inscription:

KJ 165

Figure 76: The Bülach Fibula

ᚠᚱᛁᚠᚱᛁᛞᛁᛚ·ᛚᛁᛞ·ᛞᚢ·ᚠᚢᛞ·ᚠ·ᛏ·ᛗᛁᚲ·ᛚ·ᛚ

Frifridil lid du fud f t mik L L

[your] Frifridil [who] has the member - You [who] [has] the vulva, receive me into you! (Klingenberg, 1976)

The charm states what the creator desires. Note that these leading charms are not statements of intent but describe an event as a fact.

Galdralag and Ljóðaháttr:

Galdralag and Ljóðaháttr are ancient Nordic verse forms, and Snorri describes both. While not very practical to use in amulets because of the length, this chapter would be incomplete without them. As with many subjects surrounding ancient Nordic culture, there are disagreements about what exactly constitutes Galdralag and Ljóðaháttr, here is the most popular option.

Ljóðaháttr, or chanting verse, is used when talking about the Gods or for things of religious importance, like Odin's advice for mortals in the *Hávamál.* Ljóðaháttr verse form consists of three lines; the first two lines are bound by alliteration the third line has its own alliteration. One stanza is made up of two of these verses. For example, in *Hávamál* stanza 11, it reads:

Byrði betri	A better burden
berrat *maðr* ***brautu*** *at*	may no man bear
en sé ***mannvit mikit;***	For wanderings wide than wisdom;
vegnest verra	Worse food for the journey
vegra *hann* ***velli*** *at*	he brings not afield
en sé ***ofdrykkja ols.***	Than an over-drinking of ale.

In this stanza, lines one and two are linked by alliteration just as lines four and five, lines three and six both have their own alliteration, making one stanza build from two Ljóðaháttr. The sagas are an oral tradition, stories to be told, not read. Therefore, alliteration is linked to a word's sound (phonetics), not the actual spelling. Galdralag translates to spell verse or spell meter and is used in sagas to indicate something magical or supernatural was happening. Galdralag is a subcategory of Ljóðaháttr, adding a fourth line that echoes the third line.

The following Galdralag verse comes from a standing stone in Sogn, Norway:

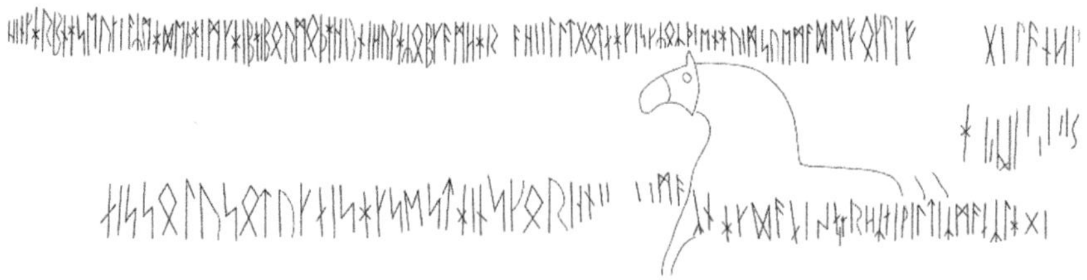

Figure 77: The Eggja grave stone

1	Hverr of kom Heráss á	As who came War-god Hither
2	Hí á land gotna	To the land of man
3	Fiskr ór Fjanda vim Svimandi	A fish from the torrents of enemies swimming
4	Fogl á Fjanda lið galandi	A bird against troops of enemies screaming. (Foote & Wilson, 1983)

The first two lines are alliterated on the H sound, with the G in Gotna's pronunciation close to the H sound. The third line has its alliteration on the F sound. The fourth line shares this alliteration but also closely echoes the structure and meaning of the third line, as seen in the translation.

Names and objects in runic amulets

Putting your name on an amulet or standing stone was a common practice to link the spell to a person. There are two possible reasons to do this, either so that the power of the caster could flow into the object or the reverse so that the power of the object could flow to the user. In a similar manner naming the object, you were applying the charm to would help bind the magic into the physical realm. Below is a two-dimensional rendering of one of the Golden Horns of Gallehus as a set of two golden Horns found in Denmark. Both horns were eventually stolen and melted down, so the originals are lost to us. However, several replicas still exist. The Shortest of the two horns bears a runic inscription on the rim.

DR 12 U

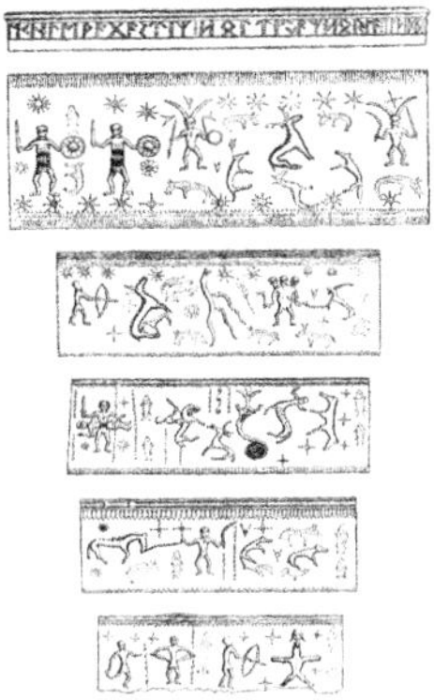

ᛖᚲᚺᛚᛖᚹᚨᚷᚨᛊᛏᛁᛉ·ᚺᛟᛚᛏᛁᛃᚨᛉ·ᚺᛟᚱᚾᚨ·ᛏᚨᚹᛁᛞᛟ·

ekhlewagastiz:holtijaz:horna:tawido:

I Hlewagastiz Holtijaz made the horn (Samnordic Rune Text database, 1993).

Figure 78: Golden Horn of Gallehus

Many theories exist that the symbols on the rest of the horn may contain Lønnruner. While several archeologists have offered wildly differing interpretations, no consensus has been reached on whether or not the horn contains Lønnruner or even what those Lønnruner would say. The horn carries with it both the name of the creator and the name of the object being consecrated.

Creating your own charm

In combination with the chapter on the runes, you should now be able to create your charms. Below you can find three examples of charms designed to have people enjoy learning the runes and illustrate how to create a charm yourself. The charms range from simple, using only a single technique, to complex, combining several different techniques.

Simple charms:

For the simple charm, I will create a bind rune.

First, pick the runes that you want to use in your charm. For example, if your goal is to have people enjoy learning about the runes, you would choose:

(ᚨ)Ansuz (Odin's rune) As Odin is the father of the runes, Ansuz is also a rune of knowledge and language (the way you are learning right now).
(ᚹ)Wunjo (The joy rune), the rune of joy, would be an essential rune in any charm meant to produce joy. Now both Wunjo and Ansuz are runes of ecstatic revelation, not necessarily book learning, and that is why I will add a third rune
(ᚱ)Raidho (the wagon rune) Raidho is a rune of structure, of following a path. A bind rune of only Ansuz and Wunjo would also have been an excellent bind rune, but Raidho helps ground the other two runes.

Second Shift the runes around until you find an aesthetically pleasing configuration; for me, the end result worked out as below. There is no one correct way to create a bind rune, as it is only used for your own ends.

Moderate Charms:

The runes used in the first charm are still the bases for this charm but with some extra things to reinforce the same theme.

First, I will add a narrative inscription. *Hávamál* stanza 142 reads:

Then began I to thrive, | and wisdom to get,
I grew, and well, I was;
Each word led me on | to another word,
Each deed to another deed

Odin gained the runes after nine nights of hanging from the world tree, fasting, and being pierced by his spear, as described in stanza 140 of the *Hávamál.* While this stanza would also synergize well with gaining the runes, the traumatic nature and how Odin gained the runes do not. Stanza 142 describes a moment after Odin is nursed back to health, and the wisdom of the runes starts growing in his mind sweeping him along to ever greater understanding. I transcribed the stanza to runes from English phonetically:

ᛏᚺᛖᚾ·ᛒᛖᚷᚨᚾ·ᛁ·ᛏᛟ·ᚦᚱᛁᚠᛖ·ᚨᚾᛞ·ᚹᛁᛊᛞᛟᛗ·ᛏᛟ·ᚷᛖᛏ·
ᛁ·ᚷᚱᛖᚹ·ᚨᚾᛞ·ᚹᛖᛚᛚ·ᛁ·ᚹᚨᛊ·
ᛖᚨᚲᚺ·ᚹᛟᚱᛞ·ᛚᛖᛞ ᛗᛖ·ᛟᚾ·ᛏᛟ·ᚨᚾᛟᚦᛖᚱ·ᚹᛟᚱᛞ·
ᛖᚨᚲᚺ·ᛞᛖᛖᛞ·ᛏᛟ·ᚨᚾᛟᛏᚺᛖᚱ·ᛞᛖᛞ·

Second, I will add two power symbols to the charm as an extra layer. Combining all of these would create the following charm.

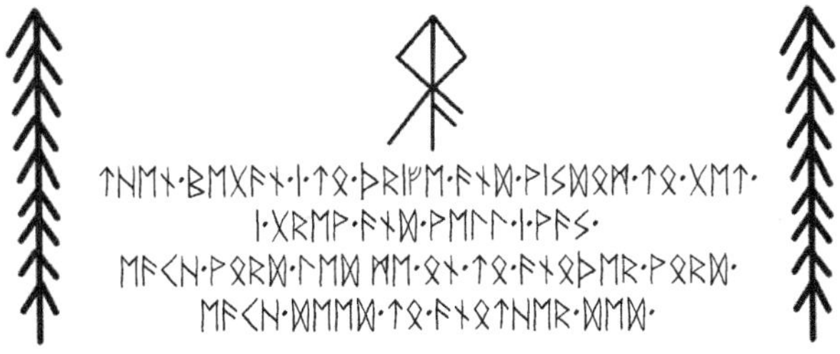

Complex charms:

First, I'm going to add a Galdralag that will also include my name and the name of the object that the charm is inscribed on, in this case, the book.

1. About **R**unes will the holder **R**ead
2. **R**eveling in the **R**esearch that you do
3. **M**cGrory says this **M**agic the holder will enjoy
4. **W**alter says this **w**ork the holder will enjoy

As can be seen, the first two lines share an alliteration on the letter R. the third line alliterates on the letter M and the final line alliterates on the letter W.
The third and the fourth line echo each other; both start with my name, thereby binding my name to the charm, and state the holder (of this book) will enjoy something. The third line names the magic, the subject of the object on which the charm is printed as something to be enjoyed. The last and fourth line gives the work (of learning the runes) as something that is enjoyed.

If we take the verse form Galdralag as a type of power symbol, this short verse alone contains all four characteristics of a charm. (1)The power symbol, (2)the statement of intent, (3)the name of the caster, and (4) a reference to the object

Transcribed in runes, this looks as follows

1· ᚨᛒᛟᚢᛏ·**ᚱ**ᚢᚾᛖᛊ·ᚹᛁᛚᛚ·ᛏᚺᛖ·ᚺᛟᛚᛞᛖᚱ·**ᚱ**ᛖᚨᛞ·
2· **ᚱ**ᛖᚡᛖᛚᛁᚾᚷ·ᛁᚾ·ᛏᚺᛖ·**ᚱ**ᛖᛊᛖᚨᚱᚲᚺ·ᛏᚺᚨᛏ·ᛇᛟᚢ·ᛞᛟ·
3· **ᛗ**ᚲᚷᚱᛟᚱᛇ·ᛊᚨᛇᛊ·ᛏᚺᛁᛊ·**ᛗ**ᚨᚷᛁᚲ·ᛏᚺᛖ·ᚺᛟᛚᛞᛖᚱ·ᚹᛁᛚᛚ·ᛖᚾᛃᛟᛇ·
4· **ᚹ**ᚨᛚᛏᛖᚱ·ᛊᚨᛇᛊ·ᛏᚺᛁᛊ·**ᚹ**ᛟᚱᚲ·ᛏᚺᛖ·ᚺᛟᛚᛞᛖᚱ·ᚹᛁᛚᛚ·ᛖᚾᛃᛟᛇ·

Second: Because the charm is already somewhat rune heavy, I want to hide this Galdralag away in Lønnruner, circling the charm using the earlier described ice rune method. So Berkana, the second rune in the second Ætt, would become 

For the full Galdralag, that would look like this.

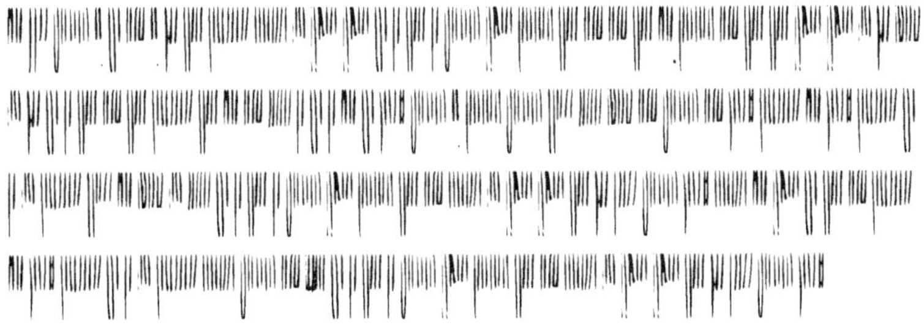

Third: I'm going to use a rune stave instead of a bind rune to create a nicer aesthetic. I again take the Wunjo (ᚹ), Ansuz(ᚨ), and Raidho (ᚱ) runes and rearrange them.

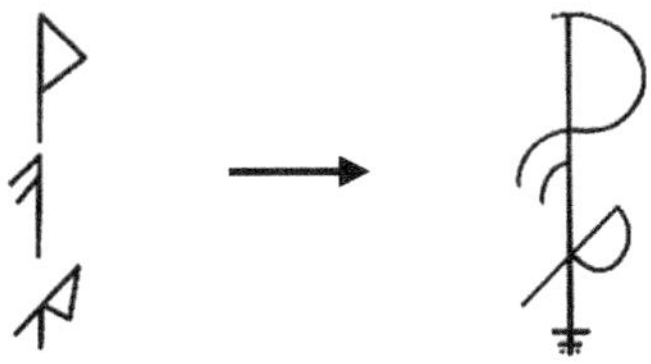

The final rune charm combining all elements would then look like this

Divination

Introduction to divination

There is a rich well of literature concerning runic divination. One would assume from the myriad of books written about runic divination that divination is the primary purpose of the runes. However, historically very little is known about whether or not runes were used in divination. The most convincing evidence for runic divination comes from Tacitus's Germania:

Augury and divination by lot no people practise more diligently. The use of the lots is simple. A little bough is lopped off a fruit-bearing tree, and cut into small pieces; these are distinguished by certain marks, and thrown carelessly and at random over a white garment. In public questions the priest of the particular state, in private the father of the family, invokes the gods, and, with his eyes towards heaven, takes up each piece three times, and finds in them a meaning according to the mark previously impressed on them. If they prove unfavourable, there is no further consultation that day about the matter; if they sanction it, the confirmation of augury is still required.

-Tacitus Germania 10

According to Tacitus, divination was an exceptionally popular activity for the Germanic tribes. That divination was done using wooden lots made from fruit-bearing trees, and the lots were inscribed with symbols. Whether or not those symbols were runes is unsure, and no surviving divination sets have been found. Given the spiritual and magical significance of the runes, it is very likely that these were used for divinatory purposes.

The method of divination is just as elusive because Tacitus is the only source we have. It seems that the gods were invoked, and the symbols were selected randomly after being thrown onto a white cloth; how the symbols were interpreted is lost to us.

In modern times rune sets can be bought, made from a wide variety of materials, including semiprecious stones, wood, and plastic. The stones are often pulled from a bag rather than cast on a white cloth, and several other methods have been devised over the years. Although it might seem more authentic to have runes made from the wood of a fruit tree cast on a white cloth while invoking Odin, we do not have enough data to determine what is historically accurate.

For instance, there is no way of knowing if stone, other types of wood, or other materials were used for divination in areas that Tacitus did not visit. The ritual for divination might also vary significantly from region to region or tribe to tribe. Because we know the meaning of each rune and their strong tie magic, I think that using runes as a divinatory tool is appropriate. This chapter will cover runic divination, how I use it today, and what works well based on my experience.

When discussing **drawing a rune,** this can be read as either drawing a rune blind from a bag or randomly selecting one from a cloth that all runes have been cast on.

In all readings, I use a system of **clarifying runes,** meaning I will draw two extra runes to add context to a rune in a difficult reading. The original rune is still leading, but the two second runes can help clarify the reading.

One rune reading

The most basic reading is the one-rune reading. This is the most straightforward reading to shed light on a question quickly. The name is slightly deceptive, as described earlier, I use a system of clarifying runes, and for the single rune reading, I almost always find myself drawing two more runes for context.

To perform this reading, ask an open-ended question and draw a single rune. This rune represents the answer to the question. If the meaning of the rune gives a clear answer to the question, then no further action is required.

If you would like to give more context to your answer, you can draw up to two more runes.

Example:

"I would like to know the dynamics of my relationship between myself and the man in my life for the rest of this year."

The rune drawn was Uruz, the ox rune:

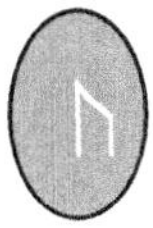

The word Uruz is a compound word meaning the primal ox. The Icelandic rune poem links Uruz to the smelting of iron and the waste products of the smelting process. Ur here has a double meaning, primal and ore, in several Germanic languages. However, the Anglo-Saxon rune poem describes the auroch a 3000lb giant bovine. Julius Caesar wrote that catching an auroch was a test of manhood for the Nordic people. Therefore Uruz is a rune of untamed potential and a tremendous primal force.

Uruz indicates a strong, almost primordial potential, but at the moment, it is undirected, just as iron ore before it is smelted and forged. This could also indicate that the couple might not yet know what they want to create out of this potential.

I will draw a second rune to see if I can get more insight into what type of potential there is. This rune will be used to clarify the meaning of the first rune. The first rune stays the heart of the answer in a one-rune reading. The second rune I drew was Gebo, the gift rune:

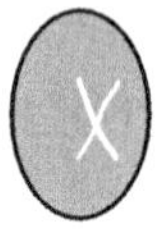

There is only one rune poem connected to Gebo, which talks unsurprisingly about the importance of giving a gift. While there are no other rune poems, exchanging gifts for the Nordic people is paramount.

The potential in this relationship is one for great balance. Both have gifts to give that the other might lack. A very favorable second rune in combination with Uruz. Imagine the same reading but with Thurisaz the troll rune as the second rune, and there would be potential for great suffering.

In conclusion, these two runes point to great potential as a couple, and they can both enrich each other's lives with their gifts. However, this potential is not yet realized, either because both are still unsure or because the exchange of gifts is one-sided. As the *Hávamál* says, "a gift for gift. "

Three rune reading

The three runes in this reading represent the three Norns: "*Urðr, Verðandi, Skuld*" or the past, the present, and the future. After the question is asked, draw three runes, the first representing the past, the second the present, and the third represents the future.

As discussed in the chapter on Naudiz, the present is formed from the choices in the past, and the future is then again formed from your choices in the present by the forces of Wyrd.

This reading is used to look at the root of the question in the past, how that past is affecting the present, and what future awaits you if you stay on this course.

Example:

"*How will my working situation evolve?*"

The three runes that were drawn were:

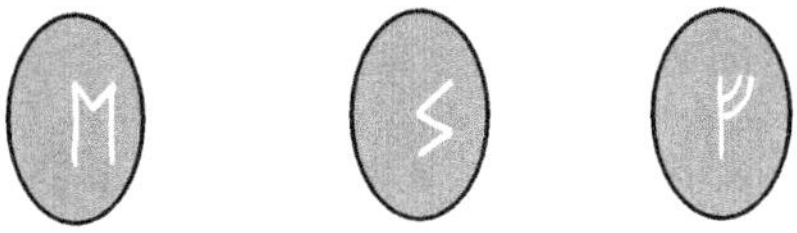

Past: Eihwaz, the horse rune - There is only the Anglo-Saxon rune poem concerning the horse rune, and it describes how great it is to have a horse. The *Hávamál* confirms this by saying "Let none be ashamed | of his shoes and hose, Less still of the steed he rides. So a steed is always desirable."

But the horse in Nordic mythology also represents the Fylgja or guardian spirit. Several amulets contain the Eihwaz symbol or the word Eihwaz to help connect the wearer with his guardian spirit.

In the case of the job, that can mean two things: the job is mostly a means, even a poor horse is better than no horse, or the job was taken for more important growth reasons. To clarify, the next rune drawn was Naudiz, the fate rune.

Naudiz is a rune of the Norns and destiny. It is used in historical magic charms to fix the desired effect of a charm into fate. The rune poems make this clear as well. The Norwegian rune poem, for example, reads: Constraint gives scant choice; a naked man is chilled by the frost.

Combined with Naudiz, I would interpret this as primarily a job taken from necessity.

Present: Sowilo, the sun rune - Sowilo is a very positive rune. The sun was a powerful symbol for the Nordic people, as the harsh winter made its power all the more critical. The Icelandic rune poem says

Shield of the clouds
and shining ray
and destroyer of ice.

Ice was destroyed by the power of the sun, and the evil trolls were also turned to stone by its power. The other rune poems describe the sun similarly as life-giving and guiding.

The interaction with the two runes representing the past is interesting here. Naudiz is a rune that freezes you into place. And the last two runes seemed to indicate that the querent was where they needed to be. Sowilo, on the other hand, is the destroyer of ice and the guiding star.

To clarify what Sowilo was referring to, an extra rune was drawn, Isa, the ice rune

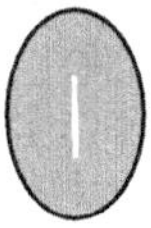

Isa means ice. The rune poems speak mostly about its danger but also about its beauty. Ice in Nordic mythology is a short suspension of the natural world; everything freezes into place and stops moving.

This seems like a strong indication that the job, at least in its current form, was a constraint, something that had to be done because there was no other way to go in the frozen path. Now the ice is melting, and Sowilo is a guiding star to new destinations. This can be either better prospects within the company or somewhere else.

Future: Fehu (cattle rune) is a rune of wealth, and the Anglo-Saxon rune poem says it best :

Wealth is a comfort to all men;
yet must every man bestow it freely,
if he wish to gain honour in the sight of the Lord.

Wealth is not without its dangers, and the other rune poems warn against hoarding wealth, a theme also prevalent in the sagas. Still, many amulets have been found with Fehu inscribed on them, meant to attract wealth.

Wealth in Viking times would be measured in cattle for most people explaining why the cattle rune is the rune for wealth.

Fehu or F is the first letter in the name of the gods Freyr and Freya, the twin gods associated with agriculture/horned beasts and gold, respectively.

Fehu, as a rune of wealth, is a good outcome for any question concerning work and seems pretty straightforward. If the past is taking a job because it was the only choice or slowly getting frozen into place at that job. Then Sowilo is burning the restraints away.

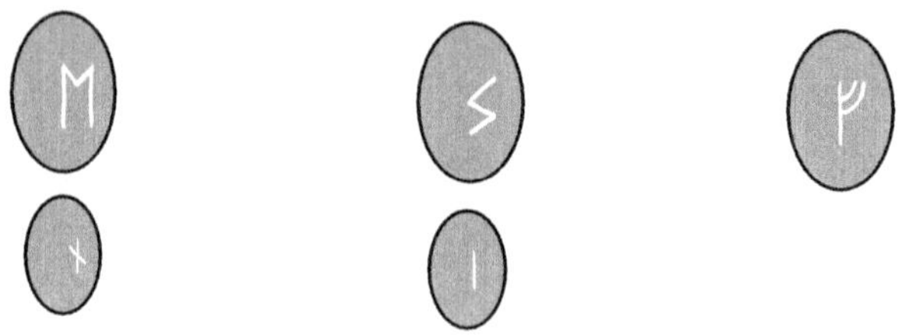

Sword reading

For the sword reading, the runes being drawn after the question is asked are laid out in a pattern resembling a sword.

1. The now / the self
2. The obstacles you face
3. The past / the cause
4. what do you need to move forward
5. the likely outcome

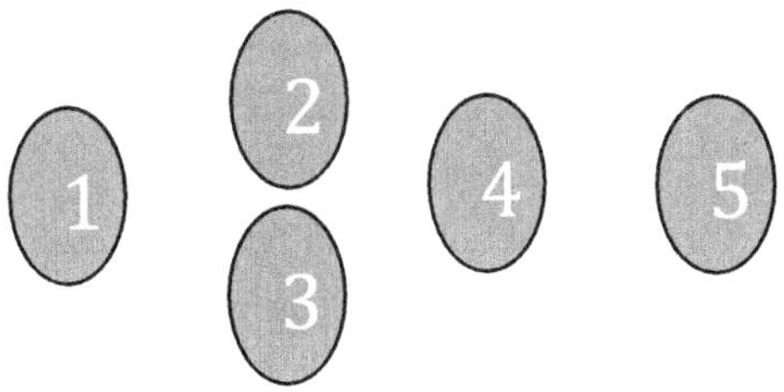

This reading can give a lot of information because it takes into account all the context of the person for whom the reading is done.

The reading starts with the role the person asking the question plays in the situation (1). It then shows what factors play a part in resolving this question, both external obstacles (2) and your past actions (3). Finally, the reading gives some guidance on how to move forward (4) and the likely outcome if you follow the advice (5) .

Example:

For this reading, I was asked to give a general reading about where life was headed.

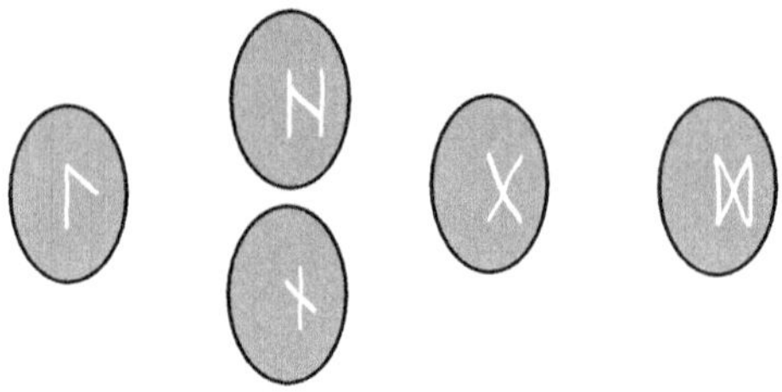

For the first rune, representing the now or self, I drew Laguz (lake rune), Laguz is a complicated rune. In the rune poems, it is described as moving waterfalls, rivers, and geysers. Powerful moving bodies of water. In historical charms and amulets, it is mainly used to represent the leek. The leek was a powerful symbol for the Vikings, meaning that many charms had the word leek or the laguz rune inscribed to increase their potency. I concluded that Laguz is a rune representing a link to another world. Just like in Celtic mythology, the fairy realm and king Arthur's sword are hidden under the waves and can only exist in our world for a limited time, so this rune represents that gate to other worlds.

Laguz, on its own, could represent a well of creativity in the context of writing a book, but as this is the core of the reading, I drew a second rune to get a clearer image. The second rune I drew was Raidho, the wagon rune.

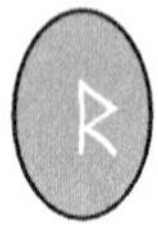

This is an interesting second rune as Laguz is also connected to Nerthus, the Goddess of lakes, and Tacitus, the roman historian, describes a statue of Nerthus that stands hidden away on an island in a lake. Once a year, the statue is covered by cloth and put on a wagon, to be driven around during the spring celebration, where the statue is all fighting prohibited. Then, in the end, the statue is returned, and the priests and priestess that accompanied it on its trip drown themselves to be with the Goddess forever.

Drawing Raidho and Laguz together resonates strongly with the yearly wagon ritual surrounding Nerthus. This might indicate a spiritual journey of some sort. I decided to draw one final rune; in this case, it was very conclusively Eihwaz, the horse rune.

Eihwaz, the rune connected to the Fylgja and the two earlier runes, speaks very strongly about an otherworldly spiritual journey.

Unless I'm not reading this enough, both Raidho and Ehwaz are runes of travel. Laguz is a rune of water, so traveling by boat could also be an interpretation, although one less connected to your question.

The second rune, the obstacle you face, is Hagalaz, the hail rune.

Hagalaz is a very destructive rune, the rune poems speak of it destroying crops, and it was used both in curses and on the tips of weapons to empower them magically

As a rune of destruction, this would indicate that before the book succeeds, some devastating life changes will happen.

The third rune, the past/the cause, is Naudiz, the constrained rune.

Naudiz is a rune of the Norns and destiny. It is used in historical magic charms to fix the desired effect of a charm into fate. The rune poems make this clear as well.

If the cause of the obstacle is Naudiz, that would indicate that the hand of fate is blocking the querent's way forward with the book project. This also resonates with the spiritual wagon journey of Nerthus; like the priests, they will have to sacrifice a lot to reach their goal and receive gifts from the other-world.

The fourth rune, What is needed to move forward, is Gebo the gift rune.

There is only one rune poem connected to Gebo, which talks unsurprisingly about the importance of giving a gift.

Exchanging gifts is, by definition, not a solitary activity, and the sagas and myths show that the Nordic people knew that no man is an island. The way past the obstacle is by accepting the help of others. This is not the same as asking for charity, you have your gifts, and others have theirs. But to weather the storm that is Hagalaz, an exchange of skills is needed.

The final and fifth rune, representing the outcome, is Dagaz, the daybreak rune.

Dagaz represents new starts, capping this journey with a positive new beginning. After the storm has ended, the sun will rise and melt the hail and ice, a favorable outcome for new ventures.

In conclusion, this is a significant journey that is spiritually fulfilling, but in making this journey, you have to break out of your comfort zone. Leaving comfort behind will lead to hard times where you will have to be able to rely on others to do what you cannot, just as they can depend on you. Behind that whole mess lies a new beginning, and if the journey is any indication, a pretty spectacular one.

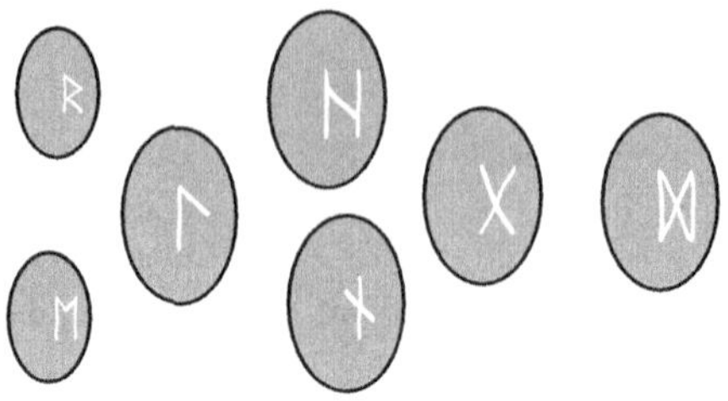

Casting the Runes

The final reading requires white cloth to cast the runes on. The cloth is divided into nine segments representing the nine realms. This reading is used for more general readings to get insight into the life of the querent

The rune caster casts the runes on the cloth; only the runes where the symbol can be seen are included in the reading, and the rest is removed from the cloth. The runes are then read based on their location on the cloth and their relation to each other.

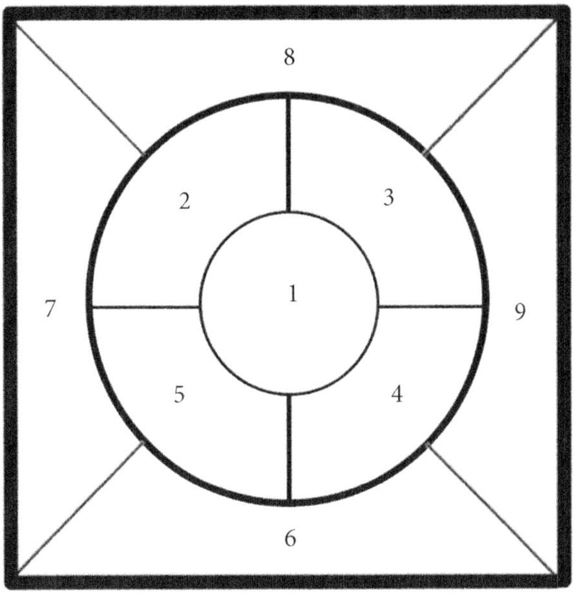

1. Midgard: This is the realm of humanity. The runes that land here represent the person asking the question as they are now.
2. Alfheim: This is the realm of the Alfar. The runes that land here represent the hopes and positive emotions of the person asking the question.

3. Vanaheim: This is the realm of the Vanir. The runes that land here represent outside influences that will have a positive or helpful effect.
4. Svartalfheim: This is the realm of the Svartalfar or dwarfs: The runes that land here represent the fears and shadow self, those feelings the person asking the question find hard to admit about them self.
5. Jötunheim: This is the realm of the Jötun. The runes that land here represent outside influences that will have a negative or hindering effect.
6. Helheim: Helheim is the realm of the dead. The runes here represent what has come before, the past.
7. Muspleheim: This is the realm of fire; it represents what you are actively working on. Things your energy is working.
8. Asgard: This is the realm of the Gods. The runes here represent your spiritual side and your connections to the supernatural.
9. Niflheim: This is the realm of ice. It represents those things in your life that are standing still but exist in potential.

Example

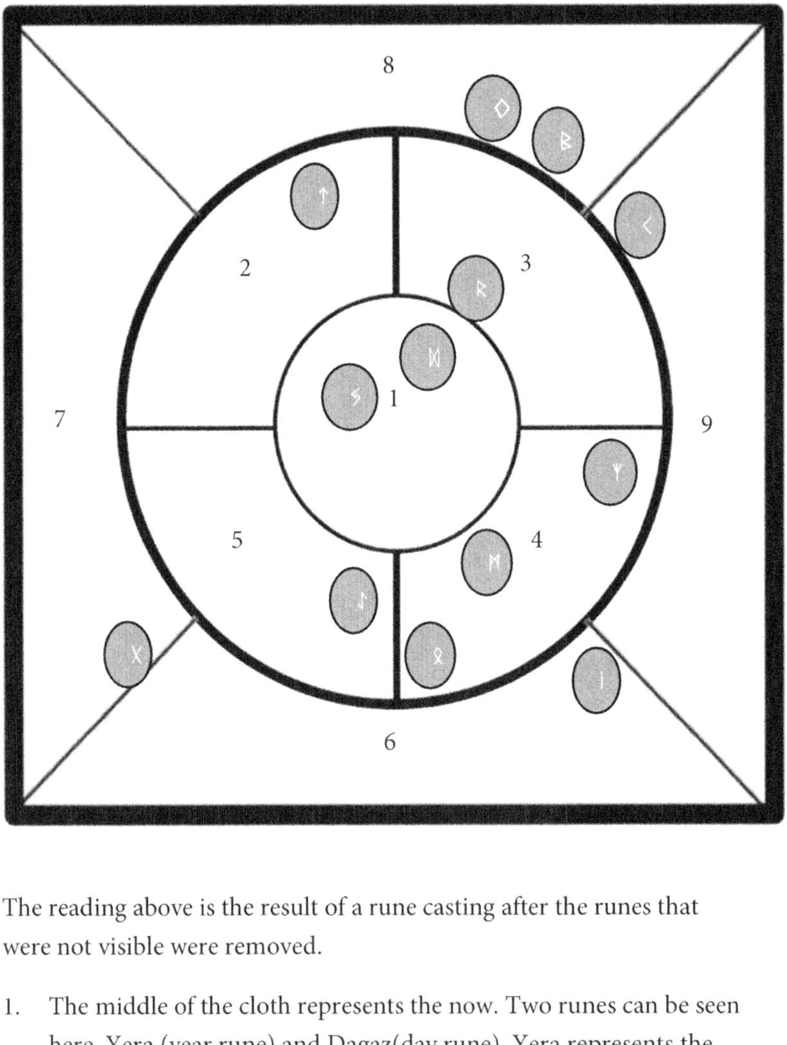

The reading above is the result of a rune casting after the runes that were not visible were removed.

1. The middle of the cloth represents the now. Two runes can be seen here, Yera (year rune) and Dagaz(day rune). Yera represents the cycle of the year and things coming to fruition. Dagaz is a rune of new beginnings. Together Dagaz and Yera show that you are finishing one project and getting ready for a new one.

2. This represents the hopes and positive emotions you have. There is only one rune Tiwaz (justice rune); this would say that the querent feels like they are acting right.
3. These are outside influences that are beneficial in life. There is only one rune here: Raidho (Wagon rune). Raidho symbolizes ordered systems, from the seasons to all well-working organizations. This, combined with Tiwaz in section two, means the system will work for the reader.
4. Here is the shadow self. Three runes are represented here. Algiz (elk rune), Mannaz (humankind rune) Othella (ancestors rune). The person struggles with feeling safe because they do not feel supported by the community in its whole family specifically. The querent finds it challenging to talk about this. It is good to note that this is the perception from the querent and not necessarily right.'
5. The negative outside influences. Eihwaz (yew tree rune) is the only rune here, representing transitional moments. This would indicate that the querent is forced into a transition they did not wish for. This can also explain the feelings of unsafety in square four.
6. This is the past. One rune is here, Isa (ice rune) representing standing still. This rune is also close to the square representing Niffelheim or potential in waiting. Combined with the other runes, this would mean that the person the reading is done for was standing still, but that is now in the past, and things are starting to move.
7. What you are actively working on. One rune is here, Gebo (gift rune), representing an exchange on edge with Helheim. This would say that the querent is pondering about something they want or because it is so close to Helheim what they recently got and what the price will be for that want.
8. The spirituality. Two runes are here close together Ingwaz (seed rune), representing potential, and Berkana (birch tree), representing growth and healing. These are two positive runes and paired, meaning that potential is opening up; these two are also on the edge of Niffelheim, frozen potential. Already seeing the Kenaz (

torch rune) close by, I see this as these two moving out of Nifelheim, not into it.

9. It means frozen potential. There is one rune here, Kenaz(torch rune). Kenaz is both the hearth fire and it is the fever. It drives away the cold of death but not always in a pleasant way.

Concluding: This reading paints a picture of a person who has been working hard and feels that they have been doing so morally. This work is finishing, and the results are a change they are not entirely comfortable with, even if it will end with growth and progress. During that change, they feel they have no control over their lives and no one to rely on. This uncomfortableness is like a fever, a part of getting better, and after it, they will have grown into their potential.

Recommended reading

Obviously, I recommend all the books in the biography of this book. But I would also recommend specific books depending on my reader's interests.

Norse Mythology

Norse Mythology, by Neil Gaiman (2017), retells the most important myths from Norse mythology clearly.

Tales of Norse mythology, by Hélène Adeline Guerber (1929), also does an excellent job retelling the old myths in an understandable fashion.

Norse Mythology: A Guide to the Gods, Heroes, Rituals, and Beliefs, by John Lindow (2001), Is an alphabetic encyclopedia containing every concept from Norse mythology.

Practicing the Norse Faith

Taking up the runes, Diana L. Paxson (2005) If you wish to include the runes in rituals with a community, then there is no better book. The second half of this book is full of suggested rituals and study tips on learning about the runes as a community.

Runic artifact

runic amulets and magic objects, Mindy MacLeod & Bernard Mees (2005), includes a wealth of runic artifacts and their historical contexts written in a very engaging way.

The Galdrabok, Stephen Flowers (1989), is not technically about artifacts, but this book contains translations of later Scandinavian magical texts and rune staves.

Bibliografy

Antonson, E. (1975). *A Concise Grammar of the Older Runic Inscriptions.* Berlin: de Gruyter.

Arntz, H. (1944). *Handbuch der Runenkunde.* Halle: M. Niemeyer.

Bellows , H. A. (1936). *The Poetic Edda's.* New York: The American-Scandinavian Foundation.

Brodeur, A. G. (1916). *The Prosse Edda.* New York: The American-Scandinavian Foundation.

Church, A. J., & Brodribb, W. J. (1876). *Germania.* Cambridge: Macmillen and Co.

Dickens, B. (1915). *Runic and Heroic Poems of the Old Teutonic Peoples.* Edinburg: Cambridge University Press.

Eriksson, M., & Zetterholm, D. (1933). amulett från Sigtuna. Ett tolkningsförsök. *Fornvännen 28*, pp. 129–156.

Flowers, S. (2006). How to do Things with Runes: A Semiotic Approach to Operative Communication. In M. L. Nielsen, B. L. Holmberg, G. Fellows-Jensen, & M. Stoklund, *Runes and their Secrets. Studies in Runology* (pp. 72–79). Copenhagen: Museum Tusculanum.

Foote, P., & Wilson, D. (1983). *The Viking Achievement.* London: Sidgwick & Jackson.

Green, W. C. (1893). *The sotry of Egil Skallagrimson.* London: Paternoster row E.C.

Kapteyn, J. M. (1937). Zwei Runeninschriften aus der Terp von Westeremden. *Geschichte der deutschen Sprache und Literatur 57*, pp. 160-226.

Klingenberg, H. (1976, april). Runenschrift, Schriftdenken, Runeninschriften. *The Journal of English and Germanic Philology vol 75.*, pp. 241-246.

Knirk, J. E. (1994). *Learning to write with runes in Medieval Norway.* Stockholm: Medeltidsseminariet och Institutionen för nordiska språk vid Stockholms universitet.

Krause , W., & Jankuhn, H. (1966). *Die Runeninschriften im älteren Futhark.* Gòttingen: Vandenhoeck u. Ruprecht.

Krause, W. (1970). *Runen.* Berlin: de Gruyter.

Lars, E. M. (2011). *The History of Runic Lore.* Stockholm: Scandinavian Heritage Publications.

Lindow, J. (2001). *Handbook of Norse Mythology.* Santa Barbara: abc-clio.

Louis-Jensen, J. (2005). Södra Kvinneby. *Reallexikon der germanischen Altertumskunde. Vol. 29*, pp. 193–196.

Louis-Jensen, J. (2010). The Norwegian Runic Poem as a Mnemonic Device. *Preprints to The 7th International Symposium on Runes and Runic Inscriptions* (pp. 1-5). Olso: International Symposium on Runes and Runic Inscriptions.

Macleod, M., & Bernard, M. (2006). *Runic Amulets and Magic Objects.* Woodbridge: the boydell press.

McDevitte, W. A., & Bohn, w. s. (1869). *Caesar's Gallic War.* New York: Harper & Brothers.

Rausing, G. (1992). The origin of the Runes. *Forn Vännen: Journal of Swedish antiquarian research 87*, pp. 200-205.

Samnordic Rune Text database. (1993). *Samnordic runetext database.* Opgehaald van Samnordic runetext database: http://www.nordiska.uu.se/forskn/samnord.htm

Sean, N., & Klaus , D. (1995). *Runeninschriften als Quellen interdisziplinärer Forschung.* Göttingen: Walter de Gruyter.

Szőke, V. (2018). The Norwegian Rune Poem in context: Structure, style and imagery. *l'analisi linguistica e letteraria xxvi*, 5 - 32.

Thorson, E. (1984). *Futhark a hand book of rune magic.* York Beach: Samuel Weiser, Inc. .

Tschan, F. (2002). *History of the Archbishops of Hamburg-Bremen.* Colombia: Columbia University Press.

Van Renterghem, A. (2014). *The Anglo-Saxon runic poem: a critical.* Glasgow: University of Glasgow.

Figures

Figures marked with an [*] are public domain. Figures marked with a [~] are licensed under creative commons or are based on images licensed under creative commons. Figures drawn by Walter McGrory are asked to give attribution to this book. Figures marked with a [c] are copy righted by their respective owners and cannot be reproduced without their consent.

Figure 1: Futhark rune row as inscribed on the Klyver stone [G88] drawn by Walter McGrory, 2022[~] 3
Figure 2: Runic alphabets comparison by Walter McGrory, 2022[~] 5
Figure 3: Ægishjálmr by Walter McGrory, 2022[~] 9
Figure 4: Floksand meatcleaver drawing by Walter McGrory, 2022, based on photo's by Universitetsmuseet i Bergen{~] 16
Figure 5: Darwing of the Gummarp rune stone by Walter McGrory , 2022, based on the drawings by Sigurd Agrell (1927) for Runornas talmystik och dess antika förebild [~] 20
Figure 6: Darwing of the Gummarp rune stone by Walter McGrory, 2022, based on the drawings by Sigurd Agrell (1927) for Runornas talmystik och dess antika förebild[~] 20
Figure 7: Freya by Johannes Gehrts for the book: "Walhall: Germanische Götter- und Heldensagen. Für Alt und Jung am deutschen Herd", 1901[*] 24
Figure 8: Cave painting of an Auroch (caves of Lascaux) drawn for this book by Walter McGrory[~] 30
Figure 9: Auðumbla licking Búri free from the ice, four rivers of milk flowing from her uthers. Photo from the page of a 18th century Icelandic edda. Original drawing by Jakob Sigurðsson edited for clarity in print by Walter McGrory[*] 34
Figure 10: Thor getting dressed up as a bride, drawing by Elmer Boyd Smith, 1902[*] 38

Printed in Great Britain
by Amazon

22629415R00169